Assembly Language Pro
For PC and Laptop Com
Contents

2 Introduction.
3 How to boot your programs with a DVD using the free software Burn Aware free.
5 How to boot your programs with a DVD using the Windows 7 program Booting-aids.
6 How to boot your programs with a USB Memory stick using Booting-aids.
7 How to boot your programs with a USB Memory stick using BIOS at the FreeDos command prompt.
15 Boot-Saving-Heading
17 A simple example of a DVD boot-loader.
22 The Bootable DVD data structures from the El Torito Specification.
26 A Windows application program: Opening a Drive instead of opening a file, to read/write specific sectors..
39 How to Enable the A20 Address line
41 Reading Inputs from the PS2 type keyboard and the mouse.
46 Conversion of PS2 keyboard scan codes into ASCII character codes.
49 Finding the higher resolution **screen memory's** address: The Physical base Pointer.
53 Drawing 8x8 pixels alphabetical characters on the graphics screen memory.
58 8x8 Character pixels
62 Windows bitmap file and picture. (.bmp)
66 A timing test and slow speed. And with xmm0 the program speeded up.
67 Configuration Space
70 Reading FAT32 files.
74 A convenient way of switching the computer's mode **to 64 bit** (long mode) and then back again.
77 An example of how to use the programs which switch modes easily
85 An example GDT or Global Descriptor Table
87 The new registers of 64 bit mode
88 About my first experiments to try to switch to 64 bit Long mode.
98 The paging table.
100 The Cmos
104 My experiment with USB.
112 Starting USB programming and reading in the Configuration space
114 Find the USB Operational base address automatically
116 Tests of the program pieces
128 Reading and writing Sectors of USB Memory sticks.
144 One Experiment with an external Samsung USB-DVD writer drive.

Daniel H. Rosenthal   1st January 2016

Introduction

This book is about Bootable Assembly Language, and this means that your computer program will be running all on its own in the computer, and there is NO operating system.

For example you can put your computer program onto a memory stick, you plug it in while the computer is completely switched off. The computer is switched on, the Boot process begins, and in a few seconds your own computer program starts running without an operating system.

Your program is completely on its own, because NO operating system of any kind is there, because the operating system never loads up.

About this book: I have left some mistakes in the book.
This book assumes that you already know a lot of basic assembly language programming. I cannot try to teach the subject from the beginning. All of the areas of program code in the book are 100% of my own writing, and they were taken from some of my experiments.

To be able to boot your programs the BIOS had to be switched into the older BIOS form, (like Legacy Bios) as BIOS is with older computers. At the actual moment when the computer is switched on, you may need to press the F2 key or the F12 key, and enter BIOS setup. Select booting from a USB memory stick to be priority on top, for example. And you need to switch off Microsoft's secure boot, by enable legacy Bios. This is because the new secure boot only allows Microsoft's own software or something with a secret product key to run.

This is about a basic form of assembly language, which is the more interesting, and bootable programming can be very frustrating and difficult.

Boot-able assembly language is sometimes called **Operating Systems Programming,** because it is sometimes claimed that when your computer program is running on its own, then the computer program is **actually** an operating system, even if it is only a very small and simple one.
So when bootable programs gradually become longer and they are improved, they can in time become new operating systems.

Bootable assembly language is sometimes very frustrating. I thought a program I have created named 'Booting-aids' removes one of the difficulties, which is getting a program to run in the first place.
Why is it difficult?
It is my opinion that during the whole period of development of personal computers, Microsoft has been controlling computer hardware design and what they wanted is to prevent other rival companies from creating new better operating systems. To prevent new operating systems from being created, what Microsoft has done is to a large extent against education, by making easy things difficult for you. Were it not for that, all the bootable programming would be very easy.

How to Boot your own programs with a DVD using the free software Burn Aware Free.

I think there is something too slow and inconvenient about using Burn aware free.
 The computer should not have Microsoft's new secure boot, since the new secure boot would prevent booting of your computer programs.

Your assembled computer program, should usually end with file name extension .bin or .com, but not .exe. (I use the FASMW assembler, and it makes a file name extension of .bin. There is a program called exe2bin, which can convert an .exe to a .bin.)

1) Erase a DVD completely or quick format it under Windows. When Windows asks which kind of quick format, click on "Like a USB".
2) Click on "Burn Aware Free", then click on the round symbol "Boot Disk".
3) Where it says "click here to add files" click to add either your longer program (if you use 2 stage booting) or
   select and add 1 small text file of any kind, but not your program. (if you wish to do 1 stage booting.)
4) Mouse click on "File" then on "Options" then on "BOOT".
5) Mouse click on the small tab next to the "Bootable Image File" strip.
6) Select your assembled computer program, the one you wish to boot, as a Boot-able image file.
   Find and select its file name. (It should be an assembled computer program, I have no idea why they would call it a bootable image). Burn Aware Free should remember its file name from then on.
7) Also, depending on the kind of BIOS which your computer has, put in "Sector Count" either a 1 for 1 DVD sector, or a 28 for 28 DVD sectors.
8) Click on "Burn". The DVD should soon be made bootable, but you may have to wait about 2 minutes for the DVD to be written onto, and maybe the DVD drive door will open and you need to re-close it.
9) BurnAware Free sometimes works slowly and I don't know why it is so slow?
10) Log off, turn the computer completely off then back on again. Your program should start running.

The BIOS on different computers is different. Some computers have a BIOS which sets a maximum length limit of 1 DVD sector, and that is 2048 Bytes. Some other computer's BIOS sets a maximum length of about 27 to 29 DVD sectors, which is approximately 60K bytes.

If you are lucky that the BIOS of the computer has a length limit of about 29 DVD sectors, then obviously quite long assembled computer programs can be booted and run with 1 stage booting. But if your computer's BIOS causes a maximum length limit of only 1 DVD sector, then you need to write a short "Boot-loader" program which fits on 1 sector, and do 2-stage booting.

If you are doing 2 stage booting you should also click on the "Sector count" spot and write a 1 in it, for 1 DVD sector. (Burn Aware free writes the sector count number into the El Torito data structure which makes the DVD boot-able. Why is it that with some computers 'sector count' has to be a 1? I found out that if it has to be a 1 then the fault is only in the BIOS.)
 Assuming that you write a boot-loader program, and want to use 2 stage booting, then click on "File, Options, Boot, then the small tab next to "Bootable Image file" and select the name of your assembled boot-loader as your bootable image file. Also this time where you see "Click here to add files" select your longer computer program, click on the plus sign to add it. With your longer computer program added as a file, Click on red button "Burn" to do the DVD.
 Log off, turn the computer off, then turn the computer back on again. Your boot-loader should immediately start running and it is then supposed to look for, and find and load a much longer computer program from the same DVD using Bios Extended Read. In this 2 stage process, you would have to mark the exact start of your longer computer program with some sort of a marking, a number, something that your boot-loader looks for and recognizes, allowing the boot loader to find your other program. I made my boot-loader look for the number 90909090h at the start of every sector until it finds my longer program. My longer programs therefore

have to start with
dd 90909090h.   (Or which is the same thing, db 90h,90h,90h,90h)

Burn Aware Free had an annoying defect which was that if you try to add another file to the DVD later, it stops being boot-able. I definitely prefer using "Booting-aids" to Burn Aware free.

When a DVD is made boot-able with Booting-aids one can save files onto it and it stays boot-able, and that is because there were certain strange symbols on the start of some DVD sectors which need to be moved up to other sectors, to avoid erasing one of them. Booting-aids moves the symbol 00,"NSR03",01 from the start of sector 11h to the start of sector 12h. And it moves the word 00,"TEA01",01 from sector 12h to the start of sector 13h. Moving up those symbols was important. (But I don't know what they are for).

If you are lucky that the version of BIOS on your computer lets you boot programs up to a long length of almost 64k bytes, then you can do lots of experiments with fairly long programs and extra-simple 1-stage booting. (put a 29 into the sector count spot. Select your assembled computer program as a boot-able image file). And at "click here to add files, select anything, or any short text file, not your program.

But to work with all computers (that do Not have Microsoft's secure boot) , including the computers where the version of BIOS allows a maximum of 1 DVD sector, you have to do 2-stage booting. Computer programmers are normally expected to create a boot-loader program, it runs in the 1st stage of 2 stage booting process.

It uses BIOS Extended Read to load your main program, and that loading is the second stage in the normal boot process.

I have written an example of a simple DVD boot-loader program. I have experimented writing several different DVD boot-loaders.

;=======--

As my programs start running they all load the stack segment register ss with zero, and put any safe number into the stack pointer.

For example a program can start running with:

dd 90909090h

mov sp,7b00h

mov ax,0

mov ss,ax

The reason for that is that for switching the mode of the computer to either 32 bit or 64 bit mode, the two calls which I commonly used, "up32" and "down16" have to run. Of course the stack pointer must steadily point to the same spot on the stack as these two calls run. It is assumed that the stack segment register ss will have zero in it, and this fits together with the zero of the base address in a GDT descriptor.

;--
;

I think the main difficulty with booting is that Microsoft's new secure boot does not let other operating systems to boot, which means that when you buy a computer to do bootable assembly language programming, make sure that you can enter Bios Setup and turn on Legacy Bios. And turn off the secure boot. You enter the Bios Setup at the moment when a computer is switched on, by pressing either the F2 or the F12 keys, or sometimes by pressing together Ctrl, Alt, Del keys. To try to make booting less difficult for myself, I created a program called Booting-aids. At first it was very good and easy to use, but then, after I made some changes it became too complicated, so I would use my earlier version.

How to Boot your programs with a DVD using the Windows 7 program Booting-aids

I wanted a better way of putting a boot loader and a boot signature onto USB Memory sticks, and I recently created a Windows application which I called booting-aids. I added to it an ability to make DVDs boot-able as well as memory sticks. I even uploaded my Booting-aids_2_.exe to the Source Forge, with its complete Source Code as one .ASM file too. It may be possible for you to download it from Source Forge. Booting-aids makes a DVD boot-able in a few seconds. It works about 20 times faster than Burn Aware free.

1) The DVD should have been formatted with Windows quick format, (but it is not necessary to keep on formatting it again.) If Windows asks what kind of quick format, click on "like a USB".
2) Click on Booting-Aids.exe
3) Click on DVD.
4) Click on DVD slot 1 (Or on one of the 3 DVD slots).
5) It asks you to select a file. Now select your longer computer program's file name.
6) Immediately in a few seconds, it should do several things: It writes a fixed Boot-loader program onto the DVD. It writes El Torito Specification data structures onto the DVD, and they include a sector number pointing to the boot-loader.
7) And it saves your longer program which you selected onto one of 3 slots on the DVD. Really the slot is a starting sector, and followed by consecutive sectors.
8) Now log off, turn the computer off then back on. The boot loader should run, and it should load and run your longer program. But you might have to press a number key 1 to 3, for which slot 1 to 3.

With Booting-aids.exe there are a few unusual rules which you have to follow: The fixed boot-loader searches for a marking-number at the start of your computer programs, and the marking should be at least 4 NOPs and at the exact start of your program. The op-code for a NOP is just the number 90h. Four NOPs can be written simply at the exact start of program code as

dd 90909090h

Or they can be written as:

NOP
NOP
NOP
NOP
Which is the same thing. (It has to be at the very start of the program.)

My boot loader looks for it. Also optionally you can write a very short text message at the start of your program. If you do so a relative jump should skip over the text, and it should start with at least 2 blank spaces typed with the space bar. Like this:
dd 90909090h
jmp skips1
db "   Two blanks then a bit of text"
skips1:
Unfortunately, my Booting-aids.exe so far sets one fixed boot-loader onto the DVD and does not let you chose other boot-loaders.

After using Booting-aids.exe one can save a few more files onto the disk with Windows, and that might or might not overlap and interfere with the slots holding a computer program. Saving some more files should not stop the DVD from being boot-able.

How to Boot your programs with a USB memory stick using Booting-aids

Booting with a memory stick and Booting-aids_2_.exe was an important improvement compared with using Burn Aware Free.

The kind of memory stick to be used for booting must not have security systems or use a password.
1)   Buy a cheap low capacity memory stick. Use Windows quick format to format the memory stick as FAT32 file system, and with the format also give it a **Volume Label** of the word **FINDING** in block capitals..

2)   This is because "**Booting-aids_2_.exe**" searches for the volume label written as the word **FINDING** and it should give you an error message when it can't find that specific volume label. The memory stick's Volume Label has to be done while formatting it, not afterwards.
3)   It was a safety precaution to be careful to prevent accidental writing onto the hard drive.

4) It has to be FAT32, because the boot loader looks for that word on its boot sector. The memory stick Must be **almost empty**. It might not work if the memory stick is not nearly empty.

5) Click on "Booting-aids_2_.exe" to run it, then on "USB Bootloader" then on "Write boot-loader onto USB memory stick". Booting-aids_2_.exe should quickly write its boot-loader program onto the memory stick's boot sector.. It can stay there permanently, and so you won't need to use Booting-aids a second time. (It also writes the boot signature 0AA55h onto the end of the boot sector.)
6)   Next you should exit from booting-aids and using Windows, with mouse drag and drop files for instance, copy a few of your computer programs onto the memory stick (as normal files, usually with file name extension .bin or .com).
7)   Preferably the memory stick should be empty before you copy your programs on to it. (the boot-loader would not find the program if it's beyond a really long file).
There is a rule to follow: Your assembled programs must start with 4 NOPs at their exact start. That can be done like this:

dd 90909090h
Or it can instead be done by writing at the exact start of your program NOP four times. Like this:
NOP
NOP
NOP
NOP
This is because the fixed boot-loader looks for the NOPs.
Optionally your programs can have a short text message close to their start, beginning with at least 2 blank spaces. Log off, turn the computer off then back on again. You might have to press number key 1 to 3.
;--
IMPORTANT:
As my programs start running they have to load zero into the stack segment register ss, and load any safe address into the stack pointer. This is necessary because the 2 important calls "Up32" and "Down16", have to run to be able to change the computer's mode. And while they load zero or a GDT index 10h into ss, the stack pointer has to continue to point to exactly the same spot on the stack. A zero in register ss at the start of the program, fits together with the zero in a GDT descriptor's base address, so that the stack pointer steadily points to the right spot of the stack. For example, my program begins with:
dd 90909090h
mov ax,0
mov ss,ax
mov esp,7b00h

How to boot your programs from a USB memory stick using BIOS at the FreeDos command prompt. (But now that I have Booting-aids, this method is not necessary)

Booting your own programs with a USB memory stick is better than using a DVD, mainly because it works quickly. This is about the way I booted my own programs with a laptop computer, until I found a better way of doing it. This chapter is about a method I consider obsolete, I don't have to use it any more.

The normal boot process is that when the computer is completely switched off and then back on again, the processor is reset and is in the 16 bit "Real Mode", and the BIOS starts running. The BIOS makes the rest of the boot process work.
To boot your programs from a USB memory stick, I think it is necessary to adjust the "BIOS Set-up" to make it able to boot from a "USB-FDD" firstly, before it tries to boot from a hard drive. FDD stands for Floppy Disk Drive, and I think choosing USB-FDD in the BIOS set-up might be what made the BIOS assign drive number 00 to the USB Memory stick.
Using only drive number 00 in the DL register must make the whole process safe, and using some other drive numbers would cause a high risk of damaging the computer, unless a specific safety precaution was carefully added to the program.
I used a system in which I saved my programs into 1 of 9 slots on the USB memory stick.
The slots were starting sectors with consecutive sectors. I wrote a very short program which I had to put above all my longer programs like a sort of a heading. I called it a boot-saver heading. I put it at the top of all my programs. I had to run the program under the old DOS system because Dos allows Bios to go on working.

Whenever I just typed the file name of a program and then pressed the return key, DOS would immediately run the program, and only the boot-saver placed above the rest like a heading ran, and it waited for me to press a key on the keyboard. Then I pressed a key for number 1 to 9, and the boot-saver saved my longer program which was just below it onto slots 1 to 9 of my memory stick. To do so, the boot-saver used BIOS Extended Write. Always using drive number 00 since only that drive number is safe. It was so important that with this laptop and with BIOS set-up set for USB-FDD firstly, it worked with drive number 00.

A second part of the system was a short program with an upper half and a lower half. It wrote the lower half onto the boot sector of a USB memory stick, but without erasing file system information. This very short program on the memory stick's boot sector can be called a "Boot-loader".

Once it was on the boot sector it could stay there permanently, and it did stay there permanently except when I had some reason to format the memory stick again. To boot my programs from one of the 9 slots on the USB memory stick, I just turned off the computer (With old DOS a computer can be turned off suddenly without harming anything) and when the computer was completely off, I turned it back on again while the memory stick was plugged in.
My boot-loader ran immediately, and it waited for me to press a key 1 to 9. And then when I pressed a key it immediately loaded and ran my longer program which was in the memory stick slot. For example, to run a program which I had saved to slot 3 I just had to press 3.
This was a nice method, and for 2 years I used it with hundreds of experiments in programming. I had thought of the possibility that if I pressed a digit for an empty slot, it would crash it. So to prevent it from trying to run a program from an empty slot, I decided to start my programs with a marking, and my boot loader would look for the marking as an indication that there was a program there in the slot. The marking I used was 4 NOP's exactly at the start of any program, and that can be written as dd 90909090h or just as "NOP" 4 times. The boot loader also always worked with drive number 00 in the DL register.
About entering BIOS set-up. You notice that in the first few seconds after you switch a computer on, a message flashes on the screen for just a second which tells you that to enter the BIOS Set-up screen you should press on a certain key, which is often the "F2" key.
You press the key quickly as the computer is switched on. In the BIOS Setup screen, select "Boot order" and adjust the BIOS so it tries to boot from a USB-FDD before trying to boot from a hard drive. Also I would adjust it so it can boot from a DVD too, just after the USB-FDD, also before the hard drive.
To boot your programs from a USB memory stick you are normally supposed to write 2 computer programs:

You are supposed to write a very short program and put it onto the boot sector of the memory stick. (That is sector 0). And you are supposed to write a longer program and write it onto some other area of the memory

stick. The very short program is called a boot-loader.
When the computer's BIOS boots, it should automatically load your boot-loader from the memory stick and run it, and this very short program is supposed to use "BIOS Extended Read" with Int 13h, to read sectors, find and to load your longer program.
The exact way your short program finds and runs your longer program is very variable as you can use any method you can think of to do it. You can think of and try different methods which all work. But I believe that in every case the very short boot loader program has to use "BIOS Extended Read" int 13h, and so it is important for you to learn about that.
 For booting it is always necessary to switch the computer completely off then back on again. If you switch the computer completely off, plug in a USB memory stick and switch the computer back on again, the BIOS normally looks at the USB memory stick's sector 00 to see whether it contains the "Boot Signature" which is the hexadecimal number 0AA55H in the sector's last 2 bytes. The last 2 bytes are at offset +1FEh. (Offset +510 in decimal). If the BIOS does not find that boot signature there, then unfortunately it may refuse to work at all with the USB memory stick.
So that boot signature is important. When I bought about 12 different kinds of USB memory sticks, only 2 of them already had that boot signature on them.
You can download a free hexadecimal editor software from the internet, and use it to write the boot signature onto your USB memory stick's boot sector. The hexadecimal editors work in Windows and they should be used very carefully to be sure that you don't accidentally write anything onto the hard drive. Especially you should be careful not to write anything accidentally onto the hard drives master boot record which is on sector 00.

When the BIOS sees that boot signature 0AA55h on the last 2 bytes of sector 0, it should automatically load sector 0 of memory sticks into the memory at a fixed address which is always 7C00h. It should then make the computer jump to 7C00h and that makes the program which was on the boot sector start running. Your own program should be on the boot sector. It then starts running.
The boot sector of a memory stick, and all sectors of a USB memory stick are only 512 bytes long. (512 is 200h in hexadecimal). Also the memory stick's boot sector has file system information on it, and it is preferable not to erase any of that, which is about 40h bytes long. Therefore your own program must be shorter than about 448 bytes.
So you are normally supposed to put 2 computer programs onto a USB memory stick. You are supposed to put a very short program of less than 448 bytes onto sector 0 of the memory stick, which then uses "BIOS Extended Read" to load a much longer program which you have saved onto another part of the memory stick. I think the process is safe with drive number 0, but typically in most computers the BIOS gives the hard drive drive number 80h. And sometimes the hard drive can be 81H. If you were to try those numbers, it could instantly destroy the computer by writing onto the computer's master boot record, erasing it.

You may save the longer program by various different methods. You can save the longer program **as a file** in the usual way using Windows or DOS, or if you want to you can save it **onto specific** sectors and consecutive sectors. The very short program on the boot sector can be designed to look for programs which have been saved as files, or it can be designed to load programs which were saved onto certain sectors instead. It could also be designed to find computer programs in the files system directory, and list the file names, but in that case I found it was too long to fit on one sector, and it had to work with 3 stages by firstly loading at least one extra sector of boot-loader.
You should preferably buy a very low-capacity memory stick and then format it as FAT16. You can also format it FAT32, but for a reason I thought FAT16 could be safer. I think only low capacity memory sticks get formatted FAT16? As the memory stick is formatted, the boot signature 0AA55h on the boot sector's last 2 bytes, will not be erased if it is already there. When it's not there try using a hexadecimal editor to put it there.

When the memory stick is formatted either FAT16 or FAT32, it is standard that the first 3 bytes of its sector 0 always contains a relative jump op-code which is normally supposed to make the computer jump over the file system information. As the BIOS boots the computer, the sector 00 is loaded to 7C00h and the computer then jumps to 7C00h. It lands exactly on the relative jump op-code, and then jumps over the file system information. So your own very short program should be on sector 0 starting just beyond the end of that file system information. It works best if you don't erase that file system information when you write your very short program onto sector 0.
So the method used to put your own very short program onto the boot sector is
(1)   Read the sector 0 into memory. (**2**) Copy your own boot-loader program onto it starting just beyond the

end of the file system information. (**3**) Write the whole thing back onto sector 0 again.

So the file system information can be preserved unchanged, and the USB memory stick can then be used as a normal memory stick for saving and loading files, as well as being used for booting your programs.

The reading and writing of sector 00 into memory can be done either using BIOS Extended Read/Write with a drive number in the DL register, or by using a Windows application program that opens a drive instead of opening a file, so that it reads and writes specific sectors.
The Windows application method is better, so when I learnt to do that with Windows, it made my earlier way of doing it obsolete for me. The rest of this writing is about the older method which I no longer use because my Windows program was better.
When I decided about 5 years ago that I wanted to boot my own programs from a USB memory stick, I read on the internet about BIOS Extended read, and then I tried to call that BIOS from Windows. Unfortunately this never worked. Windows is designed to stop the BIOS from working when it is running. Then I tried it with old fashioned DOS and it worked. It meant that you can call BIOS Extended Read with at least some types of the old fashioned DOS operating system. I downloaded a free type of DOS and booted that from a DVD. I followed instructions for doing it on the internet.
Under DOS it was possible to use BIOS to read and write sectors onto a USB Memory stick, using zero as a drive number. The drive number of 00 has to be loaded into the DL register for BIOS extended Read.

But unfortunately the BIOS only worked with the memory stick when there were 2 conditions! (**1**) the memory stick had to be plugged in to the computer at the moment when the computer booted. (**2**) the memory stick had to have the boot signature 0AA55h on its sector 00.
That meant that I had to plug in the USB memory stick so it's there plugged in at the moment when DOS booted from a DVD. Whenever I wanted to put my short boot loader program onto the memory stick, I had to firstly plug in the memory stick, then boot the computer with DOS with a DVD, **then unplug** the memory stick, then **press** on any key, or press a certain key, and **then plug** the memory stick back in again.

The action of unplugging the USB memory stick and pressing a key then plugging the same memory stick back in was always necessary. The BIOS Had to see the memory stick plugged in at the moment when the computer is switched on. The BIOS tried to boot from the USB stick. I had to unplug it, press a key. That caused the computer to run "Int 19h" or something similar, that caused the BIOS to go on to boot from something else. In that case it went on to boot DOS. The same kind of memory stick could then be plugged back in, and BIOS still recognized it. But it would not work if you plugged in a different type of memory stick, probably because different memory sticks have internally different endpoint numbers.
 I read on the internet about a way to install FreeDos as a second operating system, so that you can have a choice of booting either FreeDos or Windows. I used the software from a computer magazine disk to create a FAT32 partition on the hard drive of the laptop. I believe that before creating the new partition it was very important to run de-fragmentation software first! Without de-fragmentation, making a new partition can harm a computer, even if it is new. Following instructions from a website, I installed FreeDos as a second operating system onto the FAT32 partition, just so that I could use BIOS to install my short boot-loaders onto the USB memory sticks.
For several years I used this system. There was a sequence of actions that you have to get used to, whenever you want to write a new boot-loader onto a memory stick. It was always still necessary to plug in the USB memory stick, switch on the computer, unplug the memory stick, press on a certain key to boot from the next device or the hard drive, plug the memory stick back in again. This seems like a nuisance, but when I was used to it it seemed easy. This sequence of actions was easy when you get used to it. Under DOS or FreeDos, my short computer programs could work and put boot-loaders onto the memory stick's sector 00. I usually preserved the file system information unchanged.
I experimented with creating many different boot-loaders, and the experiments mostly worked well.

Later on when I found out how to create a Windows application that writes onto the boot sector of memory sticks, the older method became obsolete. I don't need DOS or FreeDos any more for this, I don't need BIOS extended write any more, and my Windows application program works much better.
But the actual boot-loaders that go onto the boot sector of memory sticks, still always have to use BIOS Extended Read to be able to load and run my longer programs, that will probably always be necessary.
I think these experiments are only safe because I was able to use zero as the drive number during BIOS

extended read/write. (With BIOS Extended read/write the drive number has to be loaded into the DL register, in this case always Mov DL,0.)

Because it is so very important not to accidentally write onto the computer's hard drive. Writing onto sector 00 of the hard drive would immediately damage the computer seriously and you would need to replace its hard drive or format it. It has to be avoided at all costs.

I feel drive number 00 must be safe, because the drive number for the hard drive is usually either 80h or less often 81h. The BIOS is liable to swap around those two drive numbers for no apparent reason, exchanging 80h with 81h, and therefore even trying 81h would be dangerous.

Therefore I think you should look for conditions which cause the USB memory stick to be drive number 00. But under conditions which cause the USB memory stick to be drive number 80h or 81h, it is dangerous and that must be avoided. One should not ever use drive numbers 81h without adding to the program safe safety precautions which would look at the boot sector firstly to recognize the difference between a USB memory stick and a hard drive.

In the case of a Windows application the problem is there with drive letters. (Windows uses drive letters C to F and C is nearly always the hard dive, D can be the DVD drive). Your program needs to look and recognize in a very sure way whether the sector 0 that has been read into memory is from the hard drive or from a memory stick, it should recognize a memory stick in a very safe way. And it should completely avoid and prevent BIOS Extended **Write** from ever running when the sector 0 that it read into memory could have been the hard drives.

USB memory sticks have a byte which is called 'drive number' in the file system information, but the way the BIOS uses that number seems to be varying, not reliable, and it must have been the BIOS set-up sequence being set to "USB-FDD" first which caused the drive number to be the safe zero with my laptop. (FDD must stand for Floppy Disk Drive, which normally has drive number 0. So a booting with the BIOS boot sequence as USB-FDD first caused a kind of floppy disk emulation.)

But what about the Windows application programs which writes onto sectors using a drive letter? One built-in safety precaution which I think is good, is to make your program look for the word FAT16 in the file system information. You would have to format the USB Memory stick FAT16. The only difficulty is that to be able to format it FAT16 the memory stick might have to be a really low-capacity memory stick, since high capacity memory sticks get formatted FAT32.

I bought several very cheap USB memory sticks which had a capacity of only 128 MB and I thought they were really useful. When your program tests for the words "FAT16" in the sector zero, the boot sector, and finds it, this probably makes it very safe. Because now days I don't think computer's hard drives ever have FAT16 format. But it must be a good idea to have 2 safety precautions working together.

So when you test for and find the word FAT16 it must be a memory stick. You have to remember to make the program erase the field where that word should appear before reading in sector 0, so as to be sure there won't be any false positives. One should erase an area of memory to binary zeroes, and then read the boot sector into it, and test that with several compare operations. A second safety precaution I thought of, was to get the program to find and test the Volume Label. When you format a USB Memory stick with Windows you can give it a specific volume label, chose one that a hard drive would not have. A volume label is just like the very first file name in the file directory.

When the computer boots and the BIOS jumps to 7C00h to start your program running, it is supposed to leave in the DL register the drive number of the drive which it booted from. I don't know whether that function is reliable.

So the method used to put your own very short program onto the boot sector is a bit more complicated if you are ever using a drive number that is not 00, or if you use a drive letter under Windows.

(**1**) Erase an area of memory, to prevent false-positive tests. (**2**) Read the sector 00 into memory. (**3**) Look at the sector. Test it to make sure that it definitely comes from a USB memory stick, for example, test it for the word "FAT16" in its file system information. (**4**) Copy your own boot-loader program onto it starting just beyond the end of the file system information. (**5**) Write the whole thing back onto sector 00 again.

;---

This example runs under FreeDos and uses BIOS to write a boot loader onto the boot sector of a memory stick. It always used drive number 00 in the DL register, using 00 it was safe, but it would be dangerous to try any other drive number with it because **it lacks** any method of telling apart hard drive from memory stick. It might instantly cause serious damage to the computer if you tried any other drive numbers, so only use 00. Unless one has added to it a series of tests which can tell whether its drive number is addressing the hard drive or addressing a memory stick.

This is for assembly with the FASMW assembler.

It was only possible for this to work when the memory stick was plugged in **at the moment** when the computer was switched on. And it only worked when the memory stick already has the boot signature on it. Unplug it for a second, press a key, plug it back in.
;Upper part saves lower part onto usb memory stick sector 0 and drive number 0.
;Type its file name at the DOS command prompt, to run it press return. It should run for a second and then
;return immediately to the Dos command prompt.

;Later on when the computer boots while that memory stick is plugged in, it should wait for a 1-9 key to be pressed.
;Then when a key is pressed, should load a program from slots 1-9 of the memory stick to
;the address 1000:00h and far jump to the program.
; It should only far jump to the program if that starts with at least 2 NOPs.

1) Read the boot sector or sector 0, into memory.
2) add the boot loader to it starting just beyond the end of its file system information and
3) save the boot sector back onto sector 0.

Important: The drive number in the dl register should never be any number other than **zero**.
(Use dl=0 So as to be sure that you can't damage the hard drive)

This ran from the Dos or FreeDos command prompt, and returned to that command prompt in a second.
;Start

```
        call packet
        call c7
        jmp c11

packet:  mov ax,5000h               ;First write the data packet for BIOS Extended Read/Write.
        mov ds,ax                   ;ds si point to packet in 5000:00h
        mov si,0
        mov word [si],10h           ;10h= fixed length of this packet
        mov word [si+2],01          ;1=How many sectors to do
        mov word [si+4],00          ;IP part of loading address.
                                    ;Making address where boot sector is read to = 6000:00h
        mov word [si+6],6000h       ;CS part of loading address
        mov dword [si+8],0          ;1st sector number to read
        mov dword [si+0ch],0        ;ms part of 1st sector number
        ret

  c7:   mov ax,4200h                ;42H is Bios code for READ
        jmp c9


  c8:   mov ax,4300h                ;43H in register AH is Bios code for WRITE. Drive number = zero
  c9:   mov cx,5
  c10:  mov dl,0                    ;Drive number in DL Must Always only be 0.

        push ds
        pusha
        int 13h                     ;int 13h Calls BIOS Extended read/write
        popa
        pop ds
        jnb c6
        mov word [si+2],1           ;length of 1 sector again
        dec cx                      ;cx tries again on error
        jnz c10
```

```
            mov ah,4ch                          ;4Ch and int 21h as a return to DOS or to FreeDos
            int 21h

    c6:     ret


;----------------------------------------------
; now to overwrite boot sector, only at +40h so preserving the  rest unchanged.
;the file system information was preserved unchanged

    c11:    mov ax,6000h                        ;boot sector has already been read into 6000:00h
            mov ds,ax
            mov si,00                           ; At +00 there should be EB.3C. = a jump to +03Eh
            mov ax,9090h                         ;overwrite write 2 nop's at exact target of jump
            mov [si+3eh],ax

            call c4                             ;call to C4 to get IP part of loading address
            add ax,4
            mov bx,ax                           ;CS:[bx] now points to the program just below here.

            mov cx,1b0h                         ;count length to copy in cx
    c14:    mov al,[CS:BX]                      ;[CS:BX] reads the short program below here.
            mov [si+40h],al                     ;start at 6000:40h = +40h in the boot sector.
            inc bx
            inc si
            dec cx
            jnz c14                             ;copies the boot-loader just below onto the boot sector.

;--------------------------------
            call packet                         ;rewrite the BIOS packet
            call c8                             ;Call c8 writes onto the boot sector. DL Must=0

            mov ah,4ch
            int 21h                             ;4Ch and int 21h is normal ending and return to DOS or FreeDos
            ret

    c4:     call c5
    c5:     pop ax                              ;POP the 16 bit return address that points to C5: (it then adds 4 to it)
            ret


            cli
                                ;The Boot-Loader starts just below here.
                                  ;It goes onto the boot sector starting at offset +40h
                                    ;The file system information from offset 03 to 3dh is kept unchanged.
            cli
            cli
            jmp skip0
            db "   My Name   "

  skip0:    nop
;---------------
            mov esp,7b00h
            xor ax,ax
            mov ss,ax
```

```
b0:       mov ax,5000h
          mov ds,ax                         ;ds si point to Bios packet in 5000:00h
          mov si,0
          mov word [si],10h                 ;10h is length of this packet
                                            ;How many blocks to load at once.
                                            ;80H = 128 blocks of 512 bytes each, = 64K bytes read.
          mov word [si+2],080h              ;64K was enough, but it could be lengthened.

                                            ;Address to where program is read = 1000:00h
          mov word [si+4],0h                ;IP part of the loading address.
          mov word [si+6],1000h             ;cs part of the loading address
          mov dword [si+8],0                ;First sector's number  will be over-written with another
number.
          mov dword [si+0ch],0              ;Higher part of 1st sector number was normally zero

b00:      in al,60h                         ;input a scan code from keyboard
          cmp al,80h                        ;ahead after release
          jb b00
          mov eax,0                         ;zero in extended part of eax
                                            ;wait here for a key press of 1 to 9,
                                            ;then read one of my programs from memory stick slots 1 to 9.
b4:       in al,60h                         ; input a scan code
          cmp al,1ch                        ;return key to exit loop and "not run" any of my programs
          jnz b3                            ;This was for when I wanted to unplug the memory stick and boot DOS.
          int 19h                           ;remove stick and press "return key" for a normal booting of DOS or FreeDos.

b3:       dec al
                                            ;dec scan code to make it 1-10d. waits for a key 0 to 9 to be pressed
          jz b4                             ;when 0-9 pressed, loads it from that slot. Assuming a PS2 type keyboard.
          cmp al,0bh
          jnb b4

          mov ah,al                         ;al into ah = multiplied by 256
          mov al,0                          ;multiplied by 256 so that slots are spaced apart, spaced 128 Kb apart.
          add eax,400h                      ;Start with sector 400h+100h.
                                            ;Add here **must match boot-save-heading exactly**
          mov [si+8],eax                    ;Write it into BIOS packet, as 1st sector to read, depends on 1-9 key pressed.

          mov cx,3
c15:      mov dl,0                          ;DL register has drive number 0
          mov ax,4200h                      ;42h in AH is Bios code for for Read
          push ds
          pusha
          int 13h                           ;int 13h calls BIOS Extended read.
          popa
          pop ds
          jnb c16
                                            ;how many blocks to read. (it is also an "actual length" field Bios can overwrite)
          mov word [si+2],80h
          dec cx                            ;cx try again on error
          jnz c15
          jmp b0
c16:      mov ax,1000h                      ;After reading the program, jump to run it.
          mov es,ax
          mov bx,0
```

```
        mov ax,[ES:BX]
        cmp ax,9090h            ;look for a double NOP in just loaded program
        jnz b0                  ; jmp far 1000h:00

      db  0eah,0,0,0,10h        ; Do a far jump to the newly loaded program.
                                ;the newly loaded program is at 1000:00H

   db "       My boot loader ends here with a far jump to 1000:00 H  "
   db "                                              "
```

;END of the boot loader

Now a "boot saving heading" is a short program placed just above every computer program,
and its purpose is to save the program which is immediately below it, onto a slot in a USB memory stick.
The slot is actually a simple series of consecutive sectors on the memory stick.

A Boot Saving heading, placed above programs if obsolete Dos is used.

Important: The drive number in the dl register should never be any number other than **zero**.
(Use dl=0 So as to be sure that you can't damage the hard drive)

```
;When called from DOS it waits for me to press a key of number 1 to 9 and then it saves the program
;just below it onto the slot, which is starting sectors of the memory stick.
;No file system is used for it.
;------------------------------ Write a data packet for BIOS extended read/write
            mov ax,5000h
            mov ds,ax                       ;ds si point to packet in 5000:00h
            mov si,0h
            mov word    [si],10h            ;length of packet
            mov word    [si+2],080h         ;how many blocks 128 blocks for up to 64k bytes programs.
            mov word    [si+4],0            ;IP part of ladress to be over-written and changed below.
            mov word    [si+6],0            ;cs part of laddress to be over-written and changed
            mov dword   [si+8],0            ;1st sector number to read to be over-written.
            mov dword   [si+0ch],0          ;ms part of 1st sector number

    b00:    in al,60h
            cmp al,80h
            jb b00
            mov eax,0                       ;zero in extended part of eax
    b4:     in al,60h                       ;wait here for a keyboard press then save my program onto the memory stick.
            cmp al,1ch                       ;or return key to exit loop and not save anything
            jnz b3
            mov ah,4ch                      ;Int 21h to return to Dos or Free Dos without doing anything.
            int 21h

    b3:     dec al                          ;dec scan code to make it 1-10d. waits for a key 0 to 9 to be pressed
            jz b4                           ;when 0-9 pressed, saves into that slot.
            cmp al,0bh
            jnb b4
                                            ;the add might have to be below 1.44 Mb.
            mov ah,al
            mov al,0
            add eax,400h        ;start with sector 400h+100h. The add here must match the boot-loader
exactly.
            mov [si+8],eax      ;write it into BIOS packet as 1st sector to read, depends on 1-9 key pressed.

            call c4             ;C4 to find the address.
            add ax,4            ;cs:ax must point to nop's for it to work. And preferably point to ORG 0.
            mov [si+4],ax       ;over write IP part of address
            push cs
            pop ax
            mov [si+6],ax           ;over write CS part of address.

                                ;Caution: Use drive number 0, and Never try any other drive number.
            mov cx,5
    c1:     mov dl,0            ;DL=0 for drive number 0.  Only use drive number 0.
            mov ax,4300h            ;43h in AH register is Bios code for write
            push ds
            pusha
            int 13h             ;Int 13h calls the BIOS.
            popa
            pop ds
            jnb c2
```

```
            mov word   [si+2],80h              ;length
            dec cx
            jnz c1

    c2:     mov ah,4ch
            int 21h
            ret

    c4: call c5                                 ;Find the address of program put just below here.
    c5: pop ax      ;+0
       ret          ;+1
       nop          ;+2
       nop          ;+3
          ;My older programs and programming experiments went here and started just below here.
            ;when ORG 0 is at exactly the right place, data labels can probably be used in the program.
ORG 0         ;This ORG 0 has to be exactly where the above starts saving the program.
       Nop      ;+4  is the +0 of my program just starting here.
       nop
       nop
       nop              ;For the FASMW assembler I had to write the words "offset equ" once, and then
       nop              ;If the ORG 0 is at the right spot, data labels could be used like this:
; for example "mov ax, offset label"   ; Where "label" is the label of some variable in the program
;But in reality I never used data labels in any of my programs.
;Main program started at ORG 0  and at the nop marked ;+4


;-------------------------------------------------------------
cli
mov ax,0       ;A load of Zero into ss is essential near the start, to let up32/down16 work without crashing
mov ss,ax
mov esp,7b00h
;--------------------------------------------------------------------------------------------
```

I feel the Microsoft new secure boot is something very discouraging, as it is designed to prevent operating systems other than Microsoft's from running, and that prevents normal computer programming at the same time. It must be having a bad effect on education, by making it difficult for people to do assembly language programming.

I hope that there will always be computers that don't have the secure boot!

A note about Booting-aids. It was a simple program and very easy to use, I uploaded it to Source Forge and later made some changes to it. At first it needed a USB memory stick to have the volume label of "BOOTING", but then for some reason I changed that to the word "FINDING".

Then I added a lot of unnecessary complexity to the Booting-aids, and some of its new functions were not tested properly. There is always the small risk it might damage something? If you click on "files" in Source Forge web page, you can get the older version which does not have the unnecessary complexity.

It's an example of one method of doing computer programming, making it easy to boot your programs at least if the computer does not have secure boot.

A Simple example of a DVD boot-loader.
A boot-loader is always of course for the 2 stage method.

I was able to use the software "Burn Aware Free" from the internet, to boot my own programs using a DVD. An example of a DVD boot loader is below. It is shortened and intended to be a simplest possible example. It looks at the start of sectors, one after another, until it finds a program saved onto the DVD. This boot-loader should be assembled with the FASMW assembler, and then software like Burn Aware Free would call it a "bootable image file". You could also write your own Windows application to put a boot loader like this onto a DVD. With Burn Aware Free, click on "File", then "Options" then "Boot", and then click on the small tab next to the "Bootable image" strip. Find and select this boot-loader as your "Bootable image file." Burn Aware free will remember its file name from then on.

You also select some other things. The "Sector Count" field can be made 1 for 1 sector. (of 2048 bytes). You should select "1.44 mb floppy disk emulation" (for this version of this boot-loader. 1.44 mb Floppy emulation causes the drive number to be 0.) The "load segment" should be left alone as either 0 or as 7C0h, which both mean the same thing to Bios.

Burn Aware Free writes the values you chose into its El Torito Specification data structures on the DVD. The values you chose are then on the DVD while it boots.

My example of a boot-loader can be slightly modified to make it work with No-emulation booting. If you make that adjustment, a new problem starts which is of finding the right drive number for the DL register in Bios extended read.

When you do floppy emulation booting, the drive number is always zero. So DL=0. If you select no-emulation booting, the drive number in the DL register could be a number like 0FEh or 7Fh, or maybe something near one of those.

I read that the Bios is supposed to leave the correct boot drive number in the DL register for you, and if that is true then you should simply remove from the boot loader the load of 0 into DL, and leave DL register alone. As Bios should have left the right number in it.

If that function of Bios is not reliable, you would need to add more to the beginning of this boot-loader, so that it would try reading from the DVD using a series of different possible drive numbers in the DL register, and carry out tests on the sector it reads to see whether the sector came from a DVD or not, until it finds the correct drive number for reading sectors from the DVD.

With no-emulation booting DVD sectors are the normal 2048 bytes long. With floppy emulation booting, the Bios pretends that sectors are only 512 bytes long. And it might too limit the data you can read to 1.44 MB sometimes. But even then, and a 1 in the sector count field, the Bios of my computer loaded at least 2048 bytes of the bootable image file. This means there was plenty of room for more complexity to be added to the boot-loader / bootable image file.

The example of a boot-loader which I wrote here, was not tested as I deleted complexity and simplified it, and you should check it for errors. It obviously does not work with my 1-9 slots method. It searches for an assembled program which should be saved to the DVD **as a file.** If this is done with Burn Aware free, then that longer program should be selectedwhen it says "click here to add files". This boot-loader recognizes a program by the program having been marked by the number 90909090h at its start. (Four NOPs.)

(I want to mention something else: There was an example of a boot-loader which went onto the boot sector of a USB memoy stick. The upper half of a program used Bios to save the lower half onto the boot sector of the memory stick. That lower half was the boot-loader.) The example of a DVD boot-loader can probably substitute for that one, as long as it stays adjusted for floppy emulation booting. So it should work both for DVD and for USB memory sticks.

In this case, one would have to save the longer programs onto the USB Memory sticks as files, I mean in the normal way using either Dos or Windows to save as files. Putting the boot-loader onto the Memory stick can be done either by your writing a Windows application program for it, or with BIOS at the DOS or FreeDos command prompt. But once the boot-loader is on the boot sector, Windows can save programs onto the Memory stick as normal files, and when you log off, switch the computer off and then back on again, they should run with the boot process.

The example of a program just below here was a boot loader which I wrote and which worked well, but I deleted a lot from it to make it simple as possible. I am not sure that this is free of mistakes.
Burn Aware Free would call any such program a "Bootable Image File", though it is certainly not an image. At the same time as you use this, you would have to mouse click where it says "Click here to add files" to add your other longer computer program as a perfectly normal file having a file name extension of either .BIN or .COM. But the longer program should be started with 4 NOPs, since this example of boot-loader looks for 4 NOPs at the start of sectors.

```
;when floppy emulation, sector of this program is counted as 00 and sectors are 512 byte.
;when no emulation, sectors are 2k bytes (800h.

                                            ;makes Bios read only 8 sectors in one go.
            jmp sa0
            db "DVD Bootstrap loader. "
    sa0:
            mov ax,5000h                    ;The Bios might leave the boot drive number in DL for you??
            mov ds,ax
            mov esi,0                       ;DS:SI points to a packet for Bios extended read
            mov ax,1000h
            mov es,ax

            mov esp,7b00h  ;?
            mov eax,0
            mov ss,ax                       ;a zero into stack segment register
            mov edi,1                        ;sector number in edi

load_further: mov ebx,0
            mov cx,8                        ;8 sectors read at a time while searching.
            Call write_packet2              ;uses edi = first sector's number
            call extended_read2             ;read 8 sectors to 1000h:00

compare_further:
            cmp dword [es:bx],90909090h     ;look for a marker, in this example 4 nops.
            jz found_program
            add bx,200h                     ;** move up loading address now by 200h bytes,
                                            ; (or 800h when no emulation)
            inc edi                         ;move up sector number +1 in edi
            dec cx
            jnz compare_further
            cmp edi,8000h                   ;
            jb load_further
            int 19h                         ;?? ends when an error

                                            ;To here when the marking at the start of a longer program has been found.

    found_program:                          ;Here it has found the start of a program, by its 4 NOPs.
            mov cx,40h                      ;** here in cx 10h would be for 64kb loading, when floppy emulation
            call write_packet2              ;Called with sector number in edi, sector of found program
    load_program:
            call extended_read2             ;keeping the edi=first sector number
            add edi,8
            mov [si+2],8                    ;do another 8 sectors. 8 sectors of 200h bytes = 1000h bytes
            add word  [si+6],100h           ;**  +100h to Segment part of loading address in the packet.
            mov [si+8],edi                  ;write sector number into the packet
            dec cx                          ;When no emulation booting, add +400h at +6.
```

```
                jnz load_program
                db 0eah,00,00,00,10h        ;Op-code of a real mode far jump to start of program loaded to 1000:0h
                                            ;Now write a data packet for the BIOS extended read.
                                            ;For Bios DS:SI should point to this packet.

    write_packet2:
                mov word    [si],010h               ;length of this packet is 10h bytes, DS:SI points to it
                mov word    [si+2],8                ;at 8 sectors in one go. (it gets over written with actual length.)
                mov word    [si+4],0                ;IP part of loading address
                mov word    [si+6],1000h            ;Segment part of loading address
                mov [si+8],edi                      ;edi into lower dword of Qword sector address
                mov dword   [si+0ch],0              ;upper part of qword sector number is 0.
                ret

    extended_read2:
            push cx                         ;and with edi holding sector number for hard drive.
            mov ch,12                       ;tries on error ch

    reads2:
            push ds
            push es
            pushad
            mov dx,0            ;** drive number 0 assumes floppy emulation, which causes DVD to be drive 0.

            mov al,0
            mov ah,42h                  ;42h = BIOS code for Extended Read

            int 13h                     ;Int 13h is the call to the BIOS
            popad
            pop es
            pop ds

            jnb reads1
            mov word [si+2],8           ;8 sectors try again
            dec ch
            jnz reads2
            pop cx
            ret
    reads1:
            pop cx
            ret
```

; When you want to adjust the program for No-Emulation booting, then I think there are probably just a few changes if you either know the correct drive number for the DVD drive, or if the BIOS leaves the correct drive number in DL for you?
The changes are at the asterisks ** above here.
    1)   Add to BX 800h instead of 200h for the longer sectors.
2)   Load into count-down CX 10h instead of 40h.
3)   Add word [si+6],400h instead of add word [si+6],100h to move up the loading address each time.
4)   Either remove the load of 0 into DL, if Bios leaves you the right drive number, Or add a complex test to get the program to find the correct drive number for DL by testing several numbers.   ;

;==============================

This is about the 2 stage process of booting your own longer length computer programs from a DVD. A method like this is maybe called bootstrap loading. In which you write two programs, a very short one and a longer one.

Your short program starts running when the computer boots, and then finds, loads and runs your longer program so that there is not much limit to how long your computer programs can be. In this example I made it load 256 KB.

Because DVD sectors are naturally 2048 bytes, there is plenty of room in this 1 sector program for you to add to it a Global Descriptor Table (GDT) and the calls "up32" and "down16" so that you can set 32 bit addressing mode. And you can easily copy part of the program to much higher addresses. And increase the length loaded a lot.

But I have shortened this example a lot. It was lucky at first that the BIOS of my laptop happened to have a maximum length limit of about 29 sectors, or somewhere near 60K bytes. At first I could put 29 in the "Sector count field", and Bios would load and run about 60KB of my bootable image file or program.

 If you have one of the computers where the maximum length limit is only 1 sector, then a 2-stage process would be essential. With a computer that has a 1 sector length limit, I remember that I checked by looking at the DVD data structures to make quite sure that the fault was in the BIOS, not in the Burn Aware Free software. It was definitely the BIOS that was limiting length to 1 sector, and that happens with some computers. With either Burn Aware Free software or ImgBurn, I had to specify the maximum length of my program in sectors. The program could then be any length smaller than the one specified.

Previously, with the simplest 1-stage booting, when it said "Click here to add files", I usually clicked to add any short text file which had nothing at all to do with my programming, just because it was necessary to add some file to get "Burn Aware free" working.

But with the 2-stage "bootstrap loading" process, when it says "Click here to add files" I add the important file which is my longer length assembled computer program.
It occurred to me that when the computer boots, some experts probably make their boot-loader find the longer program by understanding the complex disk directory and its filing system which must include pointers to the start of all the files. But that would have been much too difficult for me, and so I decided to do it a much simpler way, which was to make my very short program load consecutive sectors from the DVD and look at the very start of each sector looking for a marking which would allow it to recognize the start of my longer programs.

 I happened to decide to use as a marking four NOPs. That is in hex the number 90909090H. Which you can write at the exact start of the program as without the quotes "db 90909090h". Or as the letters NOP four times. (Alternatively, any short series of op-codes could have worked equally well if you know their hex numbers.) As soon as the boot-loader finds the marking, it loads the whole of the longer program and does a far jump to jump to its start. I just make my longer program begin with at least 4 NOPs, and that works.

When I used Burn Aware Free, I set it for 1.44 MB floppy disk emulation booting. (Click on "BOOT DISC" then "FILE" then "OPTIONS" then on "BOOT".) And I tried specifying 1 sector length, and that worked because the bootstrap loader is shorter than 1 sector. This method works even with those computers which unfortunately can only boot 1 sector. The example of a short bootstrap loader is adjusted to work only with the floppy disk emulation booting. But it can be modified slightly to make it able to work with "no emulation booting".

 The "1.44 MB floppy disk emulation booting" seems to mean 3 things, which all apply to what the BIOS will do when you use BIOS "Extended Read Sectors" immediately after the booting and running of your shorter program.
The 1.44 mb floppy emulation means that the BIOS will consider the DVD drive to be drive number 00 after the booting. Secondly, it means that the BIOS behaves as if the DVD has 512 bytes long sectors. (4 of them make up just 1 normal DVD sector which is normally 2k bytes) . Thirdly, the BIOS will count up the DVD sectors considering the sector where your short program starts as sector 0.
Of course the sector where your short program is starting, is not really sector 0. But immediately after floppy disk emulation booting, the BIOS will consider that boot-loader's sector to be sector 0, and it will count up sectors from that point as if sectors were 512 bytes. That means that sectors below that point are Unreachable. I know there is a way to cancel the emulation, in the El Torito specification for Bios, which should make the

lowest sectors reachable again, but I have not tried cancelling emulation yet. Floppy emulation might also sometimes mean that you can't reach more than 1.44 mb of data.

The bootable DVD data structures from the El Torito Specificaton

This is about the data structures which go onto a DVD for the BIOS, data structures which BIOS recognizes as meaning that the DVD is bootable. It gets the BIOS to run your own programs.
How To Create a Bootable DVD with writing onto sectors. In the moment when a computer is turned on the BIOS can look at the DVD to see whether it is bootable. The DVD should be considered bootable when there are 3 data structures written on 2 of its sectors, plus your program. And these 3 data structures are supposed to follow the EL TORITO Specification.
You should look up "El TORITO Specification" on Google and download that specification to print out.

Some free software such as Burn Aware Free will write the data structures and your program onto a DVD, and it works, except that it takes at least a few minutes as that free software works too slowly. But this is about how to create a bootable DVD with nothing but your own programming and when you can write onto sectors.
It is not difficult to make a DVD bootable.
Whenever I tried to do it, the BIOS accepted my data structures and made my program start running.

As well as the 3 data structures, you should save onto the DVD a short computer program that will be loaded and run by the BIOS to the usual fixed address 07C0h:00. (07C0h:00 is the address [7C00h]) This short program should start running when the BIOS boots the computer. (Your short computer program is sometimes called a "Bootable Image" though it's not an image. Or it can be called a boot-loader.)

Now the BIOS of different computers works a bit differently: The BIOS of some computers can load to 7C00h and run your program up to a maximum length of 64 K bytes, while the BIOS of other computers can load and run your program up to a maximum length of only 1 DVD sector, (2 K bytes) which is very short.

If you are lucky to have a computer where the BIOS will load and run up to 64K bytes, then experimenting with bootable programs can be easy with 1-stage booting. But 1 stage booting won't be enough with a lot of computers because their BIOS imposes a length limit of only 2K bytes.

When you want your DVD to be bootable and for it to work with most different computers, then assume the maximum length is 2K bytes and do 2-stage booting. In 2-stage booting your very short program on 1 DVD sector should use "BIOS Extended Read" to read a much longer computer program from other sectors of the DVD.
Your short program reads your long program and then jumps to it by running a far jump.
The BIOS is supposed to leave in the DL register the right drive number it used for the booting drive. I don't know whether that is reliable or not. If not, how do you find the right drive number to use in the DL register for BIOS Extended Read?
If you try floppy emulation booting, the right drive number should always be 00 so that is simple. Otherwise, the right drive number can be numbers such as 7Fh or sometimes 0FEh, and it could be a problem to get a very short program to find the right drive number.

I found out that unfortunately the BIOS of my laptop PC does not want to write anything onto DVD sectors, so I could not use BIOS, and my writing of the bootable data onto DVDs had to be done some other way. I never managed to find out how to directly program a computer's built-in DVD drive, though that is an interesting subject.
And I was able to write directly onto DVD sectors using 2 quite different methods: I managed to do EHCI programming to write sectors using a Samsung external USB-DVD writer drive, and the process was complicated.
 And later on I managed to create a Windows 7 application program which can quickly write onto DVD sectors so as to make a DVD bootable. I called my program "Booting-aids" and I even uploaded it to Source Forge. Booting-aids works a lot more quickly than Burn Aware Free.

The first data structure of the El Torito Specification always has to be written onto DVD **sector 11h.** (Which is sector 17 in decimal). It is called the "Boot Volume Descriptor" and it is supposed to include the words written in block capitals "EL TORITO SPECIFICATION" starting at offset +07. Between the 3 words there should be a blank character =20h as would be typed by the space bar.

Boot Volume Descriptor

Offset	Length bytes.	Values	
00	1	00	binary zero
1	5	"CD001"	The word as ascii text.
+6	1	01	binary 01
+7-26h	23	"EL TORITO SPECIFICATION"	
+27h - 46h		00,00,00 all binary zeroes.	
+47h	4	A sector number, absolute pointer to the Validation Entry.	
+1Bh		All zeroes from here on	

The words are written as normal ascii and can be entered as hex numbers, for the word 00,"CD001",01:
00h,43h,44h,30h,30h,31h,01h   And for the words El Torito specification in capitals:
 45h,4ch,20h,54h,4fh,52h,49h,54h,4fh,20h,53h,50h,45h,43h,49h,46h,49h,43h,41h,45h,49h,   4fh,4eh,
The next data structure is the Validation Entry. You can put the Validation Entry on any sector you want, and choose where to put it, but at offset +47H in the Boot Volume Descriptor, you must write that absolute sector number which points to it.

Validation Entry

Offset	Length Bytes	Values	
00	1	01h	Header ID
01	1	00	00 is for system 80x86
02	2	00,00	
04	up to 12?	ID String. Any words in text. Or leave it in binary zeroes.	
1Ch	2	Check Sum = sum of all 2-bytes words from 00 to +1Eh shall be zero	
1Eh	1	55h	
1Fh	1	0AAh	

Next the "**Initial Default Entry**" is on **the same sector** as the validation entry but starting at offset +20h

20h	1	88h	The 88h is means the DVD is Bootable.
21h	1	00 / 02	00=No Emulation. 02=1.44mb floppy emulation
22h	2	00 or 07C0h.	"Load Segment". 00 specially means same as 07C0h
24h	1	00	system
25h	1	00	reserved zero
26h	2	01-1Dh Sector Count. The number of sectors of your program BIOS should load.	
28h-2Bh	4	Absolute Sector Number of where Computer program starts.	

All the rest of the sector should be binary zeroes.

At +22h the "load segment" is normally 7C0h for address [7C00h]. Sometimes BIOS accepts small changes in it but can reject large changes. But if this number is zero, the zero has a special meaning to the BIOS which is 00=7C00h. So you can leave it 0.
At +26h you write the number of how many DVD sectors of your program you want BIOS to load and run. The BIOS in some computers can only accept a 01 for 1 sector here, whereas the BIOS of some other computers can accept numbers up to about 27 or a bit more, which make BIOS load and run up to nearly 64K bytes. To make it work with all computers, use just 01.
A really important number is at offset +28h and it is the 32 bit absolute sector number of the DVD sector at which your computer program starts, (or of where your boot-loader starts.) BIOS always uses this number to find your program.

You see the Boot Volume Descriptor has to be always on sector 11h. A pointer has to be written on sector 11h at offset +47h which is an 4 byte absolute sector number of the sector where the Validation Entry is.

The Validation Entry with the Initial Default Entry which are always together on the same sector, can be on almost any sector. You have to write a pointer pointing to the Validation entry's sector, in the Boot Volume Descriptor at offset +47h in sector 11h. For example I noticed that the free software "Burn Aware Free" put them on sector 1Bh, the software "ImgBurn" put them on sector 14h, and a Linux disc put them on sector 1BBh, and I tried other sector numbers which also worked.

Also, you have to write a pointer at offset +28h from the start of the Validation Entry, pointer which is the 4 byte absolute sector number of where you saved your computer program. (Your computer program was so-called "Bootable Image File" in the terminology of free software Burn Aware free).
When I tried creating bootable DVDs writing these data structures, it always worked.

Note: In the Validation Entry at offset +04 you can if you want to write a few words in text, such as your name. But if you do it, then you have to correctly calculate a check sum, and write that check sum at offset +1Ch. I usually left that area blank with binary zeroes.

At Offset +1Ch, you need to write the check sum which is 2 bytes long. The specification says that the sum of all 2 bytes numbers from offsets 00 to +1Eh shall equal zero. A sum which included the check sum itself. At +1Eh there should be a fixed boot signature of 0AA55h.
When I did not write any words in text, and when I left nearly all of the Validation Entry filled with binary zeroes, then the following 4 bytes can be OK at offset +1Ch: 0AAh,55h,55h,0AAh. The symmetrical pattern of check sum plus boot signature.
But I think that if you write some words as text at offset +4, then you can calculate the check sum by putting in a register the starting number 55ABh, and subtracting from it every 2 byte number from offset 00 to +1Ah. Then write the result at +1Ch. (And the boot signature at +1Eh).

At offset 21h, relative to the start of the Validation entry, there is the 1 byte where 0 means no emulation and 2 means 1.44 mb floppy disk emulation. If you use 0 for no emulation, DVD sectors are 2048 bytes long and the drive number for the DVD might be 7Fh or 0FEh or some number like that.
If you use number =2 for floppy emulation, then just after booting the drive number for the DVD is always 0. And as well if you chose floppy emulation, the BIOS pretends that the absolute sector where your computer program starts is sector 0, and all sectors beyond your computer program are numbered consecutively from that zero.
And lower sectors below your program become "out of reach", because to reach them you would need a sector number below zero. Also I think the BIOS makes sectors seem to be 512 bytes long. Really DVD sectors are 2048 bytes.
If your computer's BIOS will only run a program whose length is 1 DVD sector, (2 K bytes) and you want 2-stage booting, then your very short program will need to use BIOS Extended Read to load and then jump to your longer programs. How can a very short program find a longer program? There must be so many different ways of doing it, and the way I thought of was to make my longer programs start with a specific number which the boot-loader could look for. I happened to use the NOP. NOP stands for No Operation, and its op-code is the hex number 90h. So I decided to make my longer programs start with 4 NOPs,

NOP
NOP
NOP
NOP

Or these 4 NOPs can be written as data bytes like dd 90909090h. Which is exactly the same thing. The boot-loader program has to be less than 2 K bytes long, but it looks at the first 4 bytes of consecutive DVD sectors for the simple number 90909090h.

 And when it finds 90909090h, it assumes that is the start of my longer program. So it loads the longer program into memory and jumps to its start with a far jump. It is right to assume that the exact start of a longer program will be at the exact start of some DVD sector, therefore it is enough to look only at the exact start of every sector when searching for the longer program. Looking for 2 NOPs would have worked just as well, and so using 4 of them was more than really necessary. My boot loaders never tried to use a file system, as that was not necessary.

Now that I have created a Windows application program to make DVDs bootable, (Booting_Aids_2_.exe) I shouldn't ever need to use the software Burn Aware Free.
As soon as I noticed that my own Windows program worked quickly, I wondered again why Burn aware free was slow?
 Burn Aware Free also had an annoying defect, which was that whenever I made a DVD bootable with it, trying to save another file onto the DVD with Windows mouse drag and drop, always erased the DVD's boot-ability. The DVD was no longer bootable so you would have to erase it and start all over again.
I found the solution to the problem while creating Booting-aids, and my Windows program Booting-aids.exe allows you to later save more files onto the DVD without it erasing boot-ability.

With a lot of experiments I found that the problem was that when Windows quick formats a blank DVD, the quick format puts the word 00,"NSR03",01 onto the start of sector 11h, and it writes the word 00,"TEA01",01 onto the start of sector 12h.

The solution to the problem was to move the word 00,"NSR03",01 to DVD sector 12h, and to move the word 00,"TEA01",01 to DVD sector 13h. When that is done more files can be written onto the DVD without stopping its boot-ability! Which is important.

Booting Aids was better than Burn Aware free because it let you write more data without erasing bootability.

;--

A Windows application program: Opening a drive instead of opening a file, to read/write specific sectors.

While every other piece of programming was written for the FASMW assembler, this one is written for the Qeditor.exe assembler which comes in the free MASM32 package. But, if you convert it for the FASMW that will improve it. The FASMW has the ability to easily mix different 16 bit programs with 32 bit programs, by using its unusual FILE directive. And I don't know how to do that with the Qeditor.

This was about a program I wrote a year ago. To make either a DVD or a USB memory stick become bootable you need to be able to write onto specific sectors, outside of the file system, and it is better to do so using Windows than with Dos or Bios. Now that I know how to do that under Windows, I don't need Dos any more,.

In a Windows application program you can open a drive instead of opening a file in order to write onto specific sectors like the boot sector of a memory stick. I named my program Booting-aids.asm when I got it working. It can make a DVD become bootable quickly, much more quickly than the software Burn Aware Free which I had used until then. I wonder why Burn Aware free works slowly since its slow speed does not seem to have a reason?

At least Windows 7 and Windows XP lets me write onto low numbered sectors like the boot sector easily. But Windows may restrict you and prevent you from writing onto some higher sector numbers. Luckily the restricting did not affect sector 0 and the creating bootable DVDs or memory sticks,.

If you are going to write onto specific sectors of either a DVD or a USB memory stick, you should create several safety precautions to make absolutely sure that it won't accidentally write onto the hard drive. A write onto sector 0 of the hard drive would immediately seriously damage your computer. It would erase the Master Boot Record of the computer and so destroy the hard drive.

So **you need to take some safety precautions seriously**. I wanted two safety precautions in Booting-aids.asm. The drive you write on under Windows depends completely on the drive letter. And so the **safety** precautions are a matter of making sure you are using the right **drive letter.** With a USB memory stick the safety precaution must be to firstly read sector 0 into memory using a certain drive letter, look at the sector, and for the program to recognize in a safe way whether the sector 0 is from the USB memory stick or from the hard drive.

The program must be able to tell apart memory stick from hard drive in a way that won't ever go wrong. In the case of the DVD, the program should read several sectors looking for specific numbers which DVDs get when they are quick formatted. These numbers are quite different from the numbers you see on hard drives, and so should tell them apart. And a program should automatically prevent writing onto sector 0 if there is any risk that the drive letter might be for the hard drive. If there is any risk at all that the drive letter is for the hard drive, it should never write sectors, as it would immediately cause serious damage to the computer.

Under Windows operating system, if you want to read or write specific sectors without using the file system, you should open a drive instead of opening a file. You do it with invoke CreateFile, except that instead of giving the invoke CreateFile the address of a path and a file name, you give it the address of a small data structure in your .data section exactly like this: **device db "\\.\f:",0** which has these slashes in it. It should start with two slashes, a full stop, then one slash and the drive letter, and a colon, and end in a binary zero. Notice that its text part is within quotes but the binary zero is outside of the quotes. It should be in the data section of the program, and in my program it has a label such as 'device' and after the label it is started with the two letters 'db' which means data bytes follow.

The precautions are about how to find the right drive letter, since you need to avoid drive letters that go for either the hard drive or hard drive partitions, and avoiding that should be done automatically somehow. The letter "f" above was a test drive letter, often "d" is the letter for the DVD drive and "e" is often the letter for the USB memory stick, and you can try several drive letters like "g" or "f" or "e" or "d" when you want to use either a USB memory stick or for a DVD writing drive, but of course I think you should not try letter C, because C is so often the drive letter of the hard drive.

The program which reads from a specific drive sector. The special small data structure device db "\\.\f:",0 is used instead of a path and file name. Its label for the assembler is "device" in this example. It causes the invoke to open a drive instead of opening a file, so that specific sectors can be read or written.

About invoke CreateFile. It had 7 parameters separated by commas. Its first parameter is ADDR device. This is converted by the assembler into the 32 bit address of the small data structure with the label "device" in my data section. Its second parameter is GENERIC_READ. This is converted by the assembler into a constant. Its third parameter is FILE_SHARE_READ OR FILE_SHARE_WRITE. This is converted by the assembler into a constant. Its fourth parameter is zero. Its fifth parameter is OPEN_EXISTING. This is converted by the assembler into a constant. Its sixth parameter is FILE_FLAG_NO_BUFFERING. It is also converted to a constant. Its seventh parameter is zero.

When the invoke runs it returns with a handle to the drive in the EAX register. You save this handle for use in the next invokes. In my program it was saved under data label hcf.

Next the program uses invoke SetFilePointer. It is necessary to multiply the sector number of the sector which you want to read by the length of the sectors in bytes. So when you are working with a USB memory stick you have to multiply the sector number by 512 as there are 512 bytes per sector. But if you were using a DVD then you would instead have to multiply your sector number by 2048 as DVD sectors are 2048 bytes long. Anyway the multiply operation gives the result in eax.

In the invoke SetFilePointer the first parameter is "hcf", my label to a "handle" which invoke CreateFile returned in the EAX register. The assembler converts this label hcf into the right load for the invoke to get the saved handle. The second parameter of the invoke is eax, for the eax register, so the invoke will use the value in it which is the result of the multiplication. This sets a bytes-pointer which in this case has to be always an exact multiple of the sectors length, in this case an exact multiple of 512. The third parameter is zero. The fourth parameter is FILE_BEGIN, which the asembler converts into a constant.

Next there is an invoke ReadFile which has 5 parameters. In this special case Invoke ReadFile does not read a file but reads specific sectors because the drive was opened instead of opening a file. Its first parameter is hcf, the label to the drive's handle. Its second parameter is a value in register edx, which is a 32 byte address of the loading address, of where in memory you want it to read the sectors to. Its third parameter is the length of the data you want the invoke to read. As it is reading sectors of 512 bytes, this number has to be an exact multiple of the length of the sectors. In this example 512 for 1 sector. Its fourth parameter is register ecx. Before running this invoke the program has loaded into the ecx register the 32 byte address of where you want the invoke ReadFile to automatically write an "actual length" (see the operation Lea ecx,actual). After the invoke ReadFile runs, you should find an "actual length" number at data label "actual". The invoke's fifth parameter is zero.

This should read the specified sectors into memory, in this case in the data section of the program. There is next an invoke CloseHandle. It has one parameter, hcf. The handle has to be closed so that Windows operating system knows you are finished with the handle.

All these reads from sectors are perfectly safe. You can **read** as much as you want from the low-numbered sectors. But **writing** onto sectors with invoke WriteFile could immediately do serious damage to the computer if it wrote onto the hard drive by mistake. Writing of sectors **must not** be done until the program has double-checked that it has the right drive letter in that small data structure device db "\\.\e:",0 while it runs the invoke Createfile.

The first safety precautions I thought of for USB memory sticks, were, to format the memory sticks FAT16 and then make my program read its boot sector and **look for** the word "FAT16". This is a good idea because I don't think hard drives ever have FAT16 on their master boot records. A second precaution is to give the USB memory stick a specific "Volume label" when you format it under Windows, and to get the program to read the first sector of the memory stick's directory and look at the start of the directory for the specific volume label. This should make it safer, as long as you chose a volume label which people don't put onto their hard drive partitions. At first I got my program "Booting-aids.asm" to automatically look for the volume label "FINDING" in block capitals, which must be safe. It is safe because a hard drive wouldn't have that volume label. But then for some reason I changed it to "BOOTING" which might be less safe.

This is ready to be assembled with the QEDITOR.EXE assembler which comes in the free MASM32 package, which you can download free. To work the folder with the QEDITOR.EXE should be right next to the C:\ drive. With the Qeditor you just save the file then click on "console build all" and it immediately assembles.

```
    .data
 actual dd 0                                    ;'actual' where an actual length number will be saved
 hcf dd 0                                       ;'hcf' where the handle to the drive will be saved
ALIGN (10h)
    usb_boot_sector db 240h dup (0)             ;a space for reading the boot sector.
    db 80h dup (0)              ;
    usb_directory_sector  db 240h dup (0)       ;A space for reading the directory.
    db 80h dup (0)

 device db "\\.\f:",0      ;This line is Special data structure for reading sectors

; ############################################################
.code                              ;For Reading specified sectors with low sector numbers.
read_usb_sector_ax:                ;Call here with the absolute sector number in eax.
 push eax                          ;push eax saves the sector number

 invoke CreateFile,ADDR device,GENERIC_READ,FILE_SHARE_READ OR \
        FILE_SHARE_WRITE,0,OPEN_EXISTING,FILE_FLAG_NO_BUFFERING,0

    mov hcf,eax                             ;save the important handle.
    pop eax                                 ;pop eax recovers the sector number
    mov ecx,512                             ;multiply the sector number by 512
    imul ecx                                ;result is in eax
    invoke SetFilePointer,hcf,eax,0,FILE_BEGIN
    lea ecx,actual                          ;where the next invoke should give you its actual length read
    lea edx,usb_directory_sector            ;Address of an area to read the sectors into
    call align_edx                          ;do not call align_edx more than once
    invoke ReadFile,hcf,edx,512,ecx,0       ;It does read the boot sector of the USB stick.
    invoke CloseHandle,hcf                  ;necessary to close the handle
 db 0c3h
;=================================================================
 align_edx:   and dx,0ffe0h       ;I do not understand whether aligning was really necessary??
         add edx,20h          ;Align should not be called more than once since it would increase the address.
         ret
```

The above program should be able to read any low-numbered specific sector in a USB memory stick into an area in the data section.

These program parts are written to be assembled with the QEDITOR.EXE which comes with the free to download Masm32 package. The invokes are written here so that they are ready to be assembled with the Qeditor.exe

The invoke CreateFile should have as its first parameter the address of the small data structure

 device db "\\.\f",0

But the letter "f" in it might not be right so it has to be over-written with the right drive letter. The invoke CreateFile returns with a Windows handle in the EAX register, and you save it for the next operations.

The invoke SetFilePointer has this handle as its first parameter. Because of the special data structure used with invoke CreateFile, the invoke SetFilePointer works with the drive instead of with a file, and the second parameter in this invoke is a bytes-address as a pointer which has to be in multiples of the device's sector size in bytes. A memory stick has 512 byte long sectors and so it should be any exact multiple of 512. (But with a DVD it would have to be an exact multiple of 2048, the DVDs sector size).

Next the invoke ReadFile is being used to read sectors instead of files, its first parameter is the handle hcf, its second parameter is the register EDX which is holding the loading address which the sector data should be read into. The invoke's third parameter is the length to be read and it must be in exact multiples of 1 sector, in this example the length is 512 for reading 1 sector. Its fourth parameter is the number in register ECX which should be the address pointing to a variable in memory into which you want the Invoke to write an actual length of the bytes length actually loaded. The next invoke is CloseHandle which is the necessary way to end this.

Reading sectors must be totally safe, but writing sectors can be very dangerous and must be done very carefully.

The writing onto a boot sector could be extremely dangerous and could immediately damage or even destroy your computer, **and so safety precautions have to be added** to any such program to make absolutely sure it won't write anything onto the hard drives sectors. It's about the drive letter.

The program needs to know the difference between a USB memory stick's sectors and a hard drives sectors. It has to recognize when it sees the USB memory stick's sectors without any mistakes.

The following example to write onto boot sector **must not be used** without adding to it safety precautions.

```
        ;Safety precautions have to be  used to make absolutely sure it never writes onto the hard drive!
write_usb_boot_sector:
    invoke CreateFile,ADDR device,GENERIC_WRITE,FILE_SHARE_READ \
    OR FILE_SHARE_WRITE,0,OPEN_EXISTING,FILE_FLAG_NO_BUFFERING,0       ;open existing seems necessary
    mov hcf,eax
                                        ;Next, the 1st number after the handle is a bytes
                                        ;address pointer, in multiple of 512, or 1 sector's bytes
                                        ;This pointer is 0 only for the boot sector.
    invoke SetFilePointer,hcf,0,0,FILE_BEGIN
    lea ecx,actual                      ;where the invoke should give you its actual length read
    lea edx,usb_boot_sector
    call align_edx
    invoke WriteFile,hcf,edx,512,ecx,0  ;It does write onto the boot sector of the USB stick.
    invoke CloseHandle,hcf ;
    ret
```

I thought of 2 safety precautions to make this safe when intending to write upon the boot sectors of USB memory sticks. The first safety precaution was to format my memory stick FAT16 file system, and then to try to get my program to first read the boot sector and look for the words "FAT16" in the boot sector which it has just read. When a memory stick is formatted FAT16, the word "FAT16" is always there at offset +36h relative to the start of the sector. The idea was that computer hard drives are not normally FAT16 (As they are usually NTFS or FAT32 systems). So when the program reads in the boot sector of a drive, and finds in it the words FAT16, it is less likely than before to have been the drive letter for the hard drive. But this was not perfectly safe alone! The second safety precaution I thought of, was to give the memory stick a "VOLUME LABEL" while it gets formatted by Widows, which a hard drive partition would not have as its volume label. I first thought of the volume label "FINDING" which was very safe. But then I unfortunately changed it to "BOOTING" which could sometimes exist on a hard drive too. Anyway. When both precautions are working together, it should be safe?

The formula for finding the start of a FAT16 files directory, and the Volume Label at the start of the directory: When a USB memory stick is formatted FAT16 there is at offset +16h a 2 bytes number called "number of sectors per Fat" and there is usually 2 copies of Fat. There is at offset +0Eh a 2 bytes number called "number of reserved sectors". You have to take the number at offset +16h, (number of sectors per fat) and multiply it by 2 because there are 2 Fat copies. Then add to that the number at offset +0Eh, the number of reserved sectors.

The sum is the absolute sector number of the sector where the file directory starts. It should be put in a 32 bit register, and used to read the sector and the start of the directory is there. The "Volume Label" is exactly at the directory's start and is just like a first file name. My program booting-aids uses this method as shown below. I think that looking automatically for a volume label which will not be on any hard drive should make the program safer. The only difficulty is that Windows might not want to give a high capacity memory stick FAT16, so you might have to buy a cheap low capacity memory stick, one with below 2GB capacity so it can be formatted FAT16.

To explain a safety precaution with DVDs.

When I wrote my program for making a DVD bootable, I thought of 2 different safety precautions which I thought should both work together. (It was very important to be absolutely sure that the program won't damage the hard drive). I had noticed that when a DVD is given a quick format under Windows, the words 0,"CD001",01 are there in the start of its DVD sector 10h. (Binary part outside of quotes, text part in quotes). It is on sector 10h without the quotes. Therefore I made my program load sector 10h and look at the first few bytes of sector 10h for the word 0,"CD001",01 there.

If that word is found, it shows that the drive letter was OK and was for the DVD. Since I don't think a hard drive would ever have the letters 0,"CD001",01 on it. Furthermore the program can look for the words 00,"NSR03",01 at the start of either DVD sector 11h or sector 12h, and the word 00,"TEA01",01 at the start of either DVD sector 12h or 13h. Finding that in either place would mean that it was a DVD, because I noticed it were written by the Windows quick format of the DVD. The two precautions working together probably make it safe. One must remember to firstly erase the field, where the 00,"CD001",01 should appear, just before reading the sector 10h, as if you forgot to erase the field there might be a false positive.

The other safety precaution I thought of was to try a length which should not work with a DVD, to indicate that a Wrong drive letter was there. DVD sectors are 2048 bytes long, this is 512*4 bytes. My program tried reading from the DVD using a test drive letter that might or might not be the one for the DVD, but, the invoke SetFilePointer specified a pointer of 512*3, a value that should not work for a DVD. And at the same time for the precaution my invoke ReadFile specified a length to read of only 512 bytes, which is too small for a DVD, which should not work with a DVD. (Because the length you specify is supposed to be an exact multiple of the drive's sector length.)

If it succeeded in reading some sector, that would tell the program that the Wrong drive letter was being used, that the drive letter must be avoided to avoid causing damage to the hard drive. So a successful read was a sign that the drive letter was not for the DVD and writing should be inhibited and a different drive letter tried. For the second idea:

The following shows looking for the words 0,"CD001",01 in a DVD sector 10h. My second precaution. (It does not show the first.)

```
    mov dword ptr actual,0              ;erase actual length indicating.
                                        ;Then open a drive with invoke CreateFile

    invoke CreateFile,ADDR device2,GENERIC_READ OR GENERIC_WRITE,FILE_SHARE_READ \
OR FILE_SHARE_WRITE,0,OPEN_EXISTING,FILE_FLAG_NO_BUFFERING,0
    mov hcf,eax                         ;store the handle which it returns in EAX

                ;Read Sector 16 =10h to check first that there is a word similar to "CD001",01h
                ;so you know if you have the right drive letter. Once a drive has been opened
                ;it is possible to reuse the handle several times without having to reopen it every time.

    invoke SetFilePointer,hcf,2048*16,0,FILE_BEGIN    ;

    lea ecx,actual
    mov dword ptr actual,0              ;erase actual length indicating
    lea edx,see_read                    ;address of memory area where the DVD sector should be read into
    mov dword ptr [edx+4],0             ;Important to erase the field firstly

    invoke ReadFile,hcf,edx,2048,ecx,0  ;try to read from a DVD

    lea edx,see_read
    cmp actual,2048                     ;Important to make sure the drive letter is for a DVD before you write anything
    jnz nok8
    mov eax,[edx+4]                     ;A DVD normally has on several sectors including 10h and 11h
                                        ;a "xx01",01 ? Looking for it.
    and eax,0ffffffh

    cmp eax,013130h                     ;does it read the word "CD001",01 or "BEA01",01 and similar things ?
    jz ok1                              ;end if the drive might not be a dvd drive
    nok8:

    lea edx,device2                     ;the small data structure that is for opening a drive
    add edx,4                           ;point to the drive letter
    dec byte ptr [edx]                  ;decrease by 1 the drive letter
    cmp byte ptr [edx],"c"              ;if it became C it has gone too far.
    jz nok3
    jb nok3
    jmp try3                            ;try the next drive letter, avoid the hard drive,

nok3:
    call box6                           ;error message of can't find a DVD
```

```
;==== Booting-Aids.asm USB section as it is, but most of long data bytes removed

   ALIGN (10h)

     usb_boot_sector db 240h dup (0)
     db 80h dup (0)                          ;make a space between visible boot sector and visible directory sector
     usb_directory_sector  db 240h dup (0)
     db 80h dup (0)


 ;device db "\\.\physicaldrive1",0 ;This worked 00b8h=handle only when drive 0. or 1 if usb stick is plugged in.
 ;device db "\\\\.\\PhysicalDrive0",0     ;;This one did never work.

 device db "\\.\f:",0       ;This worked well (but the right drive letter needed to be found very carefully.)
        selects1 db 0

; ###########################################################

.code   ;;
;--------------------------------------------------------------

           ; NOTE the safety precaution of looking for a Volume label = BOOTING
           ; now to overwrite boot sector, so preserving an unchanged zone up to address 5eh.
 C11:            ;;IMPORTANT: As a safety precaution looking for 7 letters "BOOTING" is really necessary.

    call find_drive_that_has_volume_label_BOOTING
    cmp eax,544f4f42h                      ;WORD "BOOT" use as a volume label.
    jz find_ok
    call end_run_in_error_nofind
    ret
find_ok:
    cmp cx,99h                     ;error sign double check
    jnz find_ok2
    call end_run_in_error_nofind

    ret
find_ok2:
    jmp usb_ok_go_ahead1

   find_drive_that_has_volume_label_BOOTING:

       lea edi,device                          ;short text which has the open drive symbol "\\.\f:",0
       mov byte ptr [edi+4],"g"                ;start with drive f (might start with drive g too?)
    retries:
       lea esi,usb_boot_sector                 ;a 200h bytes area in the data section
       call align_esi
       mov dword ptr [esi+36h],0               ;erase field of "FAT16" word
       mov dword ptr [esi+52h],0               ;erase field of "FAT32"
```

```
        mov word ptr [esi+0eh],0              ;erase field
        mov word ptr [esi+16h],0                      ;erase field

        pushad
        call read_usb_boot_sector
        popad

        mov eax,[esi+36h]
        cmp eax,31544146h                     ;Look for "FAT1" in +36h.  46h="F".  41h="A".  54h=T?  33h="3"  31h="1"
        jnz not_the_right_drive
        mov ax,3631h                          ;It MUST be FAT16. This worked.
        cmp ax,[esi+39h]
        jnz not_the_right_drive

        mov eax,[esi+52h]                     ;I thought I wanted to specifically avoid fat32
        cmp eax,33544146h                     ;Avoid  "FAT3" of FAT32 in +52h
        jnz usb_check_volume_label

not_the_right_drive:

        lea edi,device
        mov al,[edi+4]
        dec al                                ;from g or f to e
        mov [edi+4],al
        cmp al,"e"
        jb drive_not_found                    ;after trying several drive numbers, its sure something was wrong.
        cmp al,"f"
        jz retries
        cmp al,"e"
        jz retries

drive_not_found:
        mov cx,99h                            ; signal
        mov eax,0 ;
        db 0c3h

usb_check_volume_label:

        mov eax,0
        mov ax,[esi+16h]                      ;read number of sectors per fat
        add eax,eax                           ;x2 assuming 2 copies of fat
        add ax,[esi+0eh]            ;add no of reserved sectors, result points to directory and volume label directly
        push esi
        lea esi,usb_directory_sector          ;An extra added safety. Volume label must be "BOOTING"
        call align_esi

        mov dword ptr [esi],0                 ;erase field in which VOLUME NAME will be
        pushad
        call read_usb_sector_ax               ;! new makes eax times 512 as pointer for invoke
```

```
        popad
        ;;Reading the  volume label is the very important safety precaution which makes the program safe enough.

        mov eax,[esi]                   ;read volume label.
        mov edx,[esi+4]                 ;read volume label the next 3 letters
        pop esi
                                        ;Volume Label has to be BOOTING  IMPORTANT
                                        ;as a safety precaution looking for word BOOTING is essential.
        cmp eax,544f4f42h               ;4 letters WORD "BOOT"
        jnz not_the_right_drive
        and edx,0ffffffh                ;keep 3 1st letters
        cmp edx,474e49h                 ; The Word part "ING"

        jnz not_the_right_drive
        ret                             ;return successfully it has found the volume label
        ;                    ;Note: it might be safer to try instead looking for a volume label like the word "FIND"
;----------------------------------------------------
view_hex2:
        pushad
        call find_drive_that_has_volume_label_BOOTING

        mov ecx,actual
        cmp ecx,512
        jz view_hex3
        mov eax,0
        cmp dword ptr which_one,1                       ;unless dvd
        jnz view_hex3
        call clear_away_input                   ;erase the view whenever no stick is plugged in.

   view_hex3:
        popad
        db 0c3h

clear_away_input:
        lea ebx,usb_boot_sector
        mov cx,240h
        mov eax,0
cle1:
        mov [ebx],al
        inc ebx
        dec cx
        jnz cle1
        lea ebx,usb_directory_sector
        mov cx,240h
        mov al,0
  cle2:
        mov [ebx],al
        inc ebx
        dec cx
```

```asm
        jnz cle2
        db 0c3h

usb_ok_go_ahead1:
        pushad
        mov eax,0                           ;0=black pixels
        call clear_away
        mov text_gone,1                     ; it does find the volume label and goes here.
        popad
usb_ok_go_ahead:
        mov edi,esi
        mov byte ptr [edi+1],5ch            ;overwrite relative jump displacement to aim it at boot loader
        mov word ptr [edi+5eh],9090h        ; Two NOPs at jump's target.
        lea ebx,my_boot_loader_code_start

        mov ecx,200h
        sub ecx,60h
        transfer:
        mov al,[ebx]                        ;read 1 byte from the boot loader program
        mov [esi+60h],al                    ;copy it to the boot sector of the usb memory stick
        inc ebx
        inc esi
        dec ecx
        jnz transfer
        mov word ptr [edi+1feh],0AA55h      ;A boot-ability signature the right way round

        mov eax,"ABCD"
        mov [edi+1fah],eax
        pushad
        call write_usb_boot_sector
        popad
        mov dword ptr [edi+1fah],"    "
        pushad
        call read_usb_boot_sector
        popad
        ;------------------ only to see the directory
          mov eax,0
          lea esi,usb_boot_sector
          call align_esi

        mov ax,[esi+16h]                    ;read number of sectors per fat
        add eax,eax                         ;x2 assuming 2 copies of fat
        add ax,[esi+0eh]                    ;add no of reserved sectors, result points to directory and volume label directly

        lea esi,usb_directory_sector        ;
        call align_esi

        mov dword ptr [esi],0               ;erase field where volume label will be
        pushad
```

```
            call read_usb_sector_ax          ; makes eax as a sector pointer times 512 for invoke
            popad
            jmp done_ok

align_esi:    and si,0ffe0h                  ;Because the Qeditor did not do align 20h??
              add esi,20h                    ;do not call this align more than once or it would increase the address
              ret
align_edx:    and dx,0ffe0h
              add edx,20h
              ret

end_run_in_error:

            mov dword ptr usb_boot,1111h
            jmp other_errors

upper:
            db "Saving boot-loader",0 ;

lower:
        db "Error:",0dh,0ah,"Did not find a Volume Label of the 7 letter word   BOOTING",0dh,0ah,0dh,0ah," and Fat 16",0

other_error:
            db " There was another error",0
no_16:
            db "Error No Fat16 drive",0
no_errors:
            db " Apparently done Ok",0

end_run_in_error_no_16:
            lea eax,no_16
            jmp mess
done_ok:
         lea eax,no_errors
         jmp mess
other_errors:   lea eax,other_error
            jmp mess
end_run_in_error_nofind:
         lea eax,lower
mess:
      mov notes_on,44

    push MB_OK                               ;;;MB_YESNO     ; alone, result goes into eax, 6=yes 7=no.
    push offset upper
    push eax
    push 0
    call MessageBox
    ret
```

```
;---------------
   ; This is for 16 bit mode and 16 bit mode bios to be used.
   ;THIS goes onto the boot sector after offset 60h. 60h not 40h
   ; from offset 0 to 5ch, kept almost unchanged.

        nop                  ; NOTE I see that the Qeditor creates E8.n.n.n.n calls. Booting needs n.n?

 my_boot_loader_code_start:              ;a label for the lea just above here. Or use b0 instead.

;----------------  it was written in 16 bit mode for running in Real Mode and converted into data bytes

        cli   ;
```

;; BOOT-LOADER should go just below here. **But this text does not show the boot-loader**

My boot-loader has to be written in the 16 bit Real mode way, and I do not know how to include a
16 bit real mode program with the Qeditor assembler, into a program which is mainly 32 bit??
Therefore when I used the Qeditor I converted my boot-loader into data bytes
and entered it all here as data bytes.
I have converted a version of my Booting-aids_2 to assemble with the FASMW assembler, and its very
interesting FILE directive can let you include an assembled 16 bit binary program right here anywhere
in the middle of your program. Just write the label, FILE, and the path and file name in single quotes without a
terminal zero. For example, (For the Fasmw assembler)

```
   my_boot_loader_code_start: FILE 'usb_loader.BIN'        ;The FILE directive will insert the 16 bit program
```

;(End of your boot-loader is here.)

;========= USB was often drive F. read sectors instead of files, open drive in stead of open file

```
read_usb_boot_sector:
  invoke CreateFile,ADDR device,GENERIC_READ,FILE_SHARE_READ OR
FILE_SHARE_WRITE,0,OPEN_EXISTING,FILE_FLAG_NO_BUFFERING,0
  mov hcf,eax

  invoke SetFilePointer,hcf,0,0,FILE_BEGIN          ;1st number after handle is a bytes address, in multiple of 1
sector's bytes
  lea ecx,actual                                    ;where the invoke should give you its actual length read
  lea edx,usb_boot_sector
  call align_edx

  invoke ReadFile,hcf,edx,512,ecx,0                        ;It does read the boot sector of the USB stick.

  invoke CloseHandle,hcf          ;when handle closed after, it produced same 0BCh handle every time run
  ret

write_usb_boot_sector:
```

```
    invoke CreateFile,ADDR device,GENERIC_WRITE,FILE_SHARE_READ OR
FILE_SHARE_WRITE,0,OPEN_EXISTING,FILE_FLAG_NO_BUFFERING,0      ;open existing seems necessary,
    mov hcf,eax

    invoke SetFilePointer,hcf,0,0,FILE_BEGIN
                ;1st number after handle in Set File pointer, is a bytes address, in multiple of 1 sector's bytes
    lea ecx,actual                          ;where the invoke should give you its actual length read
    lea edx,usb_boot_sector
    call align_edx
;Warning Danger: The invoke WriteFile would seriously damage the computer if the drive letter used to
; open the drive was accidentally the letter for the hard drive.
;Safety precautions are always essential to make sure it won't write onto the hard drive.

    invoke WriteFile,hcf,edx,512,ecx,0              ;Be very careful with this invoke!

    invoke CloseHandle,hcf ;
    ret
;------------------------------

    read_usb_sector_ax:

    push eax
    invoke CreateFile,ADDR device,GENERIC_READ,FILE_SHARE_READ OR
FILE_SHARE_WRITE,0,OPEN_EXISTING,FILE_FLAG_NO_BUFFERING,0
    mov hcf,eax
    pop eax
    mov ecx,512
    imul ecx
                ;in set file pointer, 1st number after handle is a bytes address, in multiple of 1 sector's bytes
    invoke SetFilePointer,hcf,eax,0,FILE_BEGIN
    lea ecx,actual                          ;where the invoke should give you its actual length read

    lea edx,usb_directory_sector            ;directory
    call align_edx

    invoke ReadFile,hcf,edx,512,ecx,0       ;Just Reading should be quite safe, but not writing.

    invoke CloseHandle,hcf          ;when handle closed after, it produced same 0BCh handle every time run

    ret
;================================================================
```

How to Enable the A20 Address Line.

Most computers are supposed to start running with the A20 address line in a disabled state, and one of the first things a bootable program has to do is enable the A20. I read about several different ways of doing it but only one of the methods worked when I tried them, which this one.

```
a20enable:  mov al,0d0h         ;0d0h=command "read output port"
            out 64h,al   ;
     en1:   in al,64h           ;read the status register (a read from 64h)
            test al,1           ;b0 tested, z if not ready
            jz en1              ;wait until it is ready
            in al,60h
            or al,2             ;or 2 for enable GA20 gate A20
            mov cl,al           ;save it in cl
            mov al,0d1h         ;0d1h=command
            out 64h,al
     en2:   in al,64h           ;a second wait for the controller to be ready is definitely essential!
            test al,2           ;b1=0 when input buffer is ready & empty
            jnz en2             ;this one is nz if not ready
            mov al,cl
            out 60h,al          ; The output enables the A20. Only this method ever worked.
            ret
```

The A20 is the address line of the RAM memory which carries binary bit 20 of any RAM address, and so a 1 in this address line must be worth 1 meg byte.
When a PC starts running and when it is just switched on, the A20 is supposed to be in a disabled state. Books say there is a historical reason for it, that one very old software needed the A20 disabled.
Another method of enable the A20 **Does Not work,** but it is like this:

```
in al,92h
or al,2       ;Or 2 for A20 enable.
out 92h,al
```

It is supposed to work with most modern computers, but it **did not** work with my computers.
And I have read that sometimes the BIOS can enable the A20 like this:

```
mov ax,2401h
int 15h
cli
```

What do you see when the A20 is left in a disabled state? Without the A20 the computer is incapable of using binary bit 20 of address.
I wrote a bootable program which lets me type words anywhere in the RAM memory and see them with the screen, and I arranged for an indicator of the memory address of the area being viewed to be clear as a hexadecimal number on the upper edge of the screen. The page up/ page down keys let me scroll the memory up or down quickly. I typed words on the RAM memory at an address which I think was 2 Meg bytes, then when I scrolled the screen up and reached an address of 3 meg bytes, I was surprised to see my typing reappear. Typing at 4 meg bytes also reappeared at 5 meg bytes. So there was an illusion of duplications. False

duplications seemed to be there.

I arranged for the program to enable the A20 when I pressed a certain key, and immediately when I pressed that key the illusion of duplications vanished!

Theoretically one can find out whether the A20 is enabled or disabled by testing the memory for that false illusion of duplications. I thought of an idea which you can try when in 32 bit addressing mode:

```
mov ebx,400000h            ;[ebx] to address 4 MB
mov [ebx],41h              ;write letter "A"
cmp byte [ebx+100000h],41h ;does the A appear by illusion at + 1 MB?
Jnz enabled                ;when not equal, for sure the A20 is enabled
mov [ebx],43h              ;Write letter "B", essential to try a second number
cmp [ebx+100000h],43h      ;is there an illusion of duplication 1 MB away?
Jnz enabled
mov al,"D"                 ;return with letter D for disabled
ret
enabled:
mov al,"E"
ret                        ;return with letter E for enabled
```

Call a20enable worked well with several computers, but one particular computer seemed to think a key was being held down on the keyboard, after the first method worked. Call release_key (called only once) seemed to stop that problem which I had with only one computer. It is intended to put into port 60h any number greater than 80h so as to give the impression that a key has been let go or released. It might be better not to use release_key.

```
release_key:    mov ch,82h      ; THIS called once just after enable A20 screen run problem

    akb4:   in al,64h
            test al,2  ;
            jnz akb4
            mov al,0d2h            ;note: The replacing only works after a strange delay,
            out 64h,al             ;and might wait until the vertical retrace signal ends.
    arepl1: in al,64h   ;
            test al,2   ;
            jnz arepl1  ;

            mov al,ch              ;Any number above 80h
            out 60h,al
            in al,60h
            ret
```

Reading inputs from the PS2 type keyboard and the mouse.

When the mouse is not active you read scan codes from the PS2 type keyboard with a single simple operation, which is " in al,60h."

I then use my own conversion table to make the computer convert a keyboard scan code into an ascii character code. All text in a computer is in the form of ascii code. The laptop's built in keyboard was the same as a PS2 type keyboard.

A USB type keyboard is very different with completely different codes, but sometimes when you have a USB keyboard the BIOS uses its own complex USB programming to make it seem as if you have a PS2 type keyboard. And that is useful if it happens, especially because you can then use "in al,60h" with the USB keyboard even though it is naturally quite different.

I found that the touch-pad of my laptop PC is exactly the same as a PS2 type of mouse.

If the PS2 mouse is activated, then unfortunately the mouse data inputs appear at port 60h too, that is mouse input and keyboard input both appear at exactly the same port.

Because both inputs appear at exactly the same port, two tests need to be carried out to find out which data comes from the mouse and which data comes from the keyboard. If you activate the mouse without using these two tests, all sorts of things go wrong when mouse data and keyboard data get mixed up. For example every time you move the mouse, random letters can be typed at your typing cursor. When the mouse is turned off, the wonderfully simple operation "in al,60h" is all that you need.

I solved my problem by writing **a subroutine, "keyboard"** which does the tests in its first 10 operations. Then I looked through my old program replacing every "in al,60h" with a "call keyboard". That worked well.

When the data input comes from the keyboard then "call keyboard" has exactly the same effects as the one single operation "in al,60h". But if the data input comes from the mouse/touchpad, then the subroutine detects that and instead it jumps to do mouse operations. Its jump to do mouse operations was useful to make a mouse caret and move about its co-ordinates, and detect mouse clicks. (I meant a mouse caret can be made and moved with programming.)

To tell apart the keyboard data and mouse data, **the two tests** that have to be carried out are these:

In al,64h   ;from port 64h
Test al,1   ;Its result is NZ when there is "New" data at port 60h.

The second test is:
In al,64h
Test al,20h   ;Its result is NZ if data comes from the Mouse/touch-pad, Z if coming from keyboard.

When you read input from port 60h, this changes the result you get from the first test because once it has been read the data there is "considered no longer new".

What is the mouse input?

The form of the mouse input is of 3 bytes. The first byte carries the mouse button click indication as its 2 or 3 lowest binary bits get set when you click the mouse buttons.

The second byte is the mouse X movement. It is a small number which can be either positive or negative. And it is positive when mouse moves to the right.

The third byte is the mouse Y movement, it can be either positive or negative, and moving upward is positive. I set the mouse into "Stream mode" so it sends 3 bytes of data whenever it moves or its buttons are clicked. (In front of these 3 useful bytes, there might be a byte which has a fixed unchanging value, such as FAh)

keyboard:
        in al,64h
        test al,1   ;z= nothing new,   nz= something new

```
            jnz newin
            mov al,[39420h]          ;if nothing new read a previous keyboard input and return
            ret                      ;return with a keyboard scan code in the AL register.
newin:      test al,20h              ;z=from keyboard;  nz=from mouse, (and I am trying stream mode)
            jnz mouseoperations      ;important jump to do the mouse.
            in al,60h                ;read something you know is new from the keyboard
            mov [39420h],al          ;save that somewhere, anywhere,  in memory
            ret                      ;return with a new keyboard scan code in the AL register.
```

This worked when I had set the laptop's built-in touch pad to "stream mode". Assuming that the built-in touch pad is the same thing as a PS2 mouse. Note: sometimes mouse data is in 4 bytes, and the first of the 4 is a fixed number like 0FAh which needs to be ignored.

```
mouseoperations:                     ;to this spot when the mouse is sending 3 bytes in stream mode
            push ebx
            push ecx
            push edx
            mov dx,3                 ;3 because the mouse data was 3 bytes.
            mov ecx,100000h
            mov ebx,39400h           ;[ebx]=any address you want to store the mouse input data.
    nmouse3:
            in al,60h
            mov [ebx],al             ;mouse input data.
            inc ebx
            dec dx
            jz nmouse4
    nmouse2:
            in al,64h
            test al,1
            jnz nmouse1              ;nz= something new is there
            dec ecx
            jnz nmouse2
    nmouse4:
            call mousecoordinates
            call cursor_ontocaret
            pop edx
            pop ecx
            pop ebx
            mov al,0                 ;zero in al for keyboard operations to skip
            ret
    nmouse1:
            test al,20h
            jnz  nmouse3             ;nz= it was from mouse
            in al,60h
            mov [39420h],al          ;write a keyboard input that might have been while typing.
            jmp nmouse2
```

```
                ;========================

mousecoordinates:

        mov ebx,39400h                  ;anywhere to save the mouse movement

        mov dl,[ebx+1]                  ;mouse x movements
        movsx edx,dl                    ;sign extend of 1 byte into 4 bytes
        add edx,[ebx+10h]               ;caret X
        jns mou1
        mov edx,10
    mou1:
        cmp edx,900                     ;limits of some kind on the distance the caret co-ordinates can go.
        jb mou2
        mov edx,890
    mou2:
        mov [ebx+10h],edx               ;saves changed X

        mov dl,[ebx+2]
        movsx edx,dl                    ;sign extend from dl to edx
        add edx,[ebx+14h]  ;caret Y
        jns mou3
        mov edx,10
    mou3:
        cmp edx,500
        jb mou4
        mov edx,490
    mou4:
        mov [ebx+14h],edx               ;saves changed Y
        call sqa                        ;call to draw a small mouse caret
        ret

                ;------------------------------------
```
In the above test the mouse input was in 3 bytes. In some other experiments the mouse input was of 4 bytes, but then the 1st byte was always a fixed unchanging number such as 0FAh or 01, which you can ignore, while you use the next 3 bytes.

Sqa is to draw nothing but a small square mouse caret. Just before drawing the small square, it draws it in a colour that will not be used for other things, so that a program can recognize that colour and therefore know where the caret is. That was a new idea for me.

```
  sqa:
        pushad                          ;note address of text when colour fcfc detected to be 39418h for now.

        mov esi,3a000h                  ;addresses VBE mode information, assuming it has been read into memory

        mov ecx,0
        mov cx,[esi+10h]                ;bytes per vertical intended

        mov ebx,39400h                  ;to address caret variables
        mov eax,500                     ;move down from top left corner
```

```
        sub eax,[ebx+14h]              ;caret Y correct direction subtract moves upwards on the screen
        jnb sz2
        mov eax,10
    sz2:
        imul ecx

        add eax,[ebx+10h]              ;caret x not x4 if you assume 256 colour mode
        add eax,14000000h                 ;top left corner plus X
        mov ebx,eax

        mov eax,0fdfdfdfdh             ;a colour which will be looked for to set text cursor onto caret.
        mov cl,12
        cmp ebx,14000000h
        jb sz3
        mov edx,0
        mov dx,[esi+10h]               ;Vertical. Imul erased edx
    sz: mov [ebx],eax
        mov [ebx+4],eax
        add ebx,edx                    ;Vertically downwards
        dec cl
        jnz sz
    sz3:
        popad
        ret
```

Setting stream mode.

This below **set the laptop's touch pad into stream mode,** but to activate a separate mouse some more might need to be added to this.

This stream mode start had to be called once or maybe twice to set the laptop touchpad or PS2 mouse into stream mode. After stream mode was set, the mouse was turned off and it had to be enabled to turn it on.

It might not always be enough on its own to activate a mouse?

```
            stream_start:

                mov al,0d4h
                out 64h,al
    dit6s:      in al,64h
                test al,2
                jnz dit6s
                mov al,0eah    ;
                out 60h,al                     ;0f0h=would set remote mode . 0EAh=set stream mode
                mov ecx,3000h
    we1:
                in al,60h
                dec ecx
                jnz we1
```

```
            mov al,0d4h                      ;next 0f4h does enable mouse in stream mode.
                                             ;This enable mouse has to be AFTER the setting of stream mode.
            out 64h,al
    dit4s:  in al,64h
            test al,2
            jnz dit4s                        ;The F4 has to be sent after setting into stream mode.

            mov al,0f4h                      ;f4h=enable the mouse (f5h=disable)
            out 60h,al
            mov ecx,3000h
    we2:
            in al,60h
            dec ecx
            jnz we2
        ;;  mov al,0aeh                      ;0aeh= enable keyboard is essential? ?
        ;;  out 64h,al
            Ret
```

This should be called once when a program starts if it is necessary to activate the mouse?

```
Active_mouse:
        Mov al,0A8h                  ;0A8h=enable auxiliary device
        Out 64h,al
        Mov al,0d4h                  ;0D4h=command "write to Auxiliary device"
        Out 64h,al
Ac1:
        In al,64h                    ;wait until it becomes ready
        Test al,2
        Jnz Ac1
        Mov al,0ffh                  ;0ffh=mouse internal self test? Activated the mouse.
        Out 60h,al
        ret
```

Conversion of PS2 keyboard scan codes into ascii character codes.

My bootable programs use a small conversion table to convert a scan code into an standard ascii code for the alphabetical letters, characters, since all the text in computers is stored in the form of ascii code.

(ascii stands for American standard code for information interchange. And ascii is sometimes pronounced as "Asky".)

I have always believed that it was better to avoid the Bios in this particular case and use my own conversion table. To use the conversion table is very simple. You just load into an address register the address of where the table starts, and add to it the simple keyboard scan code.

The address made by that sum is pointing exactly to the ascii character code in the table. Then you just read that byte from the table, and you have the alphabetical code which is ready for typing. In the example below here I just happened to make the scan code conversion table start in address 39500h for unshifted and 39600h for shifted.

When the touchpad or mouse is not active, you read PS2 keyboard scan codes with the simple operation "in al,60h" When the mouse or touchpad is activated in stream mode, it is better to use my short program "keyboard" or call keyboard, to get the scan code into the AL register. (to avoid typing meaningless characters every time the mouse moves).

Anyway with the example here, these 4 operations would convert a scan code into an ascii alphabetical code for unshifted letters:

```
In al,60h                ;In al60h or alternatively call keyboard.
mov ebx,39500h           ;table start address.
mov bl,al                ;scan code is as an offset
mov al,[ebx]             ;read the ascii alphabetical code.
```

A conversion table which converts a PS2 keyboard scan code into an ascii alphabetical code, has 1 byte per scan code for unshifted letters, and 1 byte per scan code for shifted letters. For that you make 2 small tables, one for shifted and one for unshifted letters.

A byte in memory should be used to keep track of whether the shift key has been pressed and whether it was let go. The keeping track of the shift key should be done with your own programming , and you can use for it the scan code of the left shift key is 02Ah when the shift key is pressed, 0AAh when the left shift key is released.

The scan code for the right side shift key is 36h when the shift key is pressed, 0B6h when the right side shift key is released. You look for those 4 numbers and record the shift key state in a 1 byte variable.

The Ps2 type keyboard gives you scan codes. For example, "Q" to "P" keys scan codes are 10h to 19h; "A" to "L" scan codes are 1Eh to 26h; "Z" to "M" scan codes are 2Ch to 32h; and "1" to "9" scan codes are 2 to 0ah; and "F1" to "F10" scan codes are 3bh to 43h. The left shift scan code is 2Ah and right shift is 36h. When a key is released the scan code has number 80h added to it, for example the "Q" key's scan code changes from 10h when pressed to 90h released. This add of 80h on release was very useful.

The keyboard scan codes have to be converted to ascii for typing to work. For example, the keys 1 to 9 on the top row of the PS2 type keyboard have scan codes 02 to 0Ah, while the ascii code for "1" is 31h and the ascii code for 9 is 39h. So the number 02 will have to be converted into 31h when you type.

One has to have 2 tables or 2 parts to a table, one for lower case letters and the other for shifted capital letters.

The principle for reading from the table is always that you use the scan code as an address displacement, which is added to the table's start address. You add the scan code to the address of where the table starts.

And then reading 1 byte from the table reads the ascii code.

The table has to contain the series of 1 byte ascii characters, in an order in which the distance from the start of this table is equal to the equivalent scan code. So that the scan code can be used as a +d address displacement or distance from the start for reading the 1 byte ascii code from the table.

There are many different ways of putting such tables in the memory, and the following method looks unnecessarily complicated. But the reason for it was that I felt the program might run anywhere in the memory after booting and so the assembler would not know exactly where the program was running or what value was in the Instructions Pointer at start. Though the method looks strange the intention was to let it work when the assembler does not know what address it will run in.

The method is intended to be called only while in real mode and it is Not necessary if you manage to tell the assembler where the program will be running. The scan code table had to be copied from wherever it happens to be to an fixed address which I know exactly.

```
copy_scan_conversion_table:
            jmp scan1
  scan3:    add bx,3                    ;exactly 3 or the whole table is shifted wrongly
            push cs
            pop es
            mov ax,3900h                ;un-shifted alphabet table to go to 3900:500h
            mov ds,ax                   ; from +d=0
            mov cx,60h                  ;need exact length because shifted table is just beyond it
            mov si,500h                 ;[si] to write scan code to asc2 converting table
  scan4:    mov al,[es:bx]
            mov [si],al
            inc ebx
            inc esi
            dec cx
            jnz scan4

            mov cx,60h                  ;shifted capitals table to go to 3900:600h from d=+60h
            mov si,600h                 ;[ds:si] to write scan code to asc2 converting table
  scan5:    mov al,[es:bx]
            mov [si],al
            inc ebx
            inc esi
            dec cx
            jnz scan5
            ret
  db "scan code to ascii convert table"
  scan1:
            call scan2                  ;call to here
  scan2:    pop bx                      ;popped return address +4 should point to tables start.
            jmp scan3                   ; NOTE: This Jump has a 1 byte displacement.

  dd  32310000h,36353433h,30393837h,00003d2dh       ;its start = 00,00,31h,32h
  dd  72657771h,69757974h,5d5b706fh,73610000h       ;
  dd  68676664h,3b6c6b6ah,23000027h,7663787ah       ;
```

```
dd  2c6d6e62h,00002f2eh,00002000h,0            ;

dd  0,0,0,0                                    ;+40h to +4fh?
dd  0,5c0000h,0,0                              ;50h to 5fh?? but in [556h] need a 5ch for the scan 56h "\"
                                               ; "~" = 7eh and scan code is 2bh +shift key.
dd  22210000h,5e25247fh,29282a26h,00002b5fh         ;+d starting= +60h?
                                                    ;7fh the £ symbol is only non standard one   ?
dd  52455751h,49555954h,7d7b504fh,53410000h
                                               ;gaps of zeroes are for the non-alphabetical keys.
dd  48474644h,3a4c4b4ah,7e000040h,5643585ah
dd  3c4d4e42h,00003f3eh,00002000h,0
dd  0,0,0,0
dd  0,7c0000h,0,0
        mov si,0656h
        mov word   [si],07ch                   ;the | key
        ret                                    ; scan codes to asky table finished

;;;;;;;;;;;;;;;;;;;;;;;;;;;;;;;;;;;;;;;;
```

Finding the higher resolution screen memory's address: The physical base pointer.

A computer has more than one access to screen memory. As a PC starts it is in a low resolution screen mode and this uses the older screen memory access starting at address B800:00 with 16 bit addressing, (Segment:IP), which is [B8000h] with 32 bits addressing. With some older screen modes, such as when you set firstly mode number 12h then number 13h, it starts at [0A0000h]. The older screen is mainly useful at the moment when the computer starts, and later on you would want to use the higher resolution screen.

Obviously the higher resolution screen usually looks better than the older screen. You normally want to set a medium or high resolution screen mode which uses the larger screen memory, and for that you need to be able to switch the computer into a 32 bit addressing mode. The Bios can both set a high resolution screen mode and also give you its starting address. But setting 32 bit addressing has to be done with your own Global descriptor table,.

The starting address of the high resolution screen is often 0d0000000h.

That is Zero "d" followed by 7 zeroes, and then the letter "h". Another common address for it is 0c0000000h.
 This is Zero "c" followed by 7 zeroes and then the letter "H". Other addresses are possible such as maybe 0b0000000h and 80000000h.

The start address of the main screen memory is also called a "physical base pointer". A number written to that exact address creates a single pixel at the very top left corner of the screen, and adding a small number to this address moves the pixel to the right across the screen.

Adding to this address a number called "bytes per scan line" moves the pixel vertically downwards by one scan line on the screen. It is useful to know the number which moves the pixel address vertically downwards.

I think the Bios which sets screen modes is called **"Vesa Bios extensions of VBE 1.2 (1991) and of VBE 2.0 (1994)** Its complete specification is easy to find with Google. Apparently the list of all its screen modes goes from numbers 4100h to 411Bh which means there are 28 of them.

To use the Bios to set one of these high resolution screen modes, is easy, you load the code 4f02h into the AX register, and you load into the BX register the number of the screen mode you want, and then you simply run Int 10h. I think when it is success the Bios returns with the carry flag clear, but if it can't set that screen mode it returns with the carry flag set to indicate an error. For example, set screen mode 4103h:

Mov AX,4f02h   ;code of the bios function of set a screen mode into AX
Mov BX,4103h   ;A screen mode's number into BX
Int 10h   ;should set screen mode 4103h and if it can't it should set the cary flag.

Every different kind of computer is capable of setting different modes. For example my laptop does only 12 of them including 4101h and 4103h and 4105h these are three examples of screen mode numbers. Note: Whenever running Int 10h, the ebp register must contain only a small number, always of less than 64K.

There are several ways to find the address of the high resolution screen memory. You can try addresses until you find the right one by chance? You can ask the Bios for the information. You can find this address by looking in the "configuration space" using the configuration space mechanism?

Asking the Bios for information about the high resolution screen modes which it can set, and for the important **screen memory start address,** is done like this:

You load the code 4f01h into the AX register, and you load a screen mode number into the CX register, and you load the Di register and the ES segment register with an address so that the address [es:di] points to any empty area of memory of at least 256 bytes size, in which you want the Bios to automatically write the information. Then run Int 10h.

For example:

```
mov AX,3000h
mov ES,AX                       ;segment part of an address into ES
Mov DI,0                        ;IP part of an address into DI (    [ES:DI] points to an area)
Mov AX,4f01h                    ;code of the bios function into AX
mov CX,4103h                    ;A screen mode's number into CX (CX this time. Not BX)
Int 10h                         ;Int 10h  should fill an area of memory of
                                    ; 256 bytes with information about the screen mode.
                                ; After the int 10h Bios call has written the information at [ES:DI]
Mov EBX,[ES:DI+28h]             ;Read the important 32 bit start address of high resolution screen into EBX
Mov EDX,0
Mov DX,[ES:DI+10h]              ;read the important bytes per scan line number (Makes pixels go Vertically down)
```

The number of scan lines (Y resolution) number is read from [ES:DI+14h]

If the screen mode number you put into CX is the number of a screen mode which the particular computer is capable of, the Bios writes a lot of information starting at the address [es:di], but personally only a small fraction of the information seemed useful.

If the number in CX was not of a screen mode that the computer is capable of, the Bios won't write anything and it will return with the carry flag set?

The information which is most useful, **is the physical base pointer,** which you find **at offset +28h.**

That is you find it at the address [es:di+28h] and this number is the start address of the high resolution screen memory, which is the address of a single pixel at the top left corner of the screen. (The physical base pointer) The number is sometimes 0d0000000h or sometimes 0c0000000h but can vary.

It is usually a 32 bit number, but it might sometimes be 64 bit.

There is at offset +10h the important number of bytes per scan line. It is a 2 byte number.

There is at offset +14h the number of scan lines, or the Y pixels resolution, it is a 2 bytes number.

And at offset +19h a one byte number, bits per pixel?

So mov dx,[es:di+10h] for example loads the bytes per scan line number into dx for example.

 (ES: inside or outside the bracket, depending on the assembler's syntax?)

There is at offset +12h the number of pixels per scan line, a 2 bytes number, and when the mode is one that has 1 byte per pixel, this number is usually but not always the same as the number at +10h. Only the number at +10h should be used to move vertically downwards, by adding it to a screen address.

The best way to use the high resolution screens is definitely to switch the computer into 32 bit addressing firstly. I don't see any purpose for the bank switching, because it is surely a lot better to reach the whole high resolution screen in one go with 32 bit addressing, starting with the physical base pointer which is often 0d0000000h or 0c0000000h or some similar value. NOTE: When you use "Int 10h" the ebp register should contain only numbers which are definitely less than 64k. If ebp contained more than 64k then "int 10h" would crash.

```
set_any_mode:                   ;Attempt to set a screen mode, trying 3 of them and hope one will be set.
mov BX,4103h
call change_mode2
jnb mode_set_ok
mov BX,4101h
```

```
call change_mode2
jnb mode_set_ok
mov BX,4107h
call change_mode2
jnb mode_set_ok
ret
mode_set_ok:
ret

    change_mode2:                       ;call in 16 bit mode with the BX register already loaded.
                                ;called with a screen mode number, such as 4103h in BX for the set mode part.
        pushad                          ;All in 16 bit mode
        push ds
        mov ebp,100h            ;only make sure ebp is below 64k. avoids crash when int 10h .

        mov ax,4f02h            ;set a screen mode code 4f02h into AX.
        Push bx                 ;save the screen mode number which is in BX register
        int 10h                 ;This Int 10h should set the screen mode if the computer's bios has it.
        pop bx                  ;screen mode number transferred to CX register for "get information"
            mov cx,bx
            jnb mode_was_set
            ret
mode_was_set:

        mov ax,3a00h            ;Make [ES:DI] point to a blank area of memory
        mov es,ax               ; That area should get filled with information about the mode
        mov ax,4f01h            ;"Get VBE mode information" code 4f01h into AX
        mov di,0
        int 10h                 ;Int 10h calls the BIOS
        nop                     ;at [es:di +10h] there should now be bytes/scan line number in 2 bytes.

        pop ds
        popad       ;
        ret
```

Another way to find the physical base pointer.
I mentioned that I think you can find the physical base pointer by reading it from the configuration space. The configuration space can be read using the configuration space mechanism, and if you copy the whole of it into the normal RAM memory you see it has 256 bytes wide zones which each belong to different integrated circuits.
I think that if your program looks at each of these zones for the class code 30000h at offset +9 relative to the start of the zone, this finds a zone which belongs to a graphics device. Then, if you read a 32 bit number from offset +18h (offset relative to the start of the zone) then this number might be the "physical base pointer".
 (The start address of the high resolution screen memory) . The lowest 3 bytes of that 32 bit number should be cleared to 0, as they don't count, for example clear them to zero by AND 0ff000000h. But I don't know if this way works with most computers?

Drawing onto the screen memory

The medium and high resolution screen modes are of 3 kinds, those which have 1 byte per pixel, and modes with 3 or 4 bytes per pixel. I think I prefer the screen modes where there are 4 bytes per pixel. The 4 bytes per pixel means that you can get perfect colours when you view bitmap pictures, and the addressing is simple too.

When there is 1 byte per pixel, there are 256 colours, and adding +1 to the screen address moves the address to the right, it draws the next pixel 1 pixel position to the right of the previous pixel on the screen. Adding the number called "bytes per scan line", to the screen address, moves the pixel vertically downwards by 1 scan line.
Technically the screen memory bytes in the 1 bytes per pixel modes, are automatically used to address one out of 256 groups of 3 DAC registers in the computer. For example a pixel made by a byte containing number 10 will automatically address the 10th group of 3 DACs and cause their colour to be seen in that pixel. These DAC registers hold 3 numbers for Blue, green, red, and there actually is a way to write into these DACs yourself, either using registers or using Bios to do it. If you change the values in some of those DACs registers, the colour of some screen bytes which will be changed by it.

I think the DACs are not used when the screen mode which you have set has either 3 or 4 bytes per pixel. This is because with those screen modes, 3 bytes of the screen memory directly specify the Blue, green and Red colours. And you get a very large number of different colours, it could be up to 256 cubed?

When there are 3 or 4 bytes per pixel, these bytes are in the order B.G.R. That is the first byte is for Blue, the second byte is for green, and the third byte is for red. When the screen mode set is one where there are 4 bytes per pixel, the 4th byte does nothing and it seems to be just a spacer. You move the pixels position by +1 to the right by adding +4 to the screen mode, if there are 4 bytes per pixel. Still adding the "bytes per scan line" number moves the pixel vertically downwards by 1 scan line down.

When there are 4 bytes per pixel, an address which is zero in its lower 2 binary bits will with +0 address the Blue colour, +1 to that address will address Green, and +2 will address the Red byte. +3 is the unused spacer byte.
You subtract -4 to move one pixel position to the Left, or subtract the bytes per scan line number to move vertically up.
One should not try to draw at addresses slightly lower in value than the start address, the physical base pointer, at the top left corner of the screen, as attempts to write into that unused area of address space might crash the computer. Writing below the bottom of the visible screen, did not crash.
You can find lots of information about BIOS screen modes with Google and VESA + BIOS
There is a list of screen modes in the pdf document "vbe20.pdf".

Examples of a few screen modes

Mode	dots	lines	Colours	Bits/pixel
4101h	640	480	256	8
4103h	800	600	256	8
4105h	1024	768	256	8
4107h	1280	1024	256	8
410Fh	320	200	16.8M	8:8:8
4110h	640	480	32k	1:5:5:5
4111h	640	480	64k	5:6:5
4112h	640	480	16.8M	8:8:8
4115h	800	600	16.8M	8:8:8
4118h	1024	768	16.8M	8:8:8
411Ah	1280	1024	64k	5:6:5
411Bh	1280	1024	16.8M	8:8:8

Drawing 8x8 pixels alphabetical characters on the graphics screen memory.

The 8x8 pixels table usually has 8 bytes for every alphabetical character. Each byte has 8 binary bits which stand for 8 pixels on the screen. The most significant binary bit of the first byte stands for the pixel at the top left corner of the alphabetical character. The least significant binary bit stands for the pixel on the top right corner of the character. The most significant bit of the second byte in the table stands for the pixel just below the top left corner of the letter. And so on. You normally test the binary bits and draw a pixel of the letter's colour when it was a binary "1", and you draw a background colour pixel when it was a binary "0". For example when you are drawing white characters on a black background you draw a black pixel when there is a binary 0, and draw a white pixel when there was a binary 1. The last pixel to be done is the bottom right corner of the character and its colour comes from the least significant binary bit of the last of the 8 bytes in the table.

You need an 8x8 pixels character pixel table. You can either use the table which is normally built into the computer's ROM, **or** you can type this table into the computer program yourself. When I tried both ways the results were almost identical. You have to know the start address of the high resolution screen memory, the so-called physical base pointer, which points to a single pixel at the top left corner of the high resolution screen. And you need to know the bytes per scan line number, and the number of bytes per pixel in the screen mode you use. Two common values for the physical base pointer are 0d0000000h and 0c0000000h. It is different with different computers.

When I typed the whole table into my program, it took a few days of work and it had to be perfectly accurate. The table I typed for all the standard alphabetical letters was 300h bytes long. It does not include lower 100h bytes for the all non-standard characters with codes below the 20h. 20h which is for a blank space, and is typed by the space bar.

To get the Bios to give to you the address of the 8x8 pixels table in the ROM, you are supposed to set a screen mode first which should get the Bios ready for giving you that address. A book said you set an old-fashioned mode such as 13h/0eh/4/5/6 for the Bios to give you 8x8 tables, or set old mode 12h/11h for 8x16 pixels tables, but when I tested a computer it worked well when you set any of the modern screen modes such as 4101h or 4013h or 4105h or 4107h so long as the computer is able to do that mode.

When you have set a screen mode, load the AX register with 1130h, and load the BH register with 3 when you want 8x8 tables or load BH with 6 when you want 8x16 tables. Then run Int 10h. For example:

Mov ax,1130h

mov bh,3

int 10h   ;Gets the address of the 8x8 character pixels table in the ROM into ES:BP registers combination.

It should return with ES:[BP] forming an address which points to the start of the character pixels tables in the ROM. What I did was to make the program copy the character pixel tables from the ROM to a fixed address in RAM. Obviously using the 8x8 character pixels table which is in the computer's ROM is much less work than typing it into your program, but I did type it into my programs as well and that took a few days of work. ("ES:" can be written into programs and it is called a segment override prefix. For different assemblers it can be written either as ES:[bp] or as [ES:bp].)

The method of using a character pixels table.

The simplest. 1) You have a byte which is assumed to be a ascii character code for text.
You multiply it by 8, because the table has 8 bytes of pixels per character.

2)   You add to it the address of where the table starts. This sum is the address of the first byte for that character, of the 8 bytes of pixels information which is for that alphabetical character.

3)   Now read the character pixels table for the character one byte at a time, each of the byte's 8 binary bits are for one screen pixel. With it write a horizontal row of 8 pixels onto the screen.

4)   Recover the screen address of the left side of the character. Move the screen address vertically down by 1 scan line. Repeat for the next 7 bytes read from the table, of 8 pixels each, to draw an 8x8 character.

How to call One_letter

;Assume that the AL register is already loaded with the assumed ascii code for a text character, and that the ESI register is already loaded with a screen address. The screen address in ESI depends on where you want the alphabetical character to appear on the screen. And assume that you know the start address of your 8x8 character pixels table. And in this example assume that the screen mode is with 1 byte per pixel, which is a 256 colour screen mode. This is a simplest case, it should draw a coloured letter on a black background. The data segment should be in its 32 bit addressing mode.

```
One_letter:                         ;call here with the DL register already loaded with a letter colour.
        Pushad                      ;and with DH loaded with a background colour such as 0 for black
        Mov ebx,0                   ;and call with ESI pointing to screen
        Mov bl,al                   ; Call with the AL register loaded with an alphabetical character code. (ascii).
        Add ebx,ebx   ;x2
        Add ebx,ebx
        Add ebx,ebx   ;x8
        Add ebx,start_address_of_pixels_table
        Mov ch,8                    ;ch to count down 8 bytes from character pixels table
One1:
        Mov al,[ebx]                ;read a byte with 8 binary bits standing for 8 pixels
        Inc ebx
        Mov cl,8                    ;count down 8 pixels
One3:
        Mov ah,dh                   ;a background colour which was stored in DH
        Add al,al                   ;add to itself shifts it to the left so bit 7 goes into the carry flag
        Jnb one2
        Mov ah,dl                   ;a letter colour which was stored in DL, whenever a binary 1 goes into carry flag
One2:
        Mov [esi],ah                ;write the pixel onto the screen memory (or sometimes onto a back screen)
        Inc esi                     ;screen address in esi is +1 ready for writing the next pixel
        Dec cl                      ;decrement countdown
        Jnz one3

        Mov [esi],dh                ;optionally erase a pixel at right hand edge of a character
        Sub esi,8                   ;recover esi then move it vertically downwards 1 scan line
        Mov eax,0
        Mov ax,bytes_per_scan_line_number   ;(this number can be found out with Bios get VBE mode info)
        Add esi,eax                 ;move vertically downwards
        dec ch                      ;count down 8 lines
        jnz one1
        Mov al,dh                   ;background colour to erase with
        Mov ah,dh
        Mov [esi],ax                ;optionally erase a few pixels just below a character
        Mov [esi+2],ax
        Mov [esi+4],ax
        Mov [esi+6],ax
        Popad
        ret
screen_full_text:
        mov ebx,start_of_bios_vbe_mode_info
        mov esi,[ebx+28h]           ;read the physical base pointer (address of screen's top left corner)
;;;mov esi,0d0000000h      ;;;mov esi,0c0000000h          ;physical base pointer common value
        Mov edi,area_to_be_viewed
        Mov DL,30h                  ;A letter's colour into DL, any colour
```

```
            Mov DH,0                      ;A background colour into DH, 0 for black background
            Mov ch,40                     ;number of rows of text count down number
Two1:
            Push esi
            Mov cl,32                     ;number of letters per each row count down
Two2:
            Mov al,[edi]                  ;read a byte which is text to be seen
            Call one_letter
            Inc edi
            Add esi,8                     ;move [esi] to the top left corner of the next character
            Dec cl
            Jnz two2
            Pop esi                       ;recover screen address after doing 1 row
            Mov eax,0
            Mov ax,bytes_per_scan_line_number
            Mov cl,9                      ;move [esi] Vertically downwards by the row spacing of either 8 or 9 pixels
Two3:
            Add esi,eax
            Dec cl
            Jnz two3
            Dec ch                        ;ch was for count down of rows
            Jnz two1
            Ret
```

To add a visible typing cursor: Note the text in memory was being read by the address In the EDI register. In a program I just happened to store the text's start address in a variable in [39000h] and store the typing cursor's address in [39004h]. This following could be added to the "one_letter" subroutine, just after a byte with 8 pixels in it is read from the character pixels table. A Not AL will invert the 1's and 0's at the typing cursor to make that cursor visible.

```
            cmp edi,[39004h]              ;cursor's address compare
            jnz one5
            not al
one5:
```

For making a screen which **shows all the memory as 2 digit hexadecimal numbers.**
The following example would convert a 1 byte number into two ascii letters for the corresponding 2 digit hexadecimal number. It can be used by "hexadecimal_screen:" subroutine.

```
    tohex:  mov ah,al                     ;call with al containing number.
            and ah,0fh                    ;returns with LS digit in ah, MS digit in al.
            add ah,30h                    ;0-9
            cmp ah,3ah
            jb tohex1
            add ah,7                      ;A-F
    tohex1: ror al,1
            ror al,1
            ror al,1
            ror al,1
            and al,0fh
            add al,30h                    ;text 0-9
```

```
            cmp al,3ah
            jb tohex2
            add al,7                    ;text A-F
    tohex2: ret


hexadecimal_screen:              ;Colours varying depending on the byte's hexadecimal value

         mov ebx,start_of_bios_vbe_mode_info
         mov esi,[ebx+28h]                        ;read the physical base pointer

   ;;;mov esi,0d0000000h      ;;;mov esi,0c0000000h          ;physical base pointer common values

         Add esi,256                ;move 8*32 pixels to the right along the top edge of the screen
         Mov edi,address_of_memory_area_to_be_viewed

         Mov DH,0                   ;A background colour into DH, 0 for black background
         Mov ch,40                  ;number of rows of text count down number
   hex1:
         Push esi                   ;push to save screen memory address
         Mov cl,32                  ;32=number of pairs of hex digit letters per each row count down
   hex2:
         Mov al,[edi]               ;read a byte which is to be seen as a 2 digit hexadecimal number
         Mov DL,7                   ;A letter's colour into DL, any colour for numbers below 20h
         Cmp al,20h
         Jb hex4
         Mov DL,30                  ;A letter's colour for values above 20h
   hex4:
         cmp al,80h
         jb hex5
         mov DL,50                  ;A any colour for numbers above ascii range
   hex5:
         Call tohex                 ;convert binary byte to 2 hexadecimal digits in ascii standard code

         Call one_letter            ;shows the more significant hex digit in AL

         Mov al,ah

         Add esi,8                  ;moves 8 pixels to the right
         Call one_letter            ;Draw the least significant hexadecimal digit

         Inc edi
         Add esi,9       ; 9 for 1 extra space. Move address [esi] to top left corner of the next 2 digit number
         Dec cl
         Jnz hex2
         Pop esi                    ;recover screen address after doing 1 row. It is now at the left hand edge.
         Mov eax,0
         Mov ax,bytes_per_scan_line_number
         Mov cl,9                   ;move [esi] vertically downwards by the row spacing of either 8 or 9
   hex3:
         Add esi,eax
         Dec cl
         Jnz hex3
         Dec ch          ;count down of rows
         Jnz hex1
```

Ret

8X8 Character pixels.

You can either load character pixels tables from the ROM or type character pixels tables into a program. Nearly all computers probably have these ROM tables. Before I knew how to load the 8x8 pixels tables from the ROM, I worked out the hexadecimal numbers for all the characters using illustrations of 8x8 character pixels which I found in an Amstrad manual for the CPC 6128, a computer which is obsolete now. When I typed the numbers into my program I got a text screen while the screen memory was in a graphics mode. When I found out how to load the ROM tables, I tried using them and I found that the result was almost exactly the same. I also tried 8x16 pixels tables from the ROM, and it worked, but it was a bit disappointing since I felt the 8x16 characters were not that much better than the 8x8 characters. I also tried writing a program that stretched the 8x8 tables into a new 8x11 pixels table, used as 8x12, and that was a slight improvement.

The method for loading the ROM tables. You should firstly set any standard screen mode. I have read that for some reason setting a screen mode first might be necessary. Then you load 1130h into the AX register. You load 3 into the BH register when you want to get 8x8 tables, or 6 into BH when you want to get 8x16 tables. Then run Int 10h, and it should return with ES:[BP] pointing to the character pixels tables from the ROM. The BIOS makes ES:[BP] point to the ROM pixels tables so that your program can use it.

In the example below, I had decided to erase an area with zeroes before starting. And I had decided to copy the ROM tables to an area of memory where I happened to be used to using character pixels tables. The useful parts of the tables start with ASCII code 20h for the blank space bar character. Because I thought the lowest part of the tables was useless, I decided to skip over it.

Since the lowest usable character was number 20h, and since there were 8 bytes in the 8x8 table per character the program skipped over the first 100h bytes (as 20hx8=100h).

```
;finds ROM pixels tables for 8x8 and 8x16

lf:     mov ax,3b00h            ; This should run while the computer is in real mode.
        mov ds,ax
        mov si,0
        mov cx,180h             ;cx for length to be erased

        xor eax,eax
lf3:    mov [si],eax            ;erase area with zero before starting
        add si,4
        dec cx
        jnz lf3

        mov ah,11h              ;always 11h?
        mov al,30h              ;always 30h?
        mov bh,6                ;bh=6 for 8x16 pixels
        int 10h                 ;returns with es:[bp] pointing to alphabet pixels table of rom

        mov ax,3b00h
        mov ds,ax
        mov si,0                ;ds:[si] to copy pixels table to a new place
        add bp,200h              ;skip over unusable part of pixels table
        mov cx,600h             ;length count

lf2:    mov al,es:[bp]          ;es:[bp] Reads Rom's table
        mov [si],al             ;Write it in a new place DS:[si]
        inc bp
        inc si
```

```
        dec cx
        jnz lf2                         ;8x16 pixels table done

        mov ah,11h                      ;always 11h?
        mov al,30h                      ;always 30h?
        mov bh,3                        ;bh=3 for 8x8 pixels
        int 10h                         ;returns with es:bp pointing to alphabet pixels table of rom

        mov ax,3800h                    ;to replace 8x8 pixels
        mov ds,ax
        mov si,100h                     ;ds:si to write pixels table in new place
        add bp,100h                      ;skip over unusable part of pixels table
        mov cx,300h                     ;length count

lf4:    mov al,es:[bp]
        mov [si],al
        inc bp
        inc si
        dec cx
        jnz lf4

        call stretching
        ret
```

;My routine which reads from an 8x8 pixels table and stretches it to create a new 8x11 pixels table
;works by duplicating three of the eight bytes, and while it reads 8 bytes from the old table it writes 11 bytes into the new table. Which three of the eight bytes have to be duplicated varies for different alphabetical characters, and the program first sets three binary bits in the ah register which control which three of the 8 bytes is to be duplicated to stretch the characters in the new table into 8x11 size. Address register DI happens to be used to read the old table, while address register BX writes the new table. It makes a slight improvement to the characters.
;The new table was used as **an 8x12 pixels table**.
; To slightly improve legibility of 8x8 characters, this was my experiment.

```
    stretching: mov bx,900h             ;3700:900h+ write new table  3800:100h+ read old table
                mov di,1100h            ;start address for asky blank of my table. I 300h bytes?
                mov ax,3700h
                mov ds,ax
                mov cx,20h              ;? letters count up from 20h

    str2:   mov ah,52h                  ;ah=three binary bits to control which 3 are duplicated
            cmp cl,67h
            jz str1
            cmp cl,70h
            jz str1
            cmp cl,71h
            jz str1
            cmp cl,79h
            jz str1

            mov ah,34h                  ;for the letter 'f'
            cmp cl,66h
            jz str1

            mov ah,4ch                  ;three binary bits are 1's to control which 3 are duplicated
            cmp cl,32h
            jz str1
```

```
                cmp cl,35h
                jz str1
                cmp cl,68h
                jz str1


                mov ah,54h              ;ah=three binary bits to control which 3 are duplicated
        str1:   mov dh,8                ;reads count down in dh
        str4:   mov al,[di]             ;read a byte from pixel table
                mov [bx],al             ;write it into new table
                inc di
                inc bx
                add ah,ah               ;shift a bit to carry. Always 3 binary bits in ah =1
                jnb str3
                mov [bx],al             ;duplicate when carry
                inc bx
        str3:   dec dh                  ;dh counts down 8 bytes read, 11 bytes written
                jnz str4
                mov al,0
                mov [bx],al             ;a 12th byte is always 0
                inc bx                  ;new table with 12 bytes spacing
                inc cx
                cmp cx,80h              ;compare to a maximum letter number
                jb str2
                ret
```

Typing the 8x8 character pixels tables into the program. The work of typing this into the program took about an hour a day for about a week.


```
        ;Note about stretching. 3700:900h+ write new table  3800:100h+ read old table
```

When I typed the 8x8 pixels tables into my program (something not really necessary since the ROM already has such a table) I wanted to copy my own table to an address which I knew exactly, as that seems better than not knowing its address. The short routine below uses a call then a POP BX, to get the instruction pointer (also called a program counter) into BX. Using CS:[BX] to read with. It then happens to search for a marking at the start of the table so it can recognize where it starts. The marking happened to be 7777h. Then it copies the table to an address which I happen to have used, using registers DS:[SI] .

```
        letters:   call letters2  ;
                   nop
        letters2:  pop bx                   ;pop return address from stack. call never needs to return
                   mov ax,7776h             ;search
                   inc ax
                   mov cx,100h
        letters5:  cmp [cs:bx],ax
                   jz letters4
                   inc bx
                   dec cx
                   jnz letters5
                   ret

        letters4:  add bx,2
                   mov ax,3800h
                   mov ds,ax
                   mov cx,400h              ;4x 256 or less lengh of table
                   mov si,100h              ;esi to write pixels
        letters6:  mov al,[cs:bx]
                   mov [si],al
```

```
        inc ebx
        inc esi
        dec cx
        jnz letters6
        ret


dw 7777h        ;at the start a visible marking searched for
dd        0,   0, 18181818h,00180018h        ; blank at 20h x8 then "!" character
dd  006c6c6ch,        00, 7cfe6c6ch,006c6cfeh    ; " character then # character
dd  3c483e18h,00187c12h, 18ccc600h,00c66630h    ; $ character then %
dd  76386c38h,0076ccdch, 00301818h,00           ; & and '
dd  3030180ch, 00c1830h, 0c0c1830h,0030180ch    ; ( and )
dd  0ff3c6600h, 00663ch, 7e181800h,01818h       ;   and +
dd         00,30001800h, 7e000000h,00000        ; ',' and -
dd         00, 181800h, 30180c06h,80c060h       ; '.' and /
dd  0d6cec67ch, 7cc6e6h, 18183818h,7e1818h      ; '0' and '1' Numbers at asky 30h
dd  3c06663ch, 7e6660h, 1c06463ch,3c6606h       ;2 and 3    was a mistake in lower half of 3
dd  98583818h, 3c18feh, 3c60627eh,3c6606h       ; 4 and 5
dd  7c60663ch, 3c6666h, 0c06467eh,181818h       ;  6 and 7
dd  3c66663ch, 3c6666h, 3e66663ch,3c6606h       ;8 and 9
dd  18180000h, 181800h, 18180000h,30181800h     ; ':' and ';'
dd  6030180ch, 0c1830h, 7e0000h,7e00h           ;< and =
dd  0c183060h, 603018h, 0c06663ch,180018h       ;> and ?
dd  0dedec67ch, 7cc0deh, 66663c18h,66667eh      ;@ and at 41h capital letter A
dd  7c6666fch, 0fc6666h,0c0c663ch,3c66c0h       ; B and C
dd  66666cf8h, 0f86c66h, 786862feh,0fe6268h     ; E and D
dd  786862feh, 0f06068h,0c0c663ch,7ec6ceh       ; F and G
dd  7e666666h,  666666h, 1818187eh,7e1818h      ;H and I
dd  0c0c0c1eh,  78cccch, 786c66e6h,0e6666ch     ; J and K
dd  606060f0h, 0fe6662h, 0fefeeec6h,0c6c6d6h    ;L and M
dd  0def6e6c6h,0c6c6ceh,0c6c66c38h,386cc6h      ; N and O
dd  7c6666fch, 0f06060h,0c6c66c38h,76ccdah      ;P and Q
dd  7c6666fch, 0e2666ch, 3c60663ch,3c6606h      ;R and S
dd  18185a7eh, 3c1818h, 66666666h,3c6666h       ;T and U
dd  66666666h,  183c66h,0d6c6c6c6h,0c6eefeh     ;V and W
dd  38386cc6h, 0c6c66ch, 3c666666h,3c1818h      ;X and Y
dd  188cc6feh, 0fe6632h, 3030303ch,3c3030h      ;Z code 5a, then '[' =5b
dd  183060c0h,   2060ch, 0c0c0c3ch,3c0c0ch      ; '\' and ']'
dd  187e3c18h,  181818h,       00,0ff0000h      ;small up arrow and '_'
dd  0c183000h,       00, 0c780000h,76cc7ch      ; '''  and then 'a' lower case letter 61h

dd  667ce0e0h, 0bc6666h, 663c0000h,3c6660h      ; b and c
dd  0cc7c0c1ch,  76cccch, 663c0000h,3c607eh     ;d and e
dd  78303c1ch,  783030h, 663e0000h,7c063e66h    ;f and g
dd  766c60e0h, 0e66666h, 18380018h,3c1818h      ;h and i
dd  060e0002h, 3c666606h, 6c6660e0h,0e66c78h    ; j and k
dd  18181838h,  3c1818h, 0fe6c0000h,0c6d6d6h    ; l and m
dd  66dc0000h,  666666h, 663c0000h,3c6666h      ; n and o
dd  66dc0000h,0f0607c66h,0cc760000h,1e0c7ccch   ;p and q
dd  6cd80000h, 0f06060h, 603c0000h,7c063ch      ;r and s
dd  307c3030h,  1c3630h, 66660000h,3e6666h      ;t and u
dd  66660000h,  183c66h,0d6c60000h,6cfed6h      ;v and w
dd  6cc60000h, 0c66c38h, 66660000h,7c063e66h    ;x and y
dd  4c7e0000h,  7e3018h, 7018180eh,0e1818h      ;z and {
dd  18181818h,  181818h, 0e181870h,701818h      ; | and }
dd      0d876h,       00,0f860663ch,0fe6660h    ;~ and £ making it 7f
dd        0,   0,        0,0
```

Windows Bitmap file and pictures (.bmp)

My bootable program was able to load and save files to USB memory sticks of either Fat16 or Fat32 format, and it was also able to load files (but not save) from a Fat32 partition on my Laptop's hard drive.

I gave it the ability to view pictures on the screen from Windows bitmap files, I mean the pictures which end with the file name extension ".bmp". The .bmp files are the only type of pictures file I understand.

Though these files are called bitmap, they have nothing to do with binary bits. On the contrary, at least one complete byte is used for one pixel.

While I was working on my bootable program improving the load and save function of files to USB memory sticks, I wanted a type of file in which you can easily see any mistakes caused by the loading and saving tests. And I used the .bmp files, since when there was any mistake in loading or saving you would immediately see something missing from the picture, or a grey distortion.

I gave my bootable program a kind of "print screen" function so when I pressed the key the visible screen was instantly made into a Windows bitmap file picture which I could then save to the memory stick. It was compatible with Windows.

Pictures under Windows can be saved in many different formats, but I noticed that many formats such as .JPG use a type of data compression which seems very difficult to understand, so I avoided them. The .bmp pictures are unusually easy to understand and simple. They either use no compression, and so picture data is simple, or they can use RLE-8 data compression, which is nearly simple and easy to understand. I thought it was important to chose the simplest. So I mainly used the no-compression .bmp pictures.

So I saved lots of pictures onto the Fat32 partition of the hard drive as .bmp, and practiced viewing the pictures with my bootable programs. (In Windows you can change the type from .jpg to .bmp when you save it).

The .bmp files are made mainly of simple picture data but at the start of the file there is a header. The header is easy to create and makes the picture compatible with the Windows operating system. The .bmp pictures data can be in several different forms.

Offset	Size	Value	Name
00	2	4d42h	The letters "BM"
2	4	Total File size in bytes	
6	4	0	Reserved binary zeroes
0Ah	4	Offset to the first byte of picture Data. (Often +36h)	
0Eh	4	28h	Size of this header section
12h	4	Image width in pixels	
16h	4	Image height in pixels	
1Ah	2	01	Fixed binary 1
1Ch	2	Binary bits per pixel. Often equals 8 or 24 or 32 (for 1 or 3 or 4 bytes per pixel)	
1Eh	4	Compression 0= No compression. 1=RLE-8 type compression	
22h	4	Data size in bytes. (slightly smaller than file size in bytes)	
26h	4	Horizontal pixels per Metre. (Windows software uses to zoom size)	
2Ah	4	Vertical pixels per Metre. "	
2Eh	4	Zero, or Number of pixels in colour Palette	
32h	4	Zero, or number of important colours in Palette	
36h		Image data often starts here, Blue byte, Green byte, Red byte, repeat B.G.R. Order.	

When the computer is in one of the screen mdes which have 3 bytes or 4 bytes per pixel, viewing the .bmp file picture is extra simple. Because you just copy the image data which starts at +36h onto the visible screen.

You have to have 3 or 4 count down numbers, while the data is being copied. One count down for the screen mode's number of pixels per screen width. One count down, for the .bmp image width in pixels. One stops and goes back to the left edge of the screen when either of those 2 count downs expires, and then start on the next scan line.

The copying of the data is ended when the count down image height in pixels expires. The colours should be perfect.

When the .bmp file has 1 byte per pixel, then the data can be copied simply onto the screen if the screen mode set is also 1 byte per pixel. But in this circumstance, the colours won't always come out right.

The .bmp file often in that case has a colour palette area, and the size of that palette is shown by the "number of pixels in the palette" field. The values in the palette, for Blue, Green, red can then be loaded into the computer's 256 groups of colour DAC registers, which could get the colours to come out just right.

In the circumstance when the computer's screen mode is 3 or 4 bytes per pixel, and when the .bmp picture has 1 byte per pixel, then if the .bmp file has a large colour palette section before the data starts, every 3 bytes in the palette correspond for B.G.R of 1 corresponding byte of pixel colour data in the .bmp file.

The value of 0-255 in the 1 byte pixel colour, should be multiplied by 3 and used as an index or offset into reading the .bmp file's palette. The way you use it is like this: Taking the address of where the palette area starts, use the actual value in the pictre data (1 byte per pixel) multiplied by 3, as an offset added to that base address which is where the palette starts, and use that new address to read just 3 bytes from the palette. Copy those 3 bytes directly from the palette to the screen memory of the computer. (In screen mode that has 3 or 4 bytes per pixel). In this case, there is no use for the computer's colour DAC registers, you don't need to load anything into them. (If 4 bytes per pixel, every 4th byte on the screen memory can be an ignored spacer).

The simplest and the best way was for the screen mode to be 3 or 4 bytes per pixel and the .bmp file to have 24 bits = 3 bytes per pixel, with no compression. Because then the colours should always come out perfect.

When both screen mode of the computer, and the bitmap file, have data as 3 bytes per pixel, the colours should naturally turn out perfect, and you never need to put a palette into the bitmap file.

But when the data in the file is 1 byte per pixel, the colours might not come out properly on the other computer because another computer might actually have different numbers in its colour DAC registers. The bitmap file should then have a palette, or 256 groups of 3 bytes, which the program can load into the other computer's colour DACs, and so make the colours come out identical on other computers. The palette has to be created by reading from the colour DACs of the first computer in that case.

This is a bit complicated. I think the following is the way I tried it in a test which worked ok.

```
;======= al=4105h color conversion to 4118h al=byte make AH=BLUE CL=GREEN CH=RED
 ;=========================================================
;To read from a color dac.
    Mov ax,1015h
      mov bx,1                    ;dac_reg_no 0 to 255?
      int 10h
                                  ;Result is CL=Blue, CH=Green, DH=Red.

;-------------------- To Read a long block of DAC registers in one go
    Mov ax,1017h
    Mov bx,0                      ;1st register in the block you want to read from
    Mov cx,255                    ;in CX the number of DAC registers you want to read from.
    Mov dx,0                      ;ES:DX points to where you want the table to appear.
    Int 10h

;-------------------- To write one dac
    mov ax,1010h
    mov bx,2                      ;register number 0-255 of dac you want to write to
    mov CL,0ffh                   ;CL=Blue
    mov ch,0                      ;ch=green
    mov dh,10                     ;DH=Red
    Int 10h
```

;=-----------

This program on the next 2 pages, was able to create a bitmap image file of the visible screen. As I take it from a much longer program, I am not sure that it is not missing something which it needs to work.
It uses a BIOS function to read a whole series of colour DACs, and writes a colour table or palette for the bitmap. That is only useful for 1 byte per pixel screen modes, since with 3 or 4 bytes per pixel 8:8:8 colour modes one never needs a palette in the bitmap file.

```
create_bitmap:  pushad                  ;Creates a non-compressed bitmap,
                call start_bitmaps
                mov edi,200436h         ; This move makes edi skip over header (36h) plus colour table (400h).
    cb6:        mov cx,[esi+86h]        ;pixels count down
                push ebx
    cb5:        mov eax,0

                mov al,[ebx]
                inc ebx
                mov [edi],al            ;( Blue is in +0; Green is in +1; Red is in +2. +3 padding

                add edi,1
                add dword [esi+88h],1

                dec cx
                jnz cb5
                pop ebx
                sub ebx,[esi+80h]       ;Vertically UP now.
                mov eax,3a028h          ;Gets the VBE mode information, it assumes you called that.
                cmp ebx,[eax]           ;The physical base pointer no at +28h.= screen memory start.
         ;;     cmp ebx,0c0000000h
                jb cb10
                dec word [esi+84h]      ;count down of lines
                jnz cb6
    cb10:
                mov eax,[esi+88h]
                mov ebx,200000h

                mov [ebx+2],eax         ;file length
                sub eax,36h
                mov [ebx+22h],eax       ;data length (some bitmap files don't have this one)

                popad
                ret
;
do_colour:  call down16                 ;This worked well.
            mov ax,5500h
            mov es,ax
            mov ax,1017h                ;Bios function code in ax, "read a block of DACs"
            mov bx,0                    ;Number of 1st DAC to be read in bx. 0 for start with DAC no 0
            mov cx,100h                 ;the number of DACs to be read from at once
            mov dx,0                    ;ES:DX = the address where you want BIOS to put the information.
            int 10h
            call up32
            mov ebx,200036h
            mov cx,100h                 ;100h for esi to read 300h bytes and ebx write 400h bytes???
            mov esi,55000h
```

```
dca:    mov eax,[esi]
        add eax,eax                     ;can that x2 make colours a bit brighter? Yes it did
        add eax,eax
        and eax,0fcfcfch                ;Now x4 and better brightness.
        mov [ebx],eax
        add esi,3                       ;only 3 for rgb
;;      mov byte [ebx+3],0              ;padding??
        add ebx,4
        dec cx
        jnz dca
        ret

;======================================
   start_bitmaps:  call do_colour       ;This worked well.
        mov ebx,200000h                 ;changed for 8 bit colour table test
        mov cx,36h
        mov al,0
    rb1: mov [ebx],al        ;
        inc ebx
        dec cx
        jnz rb1
        mov edi,3a000h                  ;edi at first to address and read vbe mode info
        mov esi,39000h                  ;esi always to variables
        mov ebx,200000h                 ;ebx at first to write bitmap header

        mov word [ebx],"BM"             ;start bitmap header with letters BM
        mov dword [esi+88h],436h        ;File length count up from here 10h bytes long color table.

        mov word [ebx+0ah],436h         ;write offset to data into bitmap header
        mov byte [ebx+0eh],28h          ;fixed length of part of the header normally necessary
        mov word [ebx+2eh],100h         ;the number of colours or zero.

        mov ax,[edi+10h]    ;VBE mode info bytes per scan line (assumes you called to get mode info)
        mov [ebx+12h],ax                ;write into header width in pixels of whole screen??
        mov [esi+86h],ax                ;prepare pixels count down

        mov ax,[edi+14h]                ;VBE mode info scan lines count
        mov [ebx+16h],ax                ;write into header height in pixels
        mov [esi+84h],ax                ;save ready count down of scan lines
        mov byte [ebx+1ah],1            ;no of planes always 1
        mov byte [ebx+1ch],8            ; 8 bits per pixel / or  20h for 4 bytes per pixel
        mov eax,0ec4h                   ;Horizontal zoom neutral number value ????
        mov [ebx+26h],eax               ;H
        mov [ebx+2ah],eax               ;V

        mov eax,0
        mov ax,[edi+10h]                ;Vertically down value, of bytes per scan line
        mov [esi+80h],eax               ;prepared v down
        mov cx,[edi+14h]                ;lines ct of mode
        mov ebx,3a000h                  ;address the BIOS mode information.
        mov ebx,[ebx+28h]               ;Read the physical base pointer assumes you got VBE mode information
    rb9: add ebx,[esi+80h]
        dec cx
        jnz rb9

        ret
```

A timing test and slow speed. And with xmm0 the program speeded up.

When I did a timing test I was surprised when it showed that the high resolution screen memory works about 8 times more slowly that the normal RAM memory. I mean a load operation like
Mov [ebx],ax
runs 8 times more slowly when [ebx] addresses the high resolution screen memory to draw pixels than when [ebx] addresses any other areas of RAM.

When I found that out I tried to rewrite my alphabetical character drawing routine so that instead of writing 1 byte at a time it wrote 4 bytes at once from eax. This worked and did speed up the program a bit.

Then I tried using an area of normal RAM memory as a "back screen", and the program draws a screen full of alphabetical characters or pictures onto the back screen which is of normal RAM first, (you don't see it) and then when drawing is finished I used the xmm0 register to quickly copy that back screen onto the high resolution screen memory.

This worked well and my whole program was speeded up a lot! The running of the program was speeded up so much that I had to readjust the flashing rate of the typing cursor.

Here the xmm0 register is used with the operation "movdqu" to copy from one area of memory to another , it copies 16 bytes of memory at a time, (128 bits) while the computer is in 32 bit addressing mode. (It has nothing to do with 64 bit mode.) Xmm0 128 bit loads can work in both 32 bit modes and 64 bit mode.

I have only used the xmm0 register to copy larger amounts of memory more quickly. And when the picture for the screen is firstly written onto a back screen of normal RAM you don't see, and then when it is copied to the visible screen memory with xmm0, that speeds up the program a lot. Because a much smaller number of actual loads to the visible screen are used then. The xmm0 register would crash the computer when certain wrong values are in the control register CR4.

```
moves1:    mov ecx,15000h           ;15000h to copy 150000h bytes  (10h times ecx)
moves2:
           movdqu xmm0,[esi]        ;xmm0 here must speed it up a lot.
           movdqu [edi],xmm0        ;It speeds up copying because it copies 16 bytes with each mov operation
           add esi,10h
           add edi,10h
           dec ecx
           jnz moves2
;-----------------------------------------------------------------------
```
I tried to time how fast these copying operations work with my laptop computer with a program loop and my watch.
  Copying a back screen onto the visible screen memory worked with 15 Meg bytes/second in the old way, when using mov [ebx],eax, which is 32 bits at a time.
It loaded 26 meg bytes/second with xmm0 and 64 bit loads.
And it loaded 47.6 Meg bytes per second when using xmm0 to do 128 bit loads!
So using xmm0 register (Or xmm1) increased the speed a lot, but the screen memory is slow compared with normal RAM.

Configuration Space

Every computer has a configuration space which in modern computers can be reached in 2 different ways. I think the configuration space might be a way for BIOS and operating systems to reach integrated circuits which are permanently in the computer so as to give them an initial configuration at the start? It is reached with the older configuration mechanism, involving inputs and outputs. And it is reached with the newer method of very high memory addresses. From the older way you see it has 256 bytes zones which each belong to a different integrated circuit in the computer.

Websites have information about so-called "class codes and sub-class codes", which are numbers at specific offsets inside each zone, and which let operating systems identify what integrated circuits are inside the computer. Unused spaces in between the zones seem to vary randomly, but the empty areas are always a multiple of 256 bytes long.

When the Configuration space is reached by the newer method, it is called the "PCI Express space". In my laptop the PCI Express space happened to start at address 0F0000000H. That is 0 "F" followed by 7 zeroes, then H. But it must be different with different computers?
That is one reaches the PCI Express space just by putting its address into an address register such as EBX, just as one reaches the normal RAM memory, by operations mov eax,[ebx] for example.
 Except that the addresses start higher above the upper end of the RAM.

When I looked at it with my hexadecimal screen, I found that all the same zones which I could see with the older configuration space method were there in the same order but spaced 10H times or that is 16 times further apart. Also some of the zones were extended to be a bit wider, and so had more registers in them.
For example with my laptop I found that a 256 byte zone for a VGA compatible controller started at the older configuration space base +1000h. And I found exactly the same zone appear at 0F0010000h. (An extra zero for 16x).
As another example, I found that in the older configuration space a zone for the EHCI started at +0d000h. And in the newer express space, exactly the same zone started at 0F00d0000h.
When the configuration space is reached that new way, it is much easier to make changes to the registers of the integrated circuits which those zone belong to: You simply write a number over them, or even type a number over them with the typing cursor, and the register values are changed when the register was read/write. But many of the registers are read only. Making random changes to any registers can crash the computer, but did no permanent harm.

The older configuration space mechanism is: Put the address you want to read/write into EAX, and set binary bit 31 of EAX. For example set the binary bit 31 with OR EAX,80000000h. Then put the port number 0CF8h into the DX register and output the address to that port with Out DX,EAX). Then put port number 0CFCh in DX register, and input into EAX by IN EAX,DX. This should read 4 bytes at a time from the configuration space. Or for writing to the configuration space first Output the address to port 0CF8h in the same way but then output to port 0CFCh with Out DX,EAX.

To Copy the Whole older Configuration Space into the RAM memory, from where I can see it with the hexadecimal screen.
(This uses the configuration mechanism which is the older method that uses inputs and outputs).

```
whole:      pushad                  ;Result: this read 4x64k ok. There were only 12 of the 256 byte zones .
            mov esi,500000h
            mov ecx,80000000h       ;bit 7 set, ecx to address the configuration space
wh1:        mov bl,4                 ;4 because using +1 to ds=+16 bytes
wh2:        mov dx,0cf8h
            mov eax,ecx
            out dx,eax              ;assembler does not allow ecx here
            mov dx,0cfch
            in eax,dx               ;it looks as if one input eax from cfc does the same as 4 1-byte inputs
            mov [esi],eax           ;from cfc / cfd / cfe / cff.
```

```
            add esi,4
            add ecx,4                   ;have to keep 2 lowest binary bits zero
            dec bl
            jnz wh2


            cmp ecx,80025000h           ;0-4 to the bus number, apparently 64kb the each bus
            jb wh1
            mov ebx,39000h
            mov eax,500000h
            mov [ebx],eax
            mov [ebx+4],eax

    wh3:    popad
            ret
```

;==

Ideas about drawing alphabet characters, and using a mouse.

Obviously there must be a million different ways to write a subroutine like 'one_letter,' or 'screen_of_text' since you can use different registers and you can also add a lot to it. You can add to it a flashing typing cursor by making a compare operation which compare the address of the text being read (in the register edi in this example) to the address of a typing cursor.
A typing cursor is nothing but an address which you store somewhere, and which you use for typing.
It is the address of where the next letter will get typed in the RAM memory. A common technique used to make a typing cursor visible is to invert the binary bits of the bytes read from the character pixels table, so that 1's become 0's and 0's become 1's, and do that whenever the two addresses become equal.
A byte somewhere in memory can be used as a timer, and that used to flash the typing cursor, as a flashing cursor is more visible.

Inverting the character pixels in AL register can be done either with an operation called "Not AL" or with "Xor AL,0ffh" which is the same thing.
A byte somewhere kept as a variable can be incremented +1 then Anded by 1fh for example, its value can determine whether the typing cursor blinks on or off. You can easily create and add a second cursor, to be used as a copy cursor, but the two cursors should then be different or else they disappear when one is exactly over the other. Another idea is that if you make a mouse caret, (something separate from the typing cursor which moves with the mouse with increments of single pixels, and so the caret moves smoothly).
I had an idea to help the program locate where the mouse caret is in relation to text in the memory.
 It was that you can choose to make your mouse caret in a particular colour which is not used for text or anything else.
The subroutine like "one_letter" can then have added to it an operation to read from the screen memory a few bytes of screen memory, and then make a comparison of their values to the special colour which you use only for your mouse caret. The mouse caret can be a character or simply a tiny grey square.
 If the compare is equal, then you know that the alphabetical character is at exactly the same spot on the screen as your mouse caret. The program can then record that text character's address (from edi in the example). That is useful as it can be used whenever you want a mouse click to move the typing cursor onto the mouse caret.

Making a hexadecimal screen.

A screen which shows all the bytes in the computer's memory as 2 digit hexadecimal numbers is very important and useful if you are doing experiments with programming the hardware!.
For example, if you are trying to learn about op-codes, or boot sector data, or about the configuration space or about the EHCI, a hexadecimal view screen is really essential!

Hexadecimal numbers are easy to understand. Each hexadecimal digit corresponds to a "nibble" of 4 binary bits. The 4 binary bits can equal 0 to 15 in decimal, or 0 to 0Fh in hexadecimal. The hexadecimal digits are the same as decimal digits from 0 to 9, but 10 to 15 are replaced with the letters A to F in the hexadecimal.

I made a screen which shows the memory as normal text on its left side, always 32 characters wide, and which shows the same area as 2 digit hexadecimal numbers, always 32 numbers wide on the right hand side.
With page up page down keys that screen can be scrolled up or down, with faster scrolling when shift was pressed too. I arranged for the screen to jump to any memory address I wanted, when I firstly typed the memory address and then pressed a certain key.

To do the hexadecimal side you can call a subroutine which converts a 1 byte binary number into two hexadecimal digits as text in standard ascii code.
Calculate how many pixels per scan line are necessary for making the split screen.

Firstly for the plain text side, my 8x8 pixels characters are 8 pixels wide, so 8x32 pixels are needed. On the hexadecimal side, you have 2 of the 8x8 number characters for each byte in the viewed memory, which means 16x32 pixels. But I wanted each hexadecimal number to be spaced apart from the others by 1 more pixel width, so they can be read easily.
This adds up to 32 pixels for the hexadecimal side of the screen. It needs 17x32 pixels.

So in total, for both normal text side and hexadecimal side, (8+17)x32 pixels per scan line are necessary. It turned out in my laptop that Bios screen mode 4103h had just barely enough pixels per scan line to make this kind of screen. A higher resolution than that screen mode makes it look smaller but has more than enough room.

;--

Reading FAT32 Files.

A Fat 32 directory entry

Offset		Length	Name
0	0	11	The File name, 8+3 bytes all in block capitals
11	0Bh	1	The attribute. 20h=archive normal file. 10h=dir 08=Volume label
12	0Ch	1	reserved zero
13	0Dh	1	tenths of a second time when created
14	0Eh	2	Time file was created
16	10h	2	Date file was created
18	12h	2	last access date, no time
20	14h	2	High word of first cluster number
22	16h	2	Time of last write
24	18h	2	Date of last write
26	1Ah	2	Lower word of first cluster number
28	1Ch	4	32 bit file size in bytes

;------------------------------------

My Emachines Laptop's FAT32 boot sector

Offset		length	Name	example value
+11	0Bh	2	Bytes per sector	200h
13	0Dh	1	sectors per allocation unit (per cluster)	20h/40h
14	0Eh	2	Number of reserved sectors	20h
16	10h	1	Number of Fats	2

;---

	1Ch	4	Number of hidden sectors (sectors preceeding partition)	
32	20h	4	Length in sectors of volume (of partition)	
36	24h	4	Number of sectors per 1 Fat	30deh
40	28h	2	Is fat mirrored??	0=it is mirrored

;-----

44	2Ch	4	First cluster number of root directory	2
48	30h	2	point to sfinfo?	1
50	32h	2	point to copy of boot record	6
	52h	5	The word "FAT32"	

;------------------------------------
Master boot record of laptop. Its 4 partition entries were at these addresses.
From +0 to + 1BEh booted running code??   Four entries for up to 4 partitions

offset	length bytes	Partition entry
+1BEh	16	"
+1CEh	16	"
+1DEh	16	
+1EEh	16	
+1FEh	2	0AA55h =bootable code

In every 16 byte primary partition entry
At offset +0   1 byte code: 80h= Bootable partition. 0=not bootable.
At offset +4   1 byte partition type code. 17H= NTFS.; 0Bh/0Ch= Fat 32 file system
At offset +8   4 bytes = first absolute sector number, of the partition
At offset +0Ch   4 bytes = partition length number in sectors

;--

I found on the internet a free paper which explains the FAT32 system clearly. Its title was:
"Hardware white paper. Microsoft extensible firmware initiative. Fat32 File System specification. Fat:General Overview of On disk format. Version 1.03. " Or "Fatgen1.03"
The program I wrote a few years ago reads and saves files to USB memory stick with Fat32 or Fat16, and it also reads files from the Fat32 partition on my laptop's hard drive. I forgot the details of how it works, and I

have looked through it to try to remember the formula that you use to read a file from a Fat32 memory stick or the hard drive partition.

These are the fields in the Fat32 Boot sector which are used for reading and writing files.

+0Bh	2	Bytes per sector. Normally 512, but could sometimes be 1024/2048/4096
+0Dh	1	Sectors Per Cluster number. Varies from 1 to 128
+0Eh	2	Number of reserved sectors. Often is 32
+10h	1	Number of Fats. Practically always equals 2
+24h	4	Sectors per one Fat number. A large variable number.
+2Ch	4	Root Directory's Cluster

For any file, the first cluster number is written in 2 parts in a directory entry. You put the two parts together to get the 32 bit first cluster number. A cluster is a group of several consecutive sectors which are used together. You use the first cluster number in 2 ways: It points to an entry in the FAT. And it points to a first sector where the file starts. That entry in the FAT will either be a number meaning EOC, which is the number 0FFFFFFFh, (7 F's) or it will be another cluster number. The other cluster number will also point both to the next FAT entry, and to the first sector of the next cluster where the file is saved. This goes on, and on, with every entry in the FAT both pointing to the next entry and also pointing to another sector of the file data.

Every entry in the FAT is really a 28 bit number, not a 32 bit number, and you should clear to zero its highest 4 binary bits. Like this: AND EAX,0fffffffh. (Use 7 F's)

When you have a cluster number, such as the first one which comes from the directory. Or one coming from the FAT, you can get it to point to the next entry in the FAT simply by multiplying it by 4 and then adding the address of where in RAM memory your copy of the FAT starts.
So cluster number*4 + base address, points to the next FAT entry. The FAT entry needs to be tested to see if it is the signal of End, .

A **Cluster-into-sector formula:** When you have a **cluster** number, the formula to get it to point to the **Sector** of the data saved on the memory stick (Or FAT32 partition on hard drive) was like this, where N is the cluster number:

((N-2)*(1 byte number at offset +0dh) + (2 bytes number at offset +0Eh) + (2*(4 bytes number at offset +24h))

(Asterisks are for multiply). These offsets are about the offsets into the Boot Sector, are relative to the start of the boot sector. This formula gets you the number of the **first sector of a cluster.** It gets the number of the first sector of where a File starts, when the cluster number was the one that was in the directory. Exactly **the same** formula written with the variable names:

((N-2)*(1 byte Sectors Per Cluster number) + (2 bytes Reserved Sector Count number) + (2*(4 bytes Sectors Per One Fat number))

Those formula have to be used constantly by the computer, and the results stored as variables.
Of course when the FAT32 area is a partition on a hard drive, and is not the first partition, the number of the first sector of the partition must be added to the result of the cluster-into-sector calculation. That is the real absolute sector number of the FAT32 boot sector has to be added to every result of the above calculation, since it is a base. In the boot sector information the 4 byte number at offset +1Ch is that number of hidden sectors.

But I think you don't need to read it from +1Ch, since you already have it. Your program would always already know it as it is the absolute sector number of the FAT32 boot sector. And to have found the FAT32 boot sector the computer must have read the number from the Master boot record entry.

I think the sector number of the start of the first FAT Copy, is simply the 2 byte number at offset +0Eh, which is called the Number of Reserved Sectors.
Start of 1st FAT = (2 byte number at offset +0Eh). (But of course, add the start of the partition's sector number if it is a partition.)

And the Cluster number of the start of the files **Directory**, is the 4 bytes number at offset +2Ch, which is called BPB_RootClus or Cluster number of the Root Directory. You can use the cluster-into-sector formula to find the sector at which the Root Directory starts.
This number is usually 02, but could be different. When it is 02, the (N-2) in the above formula would cancel out. The number 2 is the lowest cluster number that can be used and it points to the "first sector of data", which is found by this simple formula. (Which you don't need since you can use the cluster-into-sector formula)

2*(4 byte number at offset +24h) + (2 byte number at offset +0Eh) = sector of start of data.

When my program read 1 cluster at a time, it was slow. I added to the program tests to find out how many clusters were consecutive. When it could do a lot of consecutive sectors at once, it went faster.

Looking at my program I try to remember how it works. It read the boot sector first.
Then, with register EDI pointing to the boot sector, and esi pointing to an area to save some variables:

```
xor eax,eax              ;clear upper part to zero
mov ax,[edi+0Eh]         ;reads pointer to first Fat copy from boot sector = reserved sector count
                         ;The program then happened to read the Fat to address 1C0000h
;-------------------------------
Cluster-into-sector:     ;Call with ECX= Cluster number to be converted into a sector number

Mov eax,[edi+24h]        ;read sectors per one fat number, from boot sector
add eax,eax              ;Multiply by 2 as there are 2 Fats copies
xor edx,edx
mov dx,[edi+0Eh]         ;reserved sector count
add eax,edx              ;Add it. Now incidentally it points to the first sector of data.
Push eax                 ;Save result of (2 bytes at +0Eh) + (2*(4 bytes at +24h))
mov eax,ecx              ;The Cluster number from ecx
Sub eax,2                ;(N-2)
xor edx,edx
mov dl,[edi+0Dh]         ;The 1 byte long Sectors Per Cluster number
imul edx                 ;imul edx is eax*edx and gives the result in eax.
pop edx                  ;recover it, add to it the result of multiply by ((N-2)*SecPerClus)
add eax,edx              ;Cluster number from ECX should have been converted into sector number in EAX.
Ret
```

The program then happened to read the directory into address 1F0000h

When your file name is not more than 8 characters and these characters are all in block capitals, the Windows operating system switches to using the old-fashioned type of directory entry. When the program looked for a specific file name which I had typed at the typing cursor, the program turned out to be longer than I had expected. I only programmed it to work with the older form of directory entry where there is a maximum of 8 characters of file name plus 3 for the extension.

Comparing the file name I typed to the directory to find an equal matching file name, a subroutine in my program returned with EDX pointing to the start of that directory entry.
Then, read two variables from the directory entry for the file:

Mov eax,[edx+12h]   ;Read the high part of the 1st cluster number into e part of eax.
Mov ax,[edx+1Ah]   ;Read the low part of the 1st cluster number into low part of EAX.
Mov ecx,[edx+1Ch]   ;read file length in bytes from the directory entry.

When you read the file, it goes through cycles of taking a cluster number, and converting it into a sector number, reading the number of drive sectors which goes with a cluster, moving up the loading address with the number of bytes which were read, and then also using the cluster number to find the next entry in the FAT.
 The next entry in the FAT must be AND'ed with 0FFFFFFFh because the FAT entries are really 28 bits long, not 32 bits. This number from the FAT is the next cluster number to work on. But, when the next entry in the FAT is the number 0FFFFFFFh, it is the end of the file. (The EOC mark). It is also the end of the file when the length

in bytes from the directory entry goes down to zero if you use it to count down.
It worked faster when many consecutive clusters were read at a time instead of one cluster at a time.
In my program I just loaded a long length area of the FAT into the RAM memory, always from the start of the FAT. But a more complicated program would maybe read only the areas of FAT that it needs.

Whenever my bootable program read or saved a file to a Memory stick it used my programming of the EHCI, Intel's USB controller. But when it read files from the FAT32 partition on my laptop's hard drive, it used only BIOS Extended Read to read sectors. This program looked through the MBR, firstly to find an entry with the partition type code 0Bh or 0Ch which meant the entry was for a FAT32 partition. Then it read the absolute sector number of where the partition started in the hard drive. Then every time Bios Extended read was called, it had to add that absolute sector number of start of the partition to the sector number of the data in the partition. The sum being used as sector number. Most of the program ran in 32 bit addressing mode, but it had to switch down to 16 bit Real Mode every time it called BIOS Extended Read.

I find that reading Fat32 files is quite difficult, and I have not been able to try to explain it or teach it on these pages. I have only given part of the necessary information.

A convenient way of switching the computer's mode to 64 bit, (Long Mode) and then back again.

I have invented a way of switching the computer from 16 bit mode to 64 bit mode
and back again to 16 bit mode, which seems more convenient and easy to use, than the methods I had heard of. You simply call a sub-routine and the computer returns instantly from the call and is switched into a different mode when it returns. I have put on the next few pages every piece of programming which is necessary to make it work.

So it is simply a matter of calling a sub-routine whenever you want to switch between the 16 bit /32 bit /64 bit modes. The computer returns from the sub-routine switched into the new mode!

Important: For this system to work it is essential that near to the start of every program one should load a Zero into the stack segment register ss. This is necessary as the two subroutines Up32/Down16 work with zero in the stack segment register, and if ss is not holding zero they will immediately crash the program.

The FASMW assembler definitely seems to be the best assembler for this kind of programming, because with the FASMW you can combine in one program different areas for different modes. Some parts of the program can be written in 16 bit mode, some parts in 32 bit mode, and some parts in 64 bit mode, and being able to use different modes together in different areas of the same program turns out to be important. You have to be able to use different modes in different parts of the same program,.

Things written about changing modes sometimes seem to imply that one stays in one mode, but I think staying in the same mode is not a good idea, and while a bootable computer program runs it should frequently change the computer's mode. If a computer was permanently stuck in 64 bit mode or in 32 bit mode, you couldn't really use BIOS because the BIOS might only work in 16 bit mode. 64 bit mode has in it interesting new operations which you want and many new registers which are definitely useful.
Every time you need to use BIOS, the computer should be switched back again into the 16 bit so-called Real mode.

While my bootable programs run, the computer changes mode several hundred times a second, back and forth, which is in my opinion the normal and right way to make a program run.
Timing tests show that switching between 16 bit mode and 64 bit mode takes about 1 microsecond.

The complaints about Microsoft: They worked hard with an influence over Intel to make the switching between different modes seem difficult, probably because they hoped to prevent other companies from creating operating systems,.

I read that recently Microsoft invented secure boot, which prevents anything except for Microsoft Windows from booting on many new computers, and I read there have been complaints about it. When you buy a new computer, you should make sure it does not have the Microsoft secure boot, since that would prevent you from running your own bootable programs. Before that, they decided that before one can switch on 64 bit mode, one needs to firstly enable paging. Paging was intended to be very hard to understand, and it is able to scramble a computer's memory, unless you write the tables in a special way called "identity mapping".

I read in the Intel manual for the processor, and managed to write paging tables that produce "identity mapping". An example of writing these paging tables is included below here, and apart from having to run it in order to switch on 64 bit mode, I would have no interest in paging. The test is that before and after paging with identity mapping is activated the memory should stay as it was and not scramble. It is as if the paging doesn't exist, since identity mapping makes the paging do nothing.

The 64 bit mode which most computers have now is really interesting, but I have read that Intel wanted to replace it with a better 64 bit mode called "Itanium instruction set". Intel says switching to the Itanium mode will be simple. To program with it you will need an Itanium compiler? I wondered how long it will be before the older 64 bit mode is replaced by the new Itanium instruction set. But I have also read on a website that the Itanium design might never replace the older 64 bit mode after all. I think the present 64 bit mode will probably last for years.

Switching the PC computer into different modes, is normally triggered suddenly by the operations called "Far Jumps". Far jumps to some extent seem difficult or inconvenient. And I think either the difficulty or the illusion of difficulty involved with far jumps has actually prevented people from switching the computer mode. Far jumps load a number called a GDT index or selector into the code segment register or CS register. This instantly triggers several changes together.

I wanted to be able to call a sub-routine and make the actual switching of mode easy for myself, and this works because the RETF or "Far Return" operations work as a substitute for the far jump, and in this substitute you can firstly push a GDT selector and then push a return address. And then running the RETF there is the switch in mode, but less difficult.

 There is the question of how to return a computer to the 16 bit Real mode? I notice some people think you do it just with a far jump, however with most computers that cannot possibly work.
The specific reason why just running a far jump won't normally work, is connected with the default/big state and the operand size prefix 66h and the address size prefix 67h. You have to get the computer to return to the Real Mode interpretation of the operand size prefix 66h and the address size prefix 67h.

In real mode, these important prefixes, 66h and 67h, mean that an operand or an address of the next Op-code, is going to be LONGER than it's typical length, which is SHORT length by default in Real Mode.

When the computer's code segment has been switched into proper 32 bit mode (so-called protected mode) the meaning of the two prefixes 66h and 67h is the opposite, and they mean that the operand or the address is going to be SHORTER than its typical length, which is LONG by default in protected mode.

And by doing some experiments, I found out that when you simply try to return from protected mode to Real mode with a far jump, the processor's "default size" for operands and addresses, and its interpretation of the two prefixes 66h and 67h **remains** as it was in 32 bit protected mode. And this means that the computer has not returned to Real mode, and when you try to run BIOS in that mixed up mode the computer always crashes.

The solution to the problem of returning a computer to Real mode properly, is to firstly pass it through a mode so-called "Model Small Protected Mode". This switches its interpretation of 66h and 67h into the Real Mode way. And then immediately after that you can return to Real mode properly with a far jump. Or maybe with a RETF which replaces the far jump.

The computer passes through model small protected mode very quickly, so it's a "stepping stone". Model small protected mode differs from the more common Model Large protected mode, by the fact that a single binary bit, called the default-big bit in a GDT descriptor, is 0 instead of 1.

My sub-routines are only sure to be assembled properly when you use the FASMW assembler.
If you used a different assembler, some areas might get assembled wrongly, and possibly specific areas that don't assemble perfectly can be entered in the form of "Data Bytes". Anyway I assume that you use the FASMW. But even with this assembler you sometimes can enter a few data bytes in some places. (Assemblers allow you to enter any op-code as several data bytes. You start the line with the 2 letters "db" and then write the op-code as a series of one byte numbers separated by commas for example.)

You need to tell your assembler what mode the computer is in, in the different parts of the program. When using the FASMW assembler it's easy, and you need to write USE16 whenever the computer will be in 16 bit Real Mode, you write USE32 whenever the computer's code segment and Instruction Pointer has been switched into 32 bit mode. (But not when the data segments Alone are 32 bit. That is still under USE16.)
And you need to write USE64 whenever the computer will be in 64 bit mode (also called Long mode).

I am going to show here 8 sub-routines for changing the computer's mode. It's very easy to use them, all you do is call them, and the computer immediately returns from the call now switched into a different mode. These 8 sub-routines work for switching into 16 bit Real mode, 32 bit protected mode, partial 32 bit mode, and 64 bit long mode.

For the 64 bit mode a page tables writing sub-routine needs to be called, but it may be enough to call that once at the start of the program. Page tables were intended to be extremely difficult to understand. And I believe the reason for that is specific. Microsoft wanted to prevent other companies from writing operating systems, and believed difficult page tables would hinder other companies from learning to create new operating systems.

Note: there are TWO 32 bit modes. Protected mode is when the code segment and Instruction Pointer (Program Counter) becomes a 32 bit register and simultaneously with that there is the second change, which is: the processor changes in its "default size" for operands and for addresses. And the two important prefixes 66h and 67h are interpreted in an opposite way, a different way.

But another simple mode exists, and it is when ONLY the Data Segment registers and Address registers are in 32 bit mode, while the computer's Code Segment system with the Instruction Pointer (Program Counter) is still in 16 bit mode. It is interesting that individual parts of a computer's system can be switched into 32 bit mode without the other parts.
The partial 16 bit partial 32 bit mode was the best mode for me as I started programming because it works simply.
To switch on 32 bit addressing alone, only 1 descriptor is needed in your Global descriptor table. It is a data segment descriptor, 8 bytes long as all descriptors,. (Sometimes this partial 16 bit partial 32 bit mode has been called Unreal mode, but I have read that it works with all types of Intel PC computers).

In cases that you want the computer to stay in the partial 32 bit / partial 16 bit mode, you simply avoid using far jumps. Because a far jump would certainly trigger the sudden changes in the computer, a change to the Code segment and Instruction pointer and cause it to become 32 bits.
 That by itself is useful and quite harmless, but as well, another sudden change is also triggered at the same moment and it changes the operand size and the address size that the processor considers to be "Default", and this also affects the way the computer interprets the operand size prefix 66h and the address size prefix 67h, and not having separate control of these other effects is a bad nuisance.
Because of that, the FASMW assembler needs to see the word USE32 at the start of the section of the program where the Instruction Pointer becomes a 32 bit register. But in cases when you avoid the far jump so that only Data segments are 32 bit mode, and the Instruction Pointer remains 16 bits, you need the word USE16 above that area of the program as with Real mode.

If you disassemble a test program you will see that the words USE16 and USE32 more than anything affect the way the assembler automatically inserts the two prefixes 66h and 67h. While USE64 tells the assembler that it should use all the new interesting 64 bit instructions.
Before running any of these examples a call to write a Global Descriptor table is necessary. It should be enough to write the GDT just once as the program starts.

   An example of how to call a mode switching sub-routine. Assuming that you use the FASMW assembler. All the necessary pieces of programming are here. If you know the computer is in 16 bit mode and you want to switch it directly into 64 bit mode, also called Long Mode, simply call the sub-routine of label "from_16_to_64" (But firstly, when the program starts running in Real Mode, "call gdt1" is necessary to write a Global descriptor table.)

All of the pieces of programming which you need to be able to switch modes just be making a call, are here in this chapter. So if you simply include the pieces of programming in your programs you can switch modes very easily with it.

An Example of how to use the programs which switch modes easily.
(You just need the pieces of programming below here to make it work)
```
;===================================
USE16
 (A 16 bit mode program goes here)

 Call from_16_to_64
USE64

 (A 64 Bit program goes here)
 (Calls to other 64 bit programs can go from here)

;---------------------------- switch back down again ---------------------------
 Call from_64_to_16

USE16

 ( A 16 bit program can go here)
;===================================
```
It is so simple to use, just one call from_16_to_64 and then just below that the word USE64
A lot of 64 bit program or calls to 64 bit routines can go there. A whole series of calls to 64 bit programs could be put there.
Switching the computer back again from 64 bit mode to 16 bit mode is just as simple.
You just run one Call from_64_to_16, and just below that the word USE16

A Second example of how to use mode switch calls.
```
;=============================================
USE16
(A 16 bit program can be here or called from here.)
Call from_16_to_32
USE32
(A 32 bit program can be here or called from here)
Call from_32_to_64
USE64
(A 64 bit program can be here or called from here)
Call from_64_to_16
USE16
(A 16 bit program can be here or called from here)
;=============================================
```
Switching modes back and forth between 16 bit and 64 bit mode is important. You could happily
write a program that runs in both 64 bit mode and 16 bit mode, while not using 32 bit modes at all!
 But while a program runs the computer should frequently switch back and forth between modes, this is
something that works silently, without any flickering or any problems at all.
Except that some older PCs are not capable of doing 64 bit modes.
Switching to 32 bit modes is easy with the sub-routine calls I am showing below. If the Instructions Pointer has
switched to 32 bit, just write USE32 for the FASMW assembler.
Where only data segments are 32 bit, you have to write USE16.

   Important: at the very start of the whole program, I had to load the Stack segment register with zero, with
for example Mov AX,0; Mov SS,AX. Also, you have to run **Call gdt1 to write the Global descriptor Table.**

;---
You call this sub-routine while you know the computer is in 16 bit mode and it
should return immediately switched into 64 bit mode, long mode. Just below the call
that goes to this, as the computer returns, the words USE64 are needed.

```
;-------------------------------------------------------------
  USE16
    from_16_to_64:    call up32      ;this called in real mode returned in 64 bit mode properly.
            mov eax,0
            mov ax,cs          ;worked ok.
            add eax,eax
            add eax,eax
            add eax,eax
            add eax,eax
            mov ecx,0
            pop cx
            add eax,ecx
            mov ecx,18h                ;a gdt selector of 018h to set 64 bit mode.
            push ecx                   ; The GDT Selector is lower 2 bytes of 4 bytes. Retf pops 8 bytes
            push eax                   ;push ready for retf to act like a far jump.
        call write_page_tables_16      ;depending on what calls it, write page tables must be either
                                       ;assembled under use32 or under use16
            call start_page_16             ;now called start_page has to be under use16
            db 66h,0cbh                ;  retf    worked ok

; ============================ 16/9/2012
```

This sub-routine "from_64_to_16" should be called when you know the computer is in 64 bit mode and the computer should return immediately from the call switched into 16 bit Real Mode.
This one needs to be located somewhere near the beginning of a program.
Just below the call that goes to this, as the computer returns, the words USE16 are needed.

```
;-==============================21-2-2015 worked immediately
            USE64
  from_64_to_16:
            pop rcx             ;Call in 64 bit mode, pop the 64 bit return address.   This worked!

            cmp rcx,0a0000h    ;Is return possible within lower memory?
            jb dow4c
            push rcx
            ret
    dow4c:
            mov rax,rcx        ;return address to return from this sub-routine

            mov rcx,0          ;the return address has  an IP and a CS part in different proportions.
            mov cx,ax          ;so assume that the CS part is zero in its lowest 3 hex digits.
            sar rax,1
            sar rax,1          ;if not located neat the beginning of a program, maybe it can crash?
            sar rax,1
            sar rax,1
            and rax,0f000h     ;cs part of a return address made in ax
            push ax
            push cx
            mov rax,20h        ;GDT index 20h for stepping stone on the way to return to real mode.
            push rax            ;push it ready for retf to act as a far jump

            lea rax,[rip+3]    ;+3 is an exact distance to skip over, as push rax is a 1 byte opcode
            push rax           ;push it for retf to act as a substitute for a far jump
            db 48h,0cbh        ; This triggers a switch to a "stepping stone mode"
            db 90h             ;    It has not yet switched into 16 bit mode, but is in stepping stone.
            USE16
            mov eax,cr0        ;(Continued on the next page)
            and eax,07fffffeh          ; Clear to 0 the PE bit and clear the Paging enable bit.
```

```
            mov cr0,eax
;---------              End of paging was essential. The next few operations are equivalent to a call to "end_page"
            mov eax,cr4
            and al,5fh              ;clear 2 binary bits of CR4 by And FF5Fh as END PAGE should do.
            mov cr4,eax
;--------              These operations stop paging, and that is necessary, errors when paging not stopped.
            mov ecx,0c0000080h           ;ecx does address a model specific register?
            db 0fh,32h
            and ah,0feh             ;clear 100h bit used AH or and ax,0feffh  ; seems non-essential??
            db 0fh,30h              ;Now Trigger return to Real Mode.
            db 0CBh                 ;this last retf = db 0CBh causes the trigger to instantly return to Real mode.

        ;Now in Real mode. (The last retf pops the 16 bit IP and 16 bit CS which were pushed above.)


;================================================================
```

```
        ;---------------------------------
```
This sub-routine should be called while in 64 bit long mode and it should return
immediately with the computer switched into 32 bit protected mode.
Keep interrupts disabled with cli. There is 2 slightly different versions of this one.
```
            ;----------------------------------
        USE64
            from_64_to_32b:  pop rax          ;esp+8; 8 bytes rax OK
                    mov rcx,8

                    sub rsp,4              ;THIS Worked.
                    mov [rsp],ecx
                    sub rsp,4
                    mov [rsp],eax

                    db 0cbh
```
This sub-routine should be called while the computer is in 64 bit Long mode and it should return
immediately with the computer switched into 32 bit protected mode.
Keep interrupts disabled with cli. Just below the call that goes to this, as the computer returns, the words
USE32 are needed.

```
        ;----------------------------------
        USE64
            from _64_to_32:  pop rax
                    mov rcx,8           ;This worked too! 2 ways work in this case.
                    push rcx
                    push rax
                    db 48h,0cbh
```

 This sub-routine should be called while in 32 bit protected mode and it should
 return immediately with the computer switched into 64 bit long mode.
 Keep interrupts disabled with a cli. The writing of paging tables also needed to have
 been called at least once when the program starts. Just below the call that goes to this, as the computer
 returns, the words USE64 are needed.
```
            ;-----------------
        USE32                   ;Note: Before this a call to write the paging tables is also necessary.
                    ;
```

```
        from_32_to_64:
                call start_page_32      ;Plus a Call to load the paging mechanism registers,
                pop eax
                mov ecx,18h             ;This works! 18h=GDT selector for a Long Mode descriptor.
                push ecx
                push eax
                db 0cbh
```

;=======================================
Call this sub-routine when the computer is in either 16 bit real mode or in
partial 32 bit addressing mode, where the Instruction Pointer is 16 bits. It should return immediately with the computer
switched into 32 bit protected mode. (The GDT needs to have been written firstly, of course). Just below the call that goes to this, as the computer
returns, the words USE32 are needed.

```
        USE16                           ;As it's called a 16 bit return address is on the stack
        from_16_to_32:
                call up32               ; To set the PE bit.
                xor ecx,ecx
                pop cx                  ;pop the return address into cx
                mov eax,8               ;push GDT selector 8 for code segment
                push eax
                mov ax,cs               ;e part should be already zero
                add eax,eax
                add eax,eax
                add eax,eax
                add eax,eax             ; return address in ecx + 16* 16 bit CS part.
                add eax,ecx
                push eax                ;push for eip
                db 66h,0cbh             ;retf
```

This sub-routine should be called while the computer is in 32 bit protected mode
and it should return immediately switched into 16 bit Real mode.
This one should be located near the beginning of a program. If it is located lower
down there might be a risk of crashes which might happen when a relative jump or call
causes the instruction pointer go below zero. Just below the call that goes to this, as
the computer returns, the words USE16 are needed.

```
        USE32
        from_32_to_16:  ; A stepping stone is passed through called "Model Small Protected mode"

                pop ecx                 ;Call in 32 bit mode  pop 32 bit return address.   This worked!

                cmp ecx,0a0000h         ;Check Is return possible? within lower 1 MB of memory?
                jb dow9
                push ecx
                ret
    dow9:
                mov eax,ecx             ;return address is already popped into ecx

                mov ecx,0               ;the return address can be made into an IP and a CS part
                mov cx,ax               ;assume that the CS part is zero in its lowest 3 hex digits.
                sar eax,1
                sar eax,1               ;if program did not start where CS part is 00 in lowest 3 digits, it can crash?
                sar eax,1
```

```
        sar eax,1
        and eax,0f000h        ;CS part of a return address made in AX
        push ax               ;push first preparing for the second of 2 RETFs that act as far jumps.
        push cx
        mov eax,20h           ;GDT index 20h for stepping stone GDT on the way to real mode.
        push eax              ; push it ready for the first RETF to act as a far jump
        call n2               ;this call pushes a 32 bit return address that points exactly to N2
   n2:  pop eax               ; this pops the 32 bit return address which points to N2 itself
        db 83h,0c0h,6         ;=add eax,6 exactly

        push eax              ;= 50h push it for retf to act as a far jump.
        db 0cbh               ;this 1st retf pops the two 32 bit numbers pushed
        db 90h                ;land on this nop if +6
        USE16                 ;It should now be in the Model Small protected mode stepping stone as
                              ;it runs these 4 next operations
        mov  eax,cr0          ; Clear both the PE bit of CR0 and the Paging enable bit, b0 and b31.
        and eax,07fffffeh     ;this small point runs while in the Model Small stepping stone mode.
        mov cr0,eax
        db 0cbh               ;this 2nd retf pops the two 16 bit numbers pushed by ax and cx
```

;Important: In the example just above, paging is not completely stopped. So a call to end_page is necessary
; just after this mode switch!
 ;=========================
 ;---
Note: I think there is one difference between a far jump and a RETF used as a substitute. Which is that when you write a far jump, its address field needs to be in the form which is right just AFTER the far jump triggers a change in the computer's mode. But when you write a RETF, its address field (pushed onto the stack) should be in the form that is the right one for the computer's mode BEFORE the RETF switches the mode??
Also I think that this might be the reason why a return from 64 bit to 16 bit mode looks a bit less complicated if both the far jumps are completely replaced by RETF's?
           ;--

  ;==============================
This subroutine may sometimes need to be in 2 copies, one copy under USE16 and the other
copy under USE32. (Only the automatically added prefixes 66h and 67h are different then)
THIS WRITES PAGING TABLES. Starting at address [13000000h]
These paging tables are essential for the 64 bit Long Mode to be possible.
;Here should be USE16 if called to here while the computer's Code Segment is in 16 bit mode.
;Here could be USE32 instead, if called to here while the computer's Code Segment is in 32 bit protected mode.
USE16

```
 write_page_tables_16:   mov ebx,13000000h        ; This all worked well.

            mov cx,4                    ;for 4 entries in PML4 (But only a 1st one could ever be needed)
            mov eax,13001007h           ;A simple address OR7 of where the PDPT is
     wrpt3:  mov [ebx],eax

            mov dword [ebx+4],0
            add ebx,8
            add eax,1000h               ;+1000h to address next PDPT table
            dec cx
            jnz wrpt3

            mov ebx,13001000h    ;an address for writing a PDPT. 512 entries for the above only
                                 ; 512 entries for the aboce only 1 PML4 necessary
            mov cx,1000h         ;was ok as=200h  ;512 entries of 8 bytes each.
                                 ;(BUT only the first 4 entries will ever be necessary on my pc)
```

```
                mov eax,13100007h        ;PD tables will start
        wrpt4:  mov [ebx],eax            ;simple address OR 07h
                mov dword   [ebx+4],0
                add ebx,8
                add eax,1000h            ;4kb further up. (AS will address an entry in the PD table
                                         ; that is 512 x8 bytes further up)
                dec cx
                jnz wrpt4  ;

                mov ebx,13100000h        ;to write PD tables.  512 entries standing for 2MB each
                                            ;will cover 1GB, so need at least 4x512 entries.
                mov ecx,4000h
                mov eax,87h              ;first entry value 000 OR 87h

        wrpt5:  mov [ebx],eax
                mov dword   [ebx+4],0
                add ebx,8
                add eax,200000h          ;entry of value 2 MB higher up every time
                dec ecx
                jnz wrpt5

                ret                      ;Finished writing the paging tables.


    ;-===============================
;This sub-routine might have to be in 2 identical copies, one under USE16 and the
other copy under USE32.
  USE16
  start_page_16:    nop                  ;This all worked well.
            mov edx,39000h
            db 0fh,20h,0e0h              ;reads a number into eax
            mov [edx+9ch],eax            ;saved for later the number read into eax.
        ;----------------------------------------------

            mov eax,0a0h                 ;CR4 Must be loaded with 6a8h not 0a0h if using xmm0 registers
                                          ;while in 64 bit mode.
            or ax,0608h                  ;THIS was necessary for xmm0 to be used in 64 bit without crashing
            db 0fh,22h,0e0h              ;?  mov cr4,eax

            mov eax,13000000h            ;  ;PLM4 start
            mov cr3,eax                  ;= 0fh,22h,0d8h

            mov ecx,0c0000080h           ;address of MSR EFER?
            db 0fh,32h                   ;RDMSR   ;??
            or ax,100h                   ;set a bit in MSR
            db 0fh,30h                   ;WRMSR ??

            mov eax,cr0
            or eax,80000001h             ;enable paging and protected mode
            mov cr0,eax

            ret

;-   The following is used to end paging after leaving 64 bit long mode.
;       It was important to call end_page, but these operations can be built-in to mode switching instead.

  end_page:   mov edx,39000h     ;The replacing of CR4 was essential to allow xmm0 register to work.
```

```
            mov eax,[edx+9ch]              ; recover a saved number to use it now.
            db 0fh,22h,0e0h         ;mov cr4,eax    is absolutely necessary
            mov ecx,0c0000080h
            db 0fh,32h
            and ax,0feffh                  ;clear 100h bit   ; seems non-essential
            db 0fh,30h
            ret

;==================================================
      USE32
  start_page_32:   nop                     ;This all worked well.
            mov edx,39000h
              db 0fh,20h,0e0h              ;maybe mov eax,cr4 ?
            mov [edx+9ch],eax              ;
        ;----------------------------------------------

            mov eax,0a0h                   ;CR4 Must be loaded with 6a8h not 0a0h if using xmm0 registers
                                           ;while in 64 bit mode.
            or ax,0608h                    ;THIS was necessary for xmm0 to be used in 64 bit without crashing
            db 0fh,22h,0e0h                ; ?  mov cr4,eax

            mov eax,13000000h              ;PLM4 start
            mov cr3,eax                    ;= 0fh,22h,0d8h

            mov ecx,0c0000080h       address of MSR EFER?
            db 0fh,32h                     ;RDMSR   ;??
            or ax,100h                     ;set a bit in MSR
            db 0fh,30h                     ;WRMSR ??

            mov eax,cr0
            or eax,80000001h               ;enable paging and protected mode
            mov cr0,eax

            ret

;==================================================
; not to use. A test of some 64 bit opcodes worked.
    USE16
     tst2:  call from_16_to_64             ;worked ok  Call while in real mode, or 32 bit addressing.
                                           ;It returns with the computer in 64 bit mode.
    USE64
            mov rbx,200000h
            mov rax,12345678abcdef12h      ;ok
            mov [rbx+10h],rax
            mov rax,0aaabbbcccdddeeefh
            mov [rbx+18h],rax
            movdqu xmm0,[rbx+10h]   ;IMPORTANT This movdqu xmm0 crashed immediately when CR4=0a0h.
            movdqu [rbx+30h],xmm0   ; CR4 has to be =06a8h while in 64 bit mode. 0608h ok in 16/32 bit
mode.
            mov rax,[rip-6]
            mov [rbx+20h],rax

            call t64                ;call to any 64 bit test here

            call from_64_to_16_     ;Avoids going through protected mode as it seems unnecessary.
    USE16
            call up32               ;call end_page essential to allow xmm0 register to go on working.
```

```
        call end_page          ;replaces cr4 from 39054h and does a and 0feffh to msr
        nop                    ;important to call end_page
        ret
```

;===
;This up32 is very useful. But it does not switch to protected mode, unless a far jump follows it. Because up32 only sets to 1 the PE bit of control register CR0, and then sets the Data Segments, without the code segment into 32 bit mode. When I used it at first in my earlier experiments I avoided running any far jumps, and avoiding far jumps meant that the Code Segment system stays in 16 bit Mode. Whenever the Code Segment system stays 16 bits, it means that the Instructions Pointer also stays in 16 bit mode. (And the FASMW assembler should see USE16 even though data addresses can be 32 bit) (You should avoid a far jump or far call if you wish the computer to stay in this state).
A call to write the Global Descriptor Table (GDT) has to have run first before you call up32, and of course the call to write a GDT should be somewhere near the start of the program.
Both Before and After this up32 the FASMW assembler needs the word USE16 (Never USE32)
Also, **it is essental that** near the very start of the whole program the stack segment register SS needs to be **loaded with zero**. The zero in ss fits together with the base address of zero in the GDT descriptor, and it means that while "up32" or "down16" are called the stack pointer can steadily keep on pointing to the same spot in the stack. And it is essential as otherwise a call up32 would crash the program.

```
up32:   cli                    ;This call to up32 leaves the Instruction Pointer as 16 bit register.
        push eax
        mov eax,cr0
        or al,1                 ;Set the protection enable bit, called PE bit.
        mov cr0,eax            ;Setting it completely changes the effect that loading a segment register has.
        mov ax,10h             ;10h is a GDT selector, pointing to a data descriptor which should have
        mov ss,ax              ;a base address of zero,  and a default/big bit set to big, and a limit set at
        mov ds,ax              ;maximum
        mov es,ax
        mov fs,ax              ;Loads GDT selector 10h into Data segment Registers.
        mov gs,ax
        pop eax
        ret
```

 This next down16 is very useful, though it cannot possibly return the computer from protected mode to real mode. It returns the computer to 16 bit Real mode Only when far jumps were avoided so that the Instruction Pointer (the Program Counter) and the Code Segment system were still in 16 bits mode, and the Data Segments Alone were with 32 bit mode. Obviously down16: cannot change the mode from protected mode to 16 bits.
Both before and after this runs the FASMW assembler needs the word USE16.
At the very start of the whole program, the stack segment register SS needs to be loaded with zero,
as it gets reloaded with zero here too. Later you can load the other segment registers with any 16 bit values you want, remembering that in 16 bit mode those segment registers have an effect which is automatically as though multiplied by 16, as though shifted one hex digit towards the left.

```
down16:   push eax             ;To be able to Call down16 like a subroutine, it's essential that SS
          mov eax,cr0          ; should already always be Zero while the program is running.
          and eax,7ffffffeh    ; Clearing to zero the PE bit, and the paging enable bit zero too.
          mov cr0,eax   ;
          mov ax,0      ;
          mov ss,ax            ; 0 in ss fits together with the 0 in base of a GDT descriptor, allowing call/Ret.
          pop eax
          ret
```

;---
;

A Global Descriptor Table

A Global Descriptor Table has to be written in order to be able to change the mode of the computer.
When the program starts running and is in Real mode, this had to be called once.
Writes a Global Descriptor Table which can work for switching modes from 16 to 64 bit and back.
  USE16   ;USE16 suitable whenever the code segment system is still in 16 bit mode.

```
gdt1:   cli             ;You have to call here at the start of the program when in real mode.
        mov ax,0                ;[ds:bx] address to write gdt in
        mov ds,ax               ;when in real mode, EBX Must contain a value below 64k.

        mov ebx,0c00h

        mov dword   [bx],0          ;8 zeroes necessary, so called gdt null. start in [00:C00h]
        mov dword   [bx+4],0    ;

        mov dword   [bx+8],0ffffh           ;At index=08, code segment descriptor. CS.D=1  CS.L=0
        mov dword   [bx+0ch],00cf9a00h      ;Index=08. working ok cf=d/b=big

        mov dword   [bx+10h],0ffffh         ;index 10h. The useful data segment descriptor
        mov dword   [ex+14h],0cf9200h       ;92h for data seg, CS.D=1, (cfh=big), base zero

        mov dword   [bx+18h],0              ;64 bit code segment at index=18h  Works well.
        mov dword   [bx+1ch],0a09a00h       ;CS.D=0  CS.L=1 For 64 bit addressing mode.

                        ;This one for stepping-stone function, of return to Real mode, so in it CS.D=0,

        mov dword   [bx+20h],0ffffh         ;New code descriptor at index=20h  base address 0
        mov dword   [bx+24h],008f9a00h      ;stepping stone for back to real mode ;8f is CS.D=0 for small

        mov word    [bx+50h],28h            ;1word length recording 28h =length of the gdt
        mov dword   [bx+52h],0c00h          ;0:0c00h dword addr recording of where gdt is,
        mov dword   [bx+56h],0              ;prepare zero for 64 bit lgdt

                        ;4 byte simple absolute address of where gdt is
                        ;An ss of 00 in 16 bit mode will fit with the descriptor base of 00

        mov bx,0c50h            ;Make bx ready for lgdt [bx], address of gdt length and address record above

        lgdt [bx]               ;Uses [ds:bx] load with length and address records

        ret                     ; gdt register is loaded
```
;=====================
To make a GDT work it is necessary **to write a 6 bytes record in the memory near it,** in which the first 2 bytes record the length of the GDT in bytes and the next 4 bytes record the exact address at which the GDT starts, as one simple 32 bit number. You can see this 6 bytes record being made just above here at address [ebx+50h] while 0C00h was in ebx. Then with 0C50h in ebx, so DS:[BX] is aimed at the 6 bytes record, (see just above here the mov ebx,0c50h which aims [BX] at the 6 bytes record) it is necessary to run the operation LGDT [BX] which tells the computer to read in the 6 bytes record so it will know the length and addrss of your GDT.
;--------
Note: I have read that the control register CR4 should be loaded into while preserving unchanged certain binary bits called reserved bits. I am not sure that I loaded CR4 in the correct way in my test of 64 bit mode, and one could improve it so that it is preserving any reserved bits unchanged. By loading CR4 into EAX, doing

a logical OR to set binary bits or doing a logical AND to clear binary bits, and then loading EAX back into CR4.

The New Registers of 64 bit mode

These are new registers which don't exist in 32 bit mode.

Bits	8	16	32	64	128	256
				RAX		
				RCX		
				RDX		
				RBX		
	spl	SP	esp	RSP		
	bpl	BP	ebp	RBP		
	sil	SI	esi	RSI		
	dil	DI	edi	RDI		
	r8b	r8w	r8d	R8	xmm8	ymm8
	r9b	r9w	r9d	R9	xmm9	ymm9
	r10b	r10w	r10d	R10	xmm10	ymm10
	r11b	r11w	r11d	R11	xmm11	ymm11
	r12b	r12w	r12d	R12	xmm12	ymm12
	r13b	r13w	r13d	R13	xmm13	ymm13
	r14b	r14w	r14d	R14	xmm14	ymm14
	r15b	r15w	r15d	R15	xmm15	ymm15

In the table "d" must stand for doubleword, as they are 32 bits. RAX to R15 are all 64 bits general registers.
The main 64 bit new registers are R8 to R15, which can be used to hold any 64 bit addresses or data.
The operations Inc and Dec do not exist in 64 bit mode, so one uses Add 1 and Sub 1.
The operation Pushad and Popad do not exist in 64 bit mode.

USE64

```
t64:    mov rcx,200000h         ;A short test to make sure the 64 bit operations are working
        mov rax,"12345678"
        mov [rcx+10h],rax       ;It wrote the 64 bits 8 bytes of data "12345678"
        nop
        nop                     ;RIP means relative to the Instructions Pointer.
        mov rax,[rip-7]         ;This operation exactly reads itself into RAX
        mov [rcx+20h],rax
        mov rax,[rip]           ;this [rip+0] operation reads the next following opcode
        mov [rcx+40h],rax       ;(The Instructions Pointer is normally pointing to the next opcode)
        mov eax,1000h           ;any number loaded into eax gets zero extended into 64 bit rax.
        ret
```

About my first experiments to try to switch to 64 bit long mode.

Switching to 64 bit mode with my E-Machines laptop seemed very complicated at first but I managed to do it after trying to do it for a few weeks. When you read about switching to 64 bit addressing in the Intel manuals, the most obvious striking thing you notice is how things which you know should be very, very simple have been made complicated on purpose. Simply switching on 64 bit addressing should be a simple matter of running a single short and simple op-code. It should never be more difficult than running a single short and simple op-code, but the Intel manual says it is complicated.

They knew it should be simple, and yet made it complicated on purpose. Probably Microsoft wanted to prevent other companies from creating rival operating systems, and so they must have vetoed many good computer designs.

The amount of programming that is necessary to switch on 64 bit mode, to switch back again to 32 bit mode and then back to 16 bit Real mode, is luckily small enough to fit on a few pages. The Intel manuals made it seem more complicated. A timing test experiment showed that the total time for switching from 16 bit to 64 bit mode and then back again to 16 bit mode was about 2 microseconds.

My test switched from 16 bit Real mode to 64 bit long Mode then back again to 16 bit real mode 1 million times in 2 seconds.

Later on I thought it would be a good idea if I could write a sub-routine which can be called, and which would return immediately to where it was called from with the computer switched into another mode. That idea worked well.

I think you should try running the short program which I wrote which switches directly from 16 bit to 64 bit and then back again to 16 bit, as it should work. (Call from_16_to_64, and call from_64_to_16.) Obviously the computer shouldn't be stuck in the 64 bit mode, and it is important that a computer programmer should feel able to switch modes back and forth.

According to Intel manuals, you cannot switch to 64 bit mode unless you firstly enable paging. That is so wrong, paging is something horrid and people couldn't want it, it was intended to obstruct. As they knew that the switch to 64 bit mode should be something extremely simple and easy, and yet deliberately made it seem extremely difficult. For that reason I had to try to teach myself how to write paging tables for identity mapping and switch on paging. That turned out to be much less difficult than it seemed, but I find it hard to understand.

Several parts of the Intel manuals give the clear impression that they are trying to make things which are normally very simple become difficult and complicated on purpose. That is not the normal way to design a computer, because people would normally care that switching to different modes should be a very simple thing.

Paging seems to be a way to scramble the memory, so that the addressing system of the whole memory is scrambled as if in a secret code.

Luckily there is a way to enable paging without scrambling the memory at all, and this is called "Identity Mapping." The Intel manuals mention that the particular area of memory where your program is running must be "Identity Mapped" just before you turn on paging, and it is easy to understand the reason for that. When you turn on the paging, if the area of memory where your program is running was not identity mapped, then as the memory becomes badly scrambled your program would seem to disappear from underneath the processor, as if a sudden random jump had occurred.

Of course that would make the computer crash immediately. So the Intel manuals have mentioned that at first when paging gets turned on, the area where your program is running must be identity mapped, which means that that area of the memory stays where it was as paging is enabled, and that prevents an immediate crash.

But whenever you enable paging, it should be your goal to identity map the whole of the memory completely. That means that the memory is not scrambled. The scrambling of memory by paging is something really horrid and nasty, intended only to confuse companies so that they will feel that it is difficult to write a new operating system. For normal computer programming you should never want paging, as it is Microsoft's way of preventing other companies from competing and it is so useless for normal purposes.

The Intel manuals explain that to switch on 64 bit mode you have to go through several steps in the right order, You have to start with a far jump which triggers protected mode. Then your program has to write several paging tables, you have to set a binary bit in a Model Specific Register with WRMSR. The EFER LME bit. You have to load control register CR3 with the base address of where your first paging table starts. You have to set 2 binary bits in control register CR4. (I think by OR 0a0h). You have to enable paging by setting binary bit 31 of control register CR0. (While binary bit 0 of CR0 is also set.)

It explains that when you have done that the PC computer is in Long Mode. And Long Mode has 2 sub-modes, which are IA32 Compatibility mode and 64 bit long mode. At first the PC is in the IA32 compatibility mode, and you switch to 64 bit mode using a far call which indexes a GDT descriptor in which the two binary bits called CS.L and CS.D have values CS.L=1 and CS.D=0. I could not find in the manual the way to switch the computer back again to 32 bit mode, but I found out that a simple RETF does it. (This RETF should be just under the key word USE32, so that the assembler does not include a rex prefix.)

I only turned on paging because I wanted to switch on 64 bit addressing as the next step. So my goal was to "identity map" the whole of the memory at the moment when paging was turned on, and you do it with paging tables which are in a simple pattern. The scrambling or lack of scrambling is controlled by the paging tables. The Intel manuals contain useful details of the binary bit fields of entries in the paging tables. There were several different kinds of paging in the Intel manuals, and I had to be careful to choose the right one. It would be easy to choose the wrong type of paging by mistake.

When paging is enabled, the normal address which you load into an address register is called a linear address, and the series of several paging tables translate it into a physical address. The physical address is the real address which really exists without scrambling. So when you load any address into a register like EBX for example, and use [EBX] as an address, that was called the linear address. When the whole memory is identity mapped the physical address will be equal to the linear address, in every case.
I tried out 1GB page size paging but apparently my laptop PC is not capable of that. Then I tried 2MByte paging size, and that worked well. The whole of the memory is then considered to be made up of many 2Mbyte pages, which can be scrambled, but with "Identity mapping" the whole memory still works as normal, which means paging does absolutely nothing.
To figure out how to write the paging tables so as to get identity mapping of the whole memory, seems much less difficult when you are careful to start out with thinking about the lowest area of the memory, and then in thinking gradually work towards higher addresses. If you were to start with higher addresses it would get confusing.

The following is an example of a "ready to use" program which writes all of the necessary paging tables and which prepares the computer for both identity mapped paging and the interesting 64 bit mode. When you call this you must be in the 32 bit protected mode to start with. Notice that in this example the far call, with op-code 9Ah, just happens to call to an address of 300000h. Which is 3 meg bytes. In my testing I had firstly copied a part of my program to the address of 3 meg bytes, but of course if you try to use this program you can change the address.

Call write_page_tables

```
Call Start_paging
mov al,33h    ;a signal to my program
;; USE32
;; call far 18h:300000h                    ;ok

db 0 9Ah,00,00,30h,00,18h,00      ; A far call op-code, as data bytes. GDT Selector=18H To switch on 64 bit mode.
                ;You also have to write a GDT which has one entry which is suitable for 64 bit mode. The call to
;write the GDT can run only once when the program starts.
;Note. It should be enough to call this writing of page tables once when the program starts, and if the
;computer's code segment system is in 16 bit mode when you call this, the word USE16 should be just
;above this write_page_tables. But if you called it when the code segment is in 32 bit mode, use USE32.
;USE16 or USE32 here depending just on the mode of when you call this here.
;In this book 2 examples of write page tables, having different addresses, and CR3 needs to be loaded with
;the right address each time.

write_page_tables:    mov ebx,500000h   ;5mb.  Tables for 2MB pages. This all worked well.

            mov cx,4                    ;for 4 entries in PML4 . (It can probably have up to 512 entries?)
            mov eax,501007h             ;simple address of where the PDPT is then add 07.
    wrpt3:  mov [ebx],eax

            mov dword   [ebx+4],0
            add ebx,8
            add eax,1000h               ;+1000h to address the next PDPT table
            dec cx
            jnz wrpt3

            mov ebx,501000h             ;[EBX] is an address for writing a PDPT.
            mov cx,1000h
            mov eax,0600007h            ;PD tables will start at 6MB.
    wrpt4:  mov [ebx],eax               ;entries are a simple address but then add 07h
            mov dword   [ebx+4],0       ;entries are 8 bytes each.
            add ebx,8                   ;The PDPT is a simple series of increasing numbers, each 1000H higher.
            add eax,1000h               ; AS will address an entry in the PD table that is 512 x8 bytes further
            dec cx
            jnz wrpt4

            mov ebx,600000h             ;[EBX] to write PD tables.  Entries start as Zero, but all OR 87H
            move edx,0
            mov ecx,4000h               ;(512 entries which stand for 2MB each would cover 1GB.)
            mov eax,87h                 ; 4000h entries should cover 32 G bytes space. Can increase this.
    wrpt5:  mov [ebx],eax               ; The PD table is a simple series of increasing numbers, each 2MB higher.
            mov [ebx+4],edx
            add ebx,8
            add eax,200000h             ;entry 2 MB higher up every time
            adc edx,0                   ; edx to be the more significant part of the entries.
            dec ecx
            jnz wrpt5
            ret                         ;Finished writing the paging tables.
```

;Notes. Just before turning on paging, I thought it was a good idea to save the value in control register CR4 for later.
;When ending the paging and returning the computer to 16 bit real mode, it was a good idea to replace

;the previous value in CR4. (the call with label "end_page:" does that)
;I found out that if the wrong value stays in CR4, then the computer might seem to work at first but if
;you try to use the XMM0 register the computer would crash. When you replace a right value into CR4,
;you can continue using the registers XMM0 to XMM7 and that works normally.

;-===============================

```
 start_page:                              ;This all worked well.
             mov edx,39000h
             mov eax,cr4                  ;;=db 0fh,20h,0e0h  ;
             mov [edx+54h],eax
;---------------------------- Note: you are supposed to preserve CR4's reserved bits unchanged.

; Maybe this is not  really right because not preserving its reserved bits?

             mov eax,0a0h              ;CR4 Must be loaded with 6a8h not 0a0h if using xmm0 registers.
             or ax,0608h               ;THIS was necessary for xmm0 to be used in 64 bit without crashing
             mov cr4,eax               ;;=db 0fh,22h,0e0h

             mov eax,500000h           ;PLM4 table start at 5MB ?
             mov cr3,eax               ;= 0fh,22h,0d8h ;This load into CR3 triggers loading of all the tables.

             mov ecx,0c0000080h           ;address of MSR EFER in ecx register.
             db 0fh,32h                ;RDMSR   ;??
             or ax,100h                ;set a bit in MSR.
             db 0fh,30h                ;WRMSR ??

             mov eax,cr0
             or eax,80000001h     ;enable paging and protected mode together
             mov cr0,eax

             ret

 end_page:   mov edx,39000h           ;The replacing of CR4 was essential to allow xmm0 register to work.
             mov eax,[edx+54h]        ;recover a saved CR4
             mov cr4,eax              ;;=db 0fh,22h,0e0h   ;mov cr4,eax is absolutely necessary

             mov ecx,0c0000080h       ;an address of a model specific register has to be in ECX
             db 0fh,32h               ;RDMSR
             and ax,0feffh            ;clear 100h bit   ; seems non essential
             db 0fh,30h               ;WRMSR
             ret
```

 Note: I tried using the xmm0 register in some other parts of the program to copy 16 bytes of data at a time. Using the xmm0 register crashed the computer when certain wrong numbers were in the CR4 register. To be able to use the xmm0 register, the CR4 register had to have the number 608h in it during 16 bit mode, and the number 6a8h in it during 64 bit long mode. I do not understand CR4, but I have also read that the reserved bits in it should be kept unchanged.

                 I think the CR4 register can be changed with preserving its reserved bits by:
```
mov eax,CR4
or eax,0a0h                 ;set 2 bits for 64 bit mode?? 0a0h= 1010 0000b
mov CR4,eax
```
             ;And in the other direction, clear 2 bits for a return to 32 or 16 bit mode?
```
Mov eax,CR4
and AL,5Fh              ;clear the 2 bits for 32 bit mode??  05Fh = 0101 1111b
```

    mov CR4,eax

Though my paging tables worked and I have switched on 64 bit mode, I am not quite sure how large a memory you could address easily with the 64 bit mode. The reason for that is that my laptop PC has a bit less than 4 G-Bytes RAM, and so I have not been able to test the so-called 64 bit addressing on my computer with addresses higher than 4 GB. One clear diagram in an Intel manual shows that a PML4 table can have up to 512 entries, but in my own laptop 4 entries is certainly enough.
I have been able to demonstrate that with 64 bit mode my laptop PC has a new range of 64 bit registers and interesting new operations such as program counter relative MOVs, which are called RIP for Relative Instruction Pointer, and which only exist in 64 bit Long Mode. Definitely the 64 bit mode is working, and I converted some sections of my programs to 64 bit.

The only reason why I started paging, was that I wanted to turn on 64 bit long mode. And the Intel manual states that you have to enable this specific type of paging before 64 bit mode can be turned on. The 64 bit mode seems very much better than 32 bit protected mode, because it has 8 new general purpose registers and it has new Instruction pointer relative operations which could be useful. I checked that while the 64 bit mode is running the paging mechanism still works, and that makes it more important to do identity mapping so that the memory seems to be in a very simple natural state.

One experiment was of non-identity mapping.

I also did an experiment in which I started with complete identity mapping but then made one small change in the paging tables so that a single 2 meg byte area would be mapped to the main screen memory. In the experiment I changed one page directory entry which was 800087H into 0C0000087H. It worked immediately with one experiment, and any loads done to 8 meg bytes wrote onto the visible screen exactly as if the loads had been to the screen memory at its usual address of 0C0000000H. This meant that the screen memory could now be reached in 2 different ways. It is easy to get non-identity mapping in more places, but I don't think it would be useful. (Since the tables were written for identity mapping to start with, the entry which had the number 800087H in it (which stands simply for the address 800000H,) was the right entry which when changed would make any loads that normally would go to 800000H address go to somewhere else. That is loads go to the address which is specified by the new value of the entry when you have changed the entry).

But a few days later when I tried the experiment a second time, it would not work at first. I discovered that it was the loading of special control register **CR3** which was necessary to make any changes to the paging tables work. The processor must load the whole of your paging tables into a hidden area of its memory where these tables must work much more quickly than if they were left in the usual RAM memory. Whenever you make any changes to your paging tables, you need to re-load control register CR3 and the changes made to the paging tables take effect only when you have re-loaded CR3.
   It is not a question of loading a different number into CR3, because it works when you reload CR3 with the same number, which has to be the base address of your PLM4 table. So it must be just the action of loading CR3 which does it.

It is certainly not necessary to understand the details of how paging works, to be able to use the short program I wrote to enable the paging and switch to 64 bit mode. Paging is absolutely crazy, but the 64 bit mode is good. Soon after writing the program that works, I forgot about paging since paging is a system I do not like.
;------------------------   ------------------------ --------------------------------   -------------------------

I am going to describe my very first experiments for switching on 64 bit mode, because I think it was interesting.
The first step was to make a copy of the program which I wanted to try running partly in 32 bit compatibility mode and partly in 64 bit mode, to a higher part of the computer's memory, which happened to be 3 Meg Bytes.
You just have to make your program copy an area of itself to any much higher area of the memory, and then run a far jump or far call to the start of that copy in a higher area of the memory. Such tests do not necessarily involve any copying of the program to higher memory. (Later on the better way of doing it used RETF as a substitute for a far jump, and you just call a sub-routine and it switches the mode and returns). This far jump

or Retf needs to index one descriptor which you have written in your GDT, which should be suitable for switching on protected mode. The far jump itself triggers the switch to 32 bit protected mode at the same time as jumping to the start of your copy of the program, maybe in a higher area of the memory.

At the start of the experiment my program happened to make this copy of the program while it was running in plain 32 bit addressing mode. By plain 32 bit addressing I mean I had avoided running a far jump at first, so the computer's Instruction Pointer and code segment was still in its 16 bit mode, while data segments were 32 bit.

When it had made the copy of part of the program, it then used a far jump to jump to the copy of my program which was at 3 Meg bytes. This far jump, triggered a change in the Code segment and in the instruction pointer to make it 32 bit, and this state is normally called protected mode. Now about the exact form of this far jump. Specifically because the computer was at first with 16 bit code segment and so expecting the shorter form of operands, I wrote the far jump with a 66h prefix. A prefix of 66h tells the computer that the next operand is NOT of the size of the current default which it expects.

I wrote the far jump either this way
```
USE16
  db 66h,0eah,00,00,30h,00,08,00
```

Or this way
```
USE32
db 066h
jmp far 18h:300000h   ;both are the same
```

0eah is the op-code for a far jump, and 00,00,30h,00 is the address to jump to written in the "little-endian" way round, and means 0300000h which is 3 meg bytes. 08 is a GDT selector which selects the very 1st descriptor in my example of a GDT.
This method of writing an op-code as data bytes worked for both the Borland Tasm assembler and with the better FASMW assembler which I prefer using now. The processor was at that time expecting the short form of operands, and so it had the 66H operand size prefix to tell the processor that it was in the longer form at a time when it expected a shorter form. The 08,00 was the GDT selector 0008h which a far jump loads into the CS register, and it triggered a change into normal protected mode. (I had turned off interrupts by running the operation CLI .)

Now something important. Whenever the computer switches to protected mode, its code segment system switches to 32 bits, and that reverses the default size which the processor assumes of both operands and addresses, it also reverses the way in which it understands the prefixes 66h and 67h. These two prefixes go in front of other op-codes to modify their size. Assemblers automatically insert large numbers of these two prefixes into programs, and any error in the prefixes or in an assumed size anyway would crash the program of course.
Because of that switch to protected mode, the FASMW assembler had to be informed that this area of the program (which in the first experiment was copied to 3 Meg bytes,) was an area in which has the "big" default size. So the 3 MB area of the program has to have the "USE32" at its start.
So the operand size prefix 66h and the address size prefix 67h would have "an opposite meaning" to the meaning which they have in Real mode, and so it is a slight nuisance that the assembler has to be told about this. The assembler then knows that these prefixes need to be inserted into op-codes differently. With the FASMW you do that with the assembler directive USE32. USE32 reverses the way in which the FASMW inserts these two prefixes into the program from then on.
In this case
```
   USE32
    db 66h
   jmp far 8:300000h
   USE16
```
(This 66h should be there only assuming that a far jump has been avoided until now and that therefore the processor still has the "small default operand size" as it has in Real Mode. The far jump will immediately trigger a change in the "default operand size" to "big" size, and therefore any further far jumps must not have the

66h. When you write a similar far jump for when the computer is ALREADY in protected mode, then it must Not have the 66h.)
;--
The following is about my first experiment. In the part of the program which runs at 3 Meg bytes, the computer firstly did the call to write the paging tables and to enable paging in the way which according to the Intel manual should switch the computer to 32 bit compatibility mode. My program then ran in a small loop, in which it drew a hexadecimal view screen, so that you can look at all the memory in hexadecimal, and I was also able to scroll the view with the page up/page down keys. (Keyboard inputs work with the single operation in al,60h which reads a scan code.) When I pressed a certain key, my program ran a far call which instantly switched on 64 bit mode.
The reason why the far call instantly switched on 64 bit mode, is that it loaded the Code Segment register CS with the selector =18H to select my GDT descriptor which was written for 64 bit mode.

I had to write a GDT descriptor specially for 64 bit mode. The 64 bit mode GDT descriptor has to have an CS.L bit =1 and a CS.D bit=0, and its base address and upper limit fields are completely ignored in 64 bit mode. While the computer was running in 64 bit mode I did a series of simple tests to try to find out how to use the new instructions of this mode, such as the new instruction pointer relative mov instructions. And a lot of new registers.

When you use the FASMW assembler you normally have to write the assembler directive USE64 at the start of the area of 64 bit mode program, and it is better that way. But before I did that, I did something of an unusual experiment in the very first experiment. I happened to try USE32 and sometimes that did not crash. It is interesting that sometimes a program written under USE32 can run in both 32 bit and in 64 bit modes. You have to be careful to replace any Inc/Dec instructions with Add/Sub because in 64 bit mode the computer would wrongly think the Inc instruction was a Rex prefix. I found in a first experiment it was possible for the computer to run the hexadecimal view routine equally well while it was in either 32 bit or 64 bit mode if it was written in the right way. I did some changes to the routine. I am saying that if you are careful to avoid the special 64 bit instructions, there is a way to get a part of a program to run in either 32 or 64 bit mode.

Later on I wrote it so that it could run only in 64 bit mode. Under the directive USE64 the FASMW assembler automatically inserts a REX prefix 48H whenever the op-code operand should be 64 bits.
Then I tried the FASMW assembler keyword USE64. It was exciting to see proof that 64 bit data and new instruction pointer relative loads were working.

When I pressed on another key, my program should return the computer from 64 bit mode to 32 bit compatibility mode, but at first the computer kept crashing. Returning the computer to 32 bit protected mode was difficult at first because I did not know how to do it. Then after a while I found out how to do it.

To return the computer from 64 bit mode to 32 bit mode, all I needed was one RETF op-code, written as db 0CBH. So a FAR CALL triggers the change which switches the 64 bit mode on, and a RETF returns the computer to 32 bit mode. The RETF or far ret can be easily written as db 0CBH. I found out there was a problem that after the directive USE64 the FASMW assembler sees the word RETF and writes a RETF op-code as 48h,0CBh. In this the 48H is a REX prefix. In this form of the RETF makes the computer crash because the REX prefix should not be there. It seems that the FASMW assembler has a minor fault in that way. The op-code should be simply 0CBH, and it is OK to write it as data bytes. So I tried writing the directive USE32 immediately before writing RETF, and this also worked OK for the FASMW, because writing USE32 prevented the rex prefix..

Far jumps and far calls do not exist in the Intel 64 bit mode. As the Intel manual says, you cannot possibly use a far jump or far call while in 64 bit mode, because for some reason they have made it an invalid op-code in 64 bit mode. But Pushes followed by RETF can be used as a substitute for a far jump, and so I later on did experiments with pushes which were followed by RETF, and I found that you can use that as a substitute for far jumps while in 64 bit mode. I am going to give several examples of it further on. In my GDT, the descriptor which worked to activate 64 bit mode was the table's third descriptor, and therefore its index (the index is also called a selector), was 18h. In this descriptor, its CS.D bit was zero, and its CS.L bit was set to 1, as it needs to be for 64 bit mode.

The Intel manual said that in 64 bit mode the base address and the limit fields of the GDT descriptor was ignored, and so I tested that and I found that these fields in the descriptor were ignored completely and so could be zero or anything. It is true that the base address and the limit fields are completely ignored.

The following is a description of my first experiments. The far call operation which triggered the switch to 64 bit mode, had this 18H in its CS field which it loads into the CS register to trigger the change of mode. The far call which triggered the switch to 64 bit mode was written as
 db 09Ah,00,00,30h,00,18h,00 As you see this also jumped to the address of 300000h or that is 3 Meg bytes, which was the same address as where the 32 bit program started in my experiment.
So I firstly loaded a small number into the AL register just before running the far call, and at 3 Meg bytes the program began with several compare to AL and relative conditional jumps JZ.

So that the very start of the program at 3MB would jump to different places depending on the value I put into AL, and that made it jump to my 64 bit testing loop instead of going to the 32 bit loop. I tried several different loops in my program.
When the computer is switched into 64 bit mode, that area of the program should be below the assembler directive USE64. Assuming that you use the FASMW assembler since other assemblers can use a different keyword that has the same meaning.
But, a few days before I tried the FASMW assembler directive USE64, which you do need for proper 64 bit experiments, I tried making a program loop work in 64 bit mode under USE32. It is just to see that in some cases this is possible. The following are a few experiments which I tried before trying the normal keyword USE64. It sometimes worked, and in 64 bit mode the default address size was 64 bit but I had to write a REX prefix in the form db 48h in front of any operation which I wanted to have 64 bit operand. A 64 bit operand is 64 bit data in a register. This sometimes worked, for example in 64 bit mode

```
USE32              ;But with normal programming it should be USE64
db 48h                         ;db 48h is a REX prefix
mov eax,44332211h              ;IThis oaded the 64 bit RAX register with 8877665544332211H
db 55h,66h,77h,88h             ;   the second half of the same op-code is written as data bytes.

mov ebx,50000h                 ;In 64 bit mode this should automatically be zero extended.
db 48h                         ;The rex prefix to make 8 byte load rather than 4 byte load.
mov [ebx],eax                  ;This loaded RAX into memory at address in EBX, where I could see it with my view screen.
```
The above example of programming was not normal, since you should use the keyword USE64.
When I tried using the USE64 directive for the FASMW assembler, it lets you try an interesting range of new 64 bit instructions, such as 8 new general purpose registers named R8 to R15, and the interesting Instruction Pointer Relative MOV instructions.
Whenever it is in 64 bit mode, you cannot ever use the INC or DEC instructions because their op-codes are interpreted as different REX prefixes instead. My programs crashed several times when I tried using INC EBX or DEC ECX. It worked when I replaced that with an add instruction like ADD EBX,1. Or a subtract like SUB ECX,1.

The FASMW works well for 64 bit mode.
I noticed something. Before returning the computer to 32 bit mode, some of the long registers had to be cleared to 0, otherwise the program could crash a short time after returning to 32 bit mode. It was surely because of some error in my program. So before returning to 32 bit mode I loaded zeroes into some of the general purpose registers, and the crashes were prevented. But later on this might not be necessary.
```
Mov Rbx,0
Mov Rdx,0
Mov Rcx.0
db 0cbh              ; db 0cbh is a RETF which triggered a return to 32 bit.
;-------------
```
I tried out some Instruction Pointer relative movs simply to try to see it working. Instruction pointer relative is called RIP for "Relative Instruction Pointer."
It was interesting that a Mov instruction which was 7 bytes long could read its own self with [rip-7].
```
USE64
Mov rdx,51000h       ;any address which my partly hexadecimal screen view can look at.
Mov rax,[rip-7]      ;The instruction pointer relative load here reads its own op-code into rax.
```

```
    Mov [rdx],rax              ;write its own opcode where I can look at it.
```

I tried an instruction pointer relative load that added +1 to an immediate number in an op-code. When I looked at the program itself, I could see that number continually increasing!

;-----
Experiments which use a RETF as a substitute for a far jump or for a far call.

I loaded an address into the stack pointer which would let me see what it pushes with my hexadecimal view screen. I found out that whether the computer was in 32 bit protected mode or in 32 bit compatibility mode a FAR CALL always pushed 8 bytes onto the stack. A far call firstly pushed 4 bytes with a return GDT selector in the lower 2 bytes. I think the upper 2 bytes just get filled with zero. It then pushes the 4 byte return address which is the value that was in the 4 bytes Instruction Pointer. (The far call's op-code had 4+2 bytes to get pushed, and so it was a surprise that it pushed 8 bytes, not 6.)

 I found out that regardless of whether the computer is in a 32 bit mode or in 64 bit mode, the RETF which you should write as just db 0CBH firstly pops the 4 byte return address into the instruction pointer and then pops the 2 bytes return selector in the lower 2 bytes of a 4 bytes pop. So 8 bytes are popped by the RETF. This is what happens when a far call triggers the start of 64 bit mode and later a RETF returns the computer to 32 bit compatibility mode.

 I also discovered that in 64 bit mode when the RETF is written with a REX prefix 48H in front of it, then the RETF written as db 48H,0CBH always pops 16 bytes. It firstly pops 8 bytes into the instructions pointer, and then it pops another 8 bytes the lowest 2 bytes of which are the GDT selector which pops into the CS register. (The FASMW writes it with the REX prefix if it is below the assembler directive USE64, and that might be wrong since if you want to trigger the return to 32 bit mode it must not have the REX prefix).
The Intel manual says far jumps are not valid in 64 bit mode.

I found out that I can use this RETF as a substitute for a Far jump while in 64 bit mode. To do it you just firstly push 8 bytes that have your GDT selector in the lowest 2 of the 8, and then push another 8 bytes of an address for the instruction pointer. A total of 16 bytes have to be pushed. Then write either RETF or write db 48H,0CBH and it worked like a far jump. (The lowest 2 bytes of 8 bytes are the last 2 to be pushed).
I discovered that in 64 bit mode both forms of RETF can be used as a substitute for far jumps, in which the computer STAYS IN 64 bit mode after the jump takes place. For example
```
USE64
Mov Rax,18h                ; An 8 byte load
Push Rax                   ; An 8 bytes push
Mov Rax,300000h            ;address of 3 M Bytes for the instructions pointer.
Push Rax                   ;Another 8 bytes push
RETF                       ;Here  db 48H,0CBH is exactly the same thing as this RETF because of USE64.
                           ;It has the REX prefix. It pops 16 bytes.
```
The above pushes followed by RETF worked exactly like a far jump to the address of 3 Meg bytes, and the computer jumped to that address and it remained in 64 bit mode after jumping because the 18h was the GDT selector which indexes the GDT descriptor which was written for 64 bit mode.
It could be useful that though the Intel manual says that far jumps do not work in 64 bit mode, you can make the computer do a far jump by using pushes followed by a RETF.

Another example. In both examples the computer stays in 64 bit mode after the RETF has been used as a substitute for a far jump.
```
USE32                      ; A different example of a far jump to go to the same address while in 64 bits mode.
Mov eax,18h                ;In 64 bit mode a 4 byte load like this is naturally zero extended into 8 bytes
Push eax                   ; A 4 bytes push.
Mov eax,300000h
Push eax                    ;A 4 bytes push
db 0CBH                    ;Here 0CBH and RETF are exactly the same thing because of USE32. It pops 8 bytes.
```

In another test I wrote a specific address into the stack pointer just before the far call which switched on

64 bit mode. Then in order to return from my 64 bit program loop to the 32 bit program loop, I reloaded the stack pointer with that specific address minus 8, (Because as the stack pointer pushes down it gets decremented, and when the far call makes it push 8 bytes its value is decreased by 8). The Far Call was:
Mov esp,3a000h   ;this happened to be the load into the stack pointer. Here in 32 bit compatibility mode.
db 9Ah,00,00,30H,00,18H,00   ;This far call switched the computer into 64 bit mode.

Then later on returning to 32 bit mode.
Mov esp,39FF8h   ;39FF8h is equal to 3A000h Minus 8. Load the stack pointer while in 64 bit mode.
db 0CBH   ;This RETF during 64 bit mode, returned the computer to 32 bit mode.

In my experiments with a RETF used as a substitute for a far jump, it usually happened to jump to the start of the program which was at address 3 M bytes. Because I wanted the jumps to go to different directions or to program loops from there, depending of where the far jump had come from, some loops for 64 bit and some loops for 32 bit, I happened to use this technique, which was to put at the very start of the 3 Meg byte area several compare operations to the AL register, and after each compare a conditional relative jump JZ so that the computer would go to the program loop which I wanted it to go to. Just before the RETF that was used as a far jump, I loaded a number into the AL register to decide which loop the jump would end up going to.

The idea of the next experiment was that using Pushes followed by RETF as a substitute for a far call, I tried to find a way to make this substitute go only a very short distance, and land right on a nearby area of program. This experiment did it:
Assuming that you have written a GDT descriptor for 64 bit mode, and that the computer has written a GDT and run the two important calls "call write_page_tables and then call start_paging", which write the paging tables for identity mapping, and prepare control registers for paging, then under USE32, running this short program piece immediately switches the computer to 64 bit mode and the computer jumps onto a few NOP's which are just a very short distance away, and then in this example runs the jump to "loop_64_bit". (not shown) If later the computer runs a RETF in order to return to 32 bit mode, then the computer immediately returns to this area, and runs the jump to jump label "loop_32_bit". It can be interesting to think about this example to see how it works.

```
USE32
            Move cx,8            ;The 8 is a GDT selector for later on return to 32 bit mode.
            Push ecx             ;Push it for later on returning to 32 bit mode.
            Call J9              ;A call for the program to locate where it is, by popping the EIP into eax.
            Add eax,3            ;Move EIP a bit further ahead so as to skip over 2 op-codes. (to land at *2)
            Push eax             ;Push EIP for later on return to 32 bit mode
            Mov ecx,18h          ; The 18h is the GDT selector for the first jump for 64 bit mode.
            Push ecx             ;Push GDT selector of +18h to select the 64 bit mode GDT descriptor..
            Add eax,6   ;Adding 6 moves EIP further ahead so it skips over one other op-code, (land at *1.)
            Push eax             ;push EIP for first jump. (It now points to the five 90h =NOP's at (*1))
            db 0cbh              ;This RETF goes a very short distance, But switches on 64 bit addressing.
J9:         call j11             ;For the computer to locate where it is
J11:        pop eax              ;Pop the EIP into eax.
            ret
            db 90h,90h   ;(*2)  Land here later on when a retf as db 0cbh returns from 64 bit to 32 bit.

            jmp loop_32_bit      ;Go to the 32 bit program later when returned from 64 bit to 32 bit.
            db  90h,90h,90h,90h,90h     ;(*1) The first RETF jump should land within these 5 NOPs.
            jmp loop_64_bit             ;Go to the 64 bit program now.
;-------------------------------
```

The Paging Table.

The paging tables are difficult to understand, and that must be because the system of paging was intended to scramble the memory so as to protect Microsoft from competition by making it seem as though operating systems are difficult. Since my laptop PC has less than 4 GBytes of RAM memory, I have not been able to test the paging tables with a larger memory. But they are probably OK for a larger memory, because it follows a regular repeating pattern.

The following is explained clearly in the Intel manual for the processor. The number in the special control register CR3 points to the base of the PML4 table. Every entry in the PML4 paging table points to the base of a PDPT paging table. Every entry in the PDPT table points to the base of a PD table (Page Directory table). Every entry in a PD table points to the start of a 2 Meg Byte area of the computer's memory.
In my example program I wrote the PML4 table starting at address 500000h. The PDPT table starting at address 501000h, The PD tables starting at address 600000h, which is of course 6 meg bytes.
These three addresses can easily be changed, since you can write the paging tables wherever you want. But the lowest binary bits of the address have to be zero. Of course when you change the address of where you write the tables, you have to carefully change the number in the first entry of each kind of table so it points to the new base address of the next table.
Luckily for identity mapping writing the tables is less difficult than it seems, because it is better when there are no gaps at all between the PD tables. And in my example the PD tables are joined end to end and form a continuous and simple series of numbers all the way, each of those numbers is simply +200000H greater than the previous number. Each entry in these tables is 8 bytes long.
The entries in the PD tables are a normal address in their higher parts, and according to what I read in the Intel manual, should contain either the number 87h or the number 83h in their lowest binary bits, which is not a part of the address. The 87h has some other purpose and the address is just as if the 87h was not there.

Next, the PDPT tables are joined end to end with no gaps, the entries in the PDPT tables are all a simple series of ascending numbers all the way through, each number +1000h greater than the previous number. These entries are all addresses in their higher areas which point to the start of a PD table, while in their lower binary bits, they should contain either a 7 or a 3, which is not part of the address.
The entries in the PML4 table are each an address which points to the start of a PDPT table.
 Their lowest binary bits should contain either a 7 or a 3 which is not part of the address. But since I have written the whole lot of the PDPT tables joined up as a simple series of numbers, each entry is simply +1000h greater than the previous entry. But PML4 table only has 4 entries. It can probably have up to 512 entries, but the memory of my computer is much too small for me to test it. If your computer had a much bigger RAM memory, you could try increasing the count-down numbers in the ECX register to make the program just write longer tables. Just writing longer tables should work with a computer which has a much bigger RAM memory.

The lowest of the entries in the PML4 table has to simply point to the start of the first PDPT table, so this first entry is 501007h. (Since I happened to start the PDPT table at address 501000h).The lowest entry in the series of PDPT tables has to simply point to the start of the lowest entry in the PD tables, so this lowest entry is 600007h. (Since I happened to start the PD table at address 600000h.) The lowest entry in the very start of the PD tables is simply a zero which stands for zero memory address, with an 87h (or 83h), in its lowest binary bits which has some other meaning and is not part of the address. 000087h. This points to the zero address of the very lowest part of the computer's RAM memory. The second entry in the PD table is 200087h, which is for 2 meg bytes. The third entry is 400087h, which stands for 4 meg bytes, the fourth entry is 600087h, and so on.
 I think it identity mapped the whole memory.

You can change a few entries in the PD tables so as to create non-identity mapping in just one or several of the 2 meg byte areas of memory at a time, but when you do that you have to reload the special register CR3 again with the same address of where the PML4 table starts, because I have noticed that the action of loading CR3, makes the computer register the new changes that you have made to the tables. In my experiment the computer did not notice that I had made changes to the tables, until the instant when it reloaded CR3.
You can do this with:
Mov eax,500000   ;address of start of PML4 table (in other example paging tables were at different ad
Mov CR3,eax

When a table is changed so that a part of the memory is no longer identity mapped, this has no effect on any data that was already in the memory, but it affects any loads which you make to that address afterwards.
;--
I have read that the reserved binary bits of control register CR4 should be preserved unchanged, and I am not sure that my experiments did that the right way?

I have read in the manual for the processor that in 64 bit mode the segment registers DS;ES;SS are not used at all, and would be ignored. The 64 bit mode was definitely set and all worked without loads into those segment registers.

END

;--

The Cmos

I think this is where my program reads from the Cmos and writes a visible time and date onto the memory at an address of 1ffff0h or just below 2 MB, where I could see it on the screen.

I have read in a book that one should never write into certain areas of a Cmos because the areas are guarded by a check-sum, and if any small change were made to those areas then next time the computer starts, the BIOS would see the error in the check-sum and the BIOS would then refuse to boot the computer. In fact the computer would need to be repaired.

The time and date area is just outside of the check sum area.

I think, but am not sure, that one of the check-sums is the simple sum of Cmos bytes +10h to +2dh, and the sum has to be written in a Big-Endian way round at offset +2eh, as a 2 byte number?

I never tried writing into the Cmos because I felt it would not be safe and might damage my computer.

My bootable program displays time and date and I think it does it with this program.

```
;-------------------------------------------------
cmos10:     in al,70h           ;Read a byte from the CMOS
            and al,080h         ;preserve b7 which is for nmi
            or al,cl
                                ;lowest 6 bits can select a cmos byte, bit7 has to be preserved
            out 70h,al          ;select cmos byte
            in al,71h           ;read the selected cmos byte
            ret

unpack:     mov ah,al           ;call with al=BCD number to unpack and to make ascii
            and al,0fh
            add al,30h
            shr ah,1
            shr ah,1
            shr ah,1
            shr ah,1
            add ah,30h
            ret
;-----------------------------------------------------------------------
to_bin:     push cx             ;call here with one two digit number in AL only.
                                ;(AL can't go above 99.
            mov cl,al           ;call with al= 2 bcd digits to convert to binary.
            and al,0fh          ;to return with ax = binary in AL

            and cl,0f0h         ;in binary the left bcd digit is to start with x16

            shr cl,1            ;zeroes in the left. from x16 to x8
            mov ah,cl           ;ah is x8
            shr cl,1            ;to x4
            shr cl,1            ;to x2
            add cl,ah           ;x8+x2=x10
            mov ah,0
            add al,cl           ;upper digit x10 + lower digit x1.

            pop cx
            ret

;====================================
;-----------------------------------
seconds:    mov ebx,1ffff0h     ;1fffd0h is one row higher
            mov cl,4            ;address cmos hours  This all worked well.
            call cmos10         ;gets one cmos byte into AL
            call unpack         ;the cmos byte is simply 2 decimal digits, 0-9 each in a 4 bits nibble.
            mov [ebx],ah
```

```
            mov [ebx+1],al
            mov byte [ebx+2],":"        ;between hours and minutes
            add ebx,3
            mov cl,2                    ;address cmos minutes
            call cmos10
            call unpack
            mov [ebx],ah
            mov [ebx+1],al
            mov byte [ebx+2],":"
            add ebx,3

            mov cl,0                    ;cl to address a cms seconds byte.
            call cmos10                 ;after read cmos byte, either call to binary or call unpack to ascii
            call unpack
            mov [ebx],ah
            mov [ebx+1],al
;-------------

            mov ebx,1fffd0h
            mov cl,7                    ;+6=day of week, +7= day of month
            call cmos10
            call unpack
            mov [ebx],ah
            mov [ebx+1],al
            mov byte [ebx+2],2fh
            add ebx,3
            mov cl,8                    ;month
            call cmos10
            call unpack
            mov [ebx],ah
            mov [ebx+1],al
            mov byte [ebx+2],2fh
            add ebx,3
            mov cl,9                    ;=9 to address cmos year.
            call cmos10
            call to_bin                 ;once converted to binary, I can add 2000d
            add ax,2000d                ;book said add 1980d but book is wrong. ;add year 2000d
            call to_decimal
            mov [ebx],dh
            mov [ebx+1],dl              ;you have to add 2000d to what's in the cmos, to get 2013d, so
            mov [ebx+2],ah              ;after adding 2000d you have to subtract 1980d
            mov [ebx+3],al              ;to get value that goes into the directory word at +18h
                                        ; That sum is overall adding 20d to value in cmos +9, and then it goes into +18h

      ret
```

;------------------

A worry about the drive number.

When you put a boot loader onto a USB memory stick, it goes onto its sector 0. As the boot sector is usually sector 0, though one USB memory stick had, before I formatted it a system similar to the master boot record on its sector zero, and that has entries which point to the sector which is the start sector of a partition. I have put my own boot loaders onto memory stick boot sectors so many times, using several methods. You can use BIOS int 13h from "Free Dos" to do that, and I have also used my own EHCI programming to do it many times. And I have also created a windows 7 program which puts my boot loader onto sector 0 of the USB memory stick from windows. I have always been very careful when I used either Bios Int 13h or Windows, because there is a danger which you have to be careful of.

There is something that worries me about the drive numbers. Sector 0 of the computer's hard drive is its master boot record, and if you wrote anything over the master boot record the computer would be damaged, completely ruined in an instant. The problem is that when you use bios int 13h you have to put the right drive number into the DL register, and the right drive number is sometimes unpredictable. When I used Free Dos operating system and my laptop's BIOS boot sequence set to boot USB-FDD, the drive number was always zero, and so it was not a problem. But a serious problem might exist if I tried using a certain desktop PC.

 A few years ago I wrongly assumed that the drive number for the hard drive was with no exceptions 80h and that when FreeDos was not there or when the BIOS setup was not set for USB-FDD, the drive number for a USB memory stick was 81h, because this seemed to be so for several computers. This was the case for a certain desktop PC, but then a week later when I tested a program on the same PC suddenly the drive numbers were the opposite way round! Now drive number 81h was the hard drive, and drive number 80h was for my Usb memory stick!.

So without warning the Bios had swapped around the two drive numbers. The number 81h used to be the memory stick, but suddenly 81h was the hard drive! The Bios did this for no reason that I could think of. So if I had assumed that number 81h was permanently right for the memory stick, and if I had tried to write onto the memory stick boot sector with that drive number of 81h, it would have been very dangerous and it would have instantly caused serious damage by writing over the master boot record of the hard drive. How strange that the BIOS swapped over the two drive numbers and interchanged them with no warning. So when you try to write a boot-loader over the memory stick's sector 0 using Int 13h, you have to take precautions to make absolutely sure you won't write onto the hard drive by mistake, and that is important as a mistake would wreck the computer. I think maybe the drive number becomes a safe 00 when USB-FDD (floppy) is in the start of the BIOS boot sequence?

When you create a boot-loader, it should use BIOS extended read to read your whole program from the memory stick into the memory, and the whole thing is actually simple if you know what drive number the memory stick will have to the BIOS at the time when the computer starts running.

I don't know yet whether it is true that when booting the BIOS leaves for you the right boot drive number in the DL register?? If not, then one would want to make a boot-loader automatically try out several different drive numbers in DL register until it can find the right one? I did that by formatting the memory stick so it would have a specific "Volume label", (A volume label appears in the place of the first directory entry. The Volume Label is therefore like the very first file name in the file directory.)

The boot loader had to try several different drive numbers in turn, calculate the sector number which would have the Volume label at its start, and looking each time for the volume label. So it is so much easier to make a boot loader when it works for just one computer and you know the right drive number, but you can get a boot loader to try several different drive numbers and look for the volume label which you gave the memory stick as you formatted it.

(Of course there is no danger when you use EHCI programming to write sectors since the EHCI does not use drive numbers and never writes on the hard drive anyway). Of course when a boot-loader is only using Bios extended read there is no risk in that. The method I thought of is to try reading from a drive looking for certain specific words which I know are there on my memory stick only, numbers that I am sure won't be on a hard drive, and when those specific words are there you can assume your test drive number is for the memory stick. When you format a memory stick as fat16, the text words "fat16" will be on a USB memory stick at offset + . This should make it relatively safe since computer hard drives do not often or normally start with a single fat16 partition?

You can also deliberately put words on a memory stick as a Volume label. You can easily format a USB memory stick in windows, and when you do it you have the chance to type a "Volume label." A volume label goes onto the very beginning of the drives file directory, where the first file name would be. I gave my usb memory stick a specific volume label such as the words "FIND" or the words "BOOTING" in capitals, and I got my boot loader program to search for the volume label with several different drive numbers in the DL register, testing the different drive numbers with bios int 13h extended read. When the boot loader finds that volume label, you can be absolutely sure that it has the right drive number for the memory stick, and this idea can be used to make sure a program won't write onto the hard drive.

Also an idea is that a hard drive is hardly ever formatted in FAT16 since FAT16 is suitable for low-capacity, and a hard drive usually starts with a master boot record which does not have the word FAT in it. So if your program searches with a test drive number for the word FAT16, and finds the word FAT16, then it probably has the correct drive number for the memory stick. I have noticed that with some computers the DVD drive has drive number 7Fh (which is 127 in decimal) and in some other computers the DVD drive is drive number 0EFh. Probably lots of other numbers are used.

My experiment with USB.

I have mostly programmed the EHCI, (Extended Host Controller Interface) in my laptop. The most important document **is the Intel Specification for the EHCI.** It is a .pdf document. You should download it, as it has all the interesting information about the registers, and the Queue Heads in detail.

You also need to download at least several other USB Specifications, as they contain information which is important about descriptors and about setup packets. In USB specifications they call "setup packets" by the name "standard device requests".

I did literally thousands of experiments with the laptop, just for fun. I wanted to self-teach myself a way to get USB devices to work. I found that they can't work immediately, as they have to be enumerated first.

I wrote a long bootable program (may4.asm) which was able to read and write files to USB memory sticks, using the EHCI programming to read and write sectors, and in that way save and load whole files. I did thousands of those experiments which did not always work, and gradually I got the program to work faster, until it was able to load and save files to memory sticks nearly, but never quite, as quickly as Windows could.

Another of my bootable programs was able to add together sine waves and send sound to a USB headset. And record from the headset microphone. I am not going to give details of that program here, but it is interesting that the way it worked was that it first went in a loop drawing 1024 isochronous transfer descriptors. The frame list pointed at the transfer descriptors, and they worked to send sound to the headset. As they were used up I did not rewrite them, instead my program re-wrote the buffer pointer fields of all the transfer descriptors, for the correct loading address along the sound trak data, and re-wrote their total length fields, and then, reactivated them by setting their active binary bit.

Here I have rearranged parts of this program, but unfortunately I have not tested the result, and **there could be some errors or something left out** in the programs in this writing.

Obviously most of the information about how to program the USB system should come from the Intel specification for the EHCI, and from a lot of other USB specifications which you can easily find and download.

Usb devices are things like usb memory sticks, usb headphones or headsets, and usb keyboards or mice, and hubs. When the usb device is plugged in to the computer, it at first contains a device address of zero. Before you can get it ready to work, you are supposed to go through several steps called enumeration which you can't avoid since they are designed so that these steps have to be done.

Firstly you need to read from the usb device's endpoint zero, a "device descriptor". The usb devices all contain permanently in themselves some information about themselves called descriptors. You can download with Google the free USB 2.0 specifications which explain all details of the descriptors.

After reading the 8 bytes long first part of the device descriptor from the device, loading it into the computer's RAM memory, you get from that descriptor a piece of information called the "max packet size for endpoint zero." Usually that number is either 08 or 40h. Next you should put that number, 08 or 40h, into a queue head's max packet size field and use it when reading the rest of the descriptors.

Next you are supposed to read, also always from the device's endpoint zero, a "Configuration descriptor" and several string descriptors. The configuration descriptor is easy with some devices, but is extremely long and difficult in headsets. The complexity of a headset's configuration descriptor can be incredible, so it looks as if they have made understanding it difficult on purpose. A USB memory stick has a relatively simple descriptor which you can learn to understand. Then you can read the 'string' descriptors which can often contain a few words in English, such as the device's name, manufacturer or a serial number.

As a usb device is plugged in, it's not ready to work yet and it has at the start a "device address" of zero. And a configuration of zero. And you are supposed to quickly give it a non zero device address, and a configuration of always 01. Using a queue head, I experimented by giving many usb devices a device addresses. When several usb devices are plugged in to a computer, each should be given a separate device address,.

You send it a device address by sending it an 8 bytes long "setup packet" to its endpoint 0, and the new device address is in the correct byte of that setup packet. It should be a small number usually in the range of 3 to 120,. Setup packets are always 8 bytes long, and setup packets are always sent to a device's "endpoint zero" which is called its control endpoint. That involves having a zero in the endpoint field of a queue head. Since the device address is zero when a USB device has just been plugged in, a zero should be in the queue head's device address field during this operation of sending that setup packet.

After the usb device, whatever it may be, has been given a device address it is still not ready to work, because you have to send it something that seems pointless, you have to send it an 8 bytes long setup packet called 'set configuration' containing the number 01. This is called "giving it a configuration of 01". One always gives any usb device that configuration of 01. And then if it is not an audio device it is supposed to be ready for work!

But one needs to double check that it has received and accepted its configuration of 01. And to double check it, you have to send it another setup packet called "get configuration" and then read an input of 1 bytes length from its endpoint zero. As you read that one byte of input from it, if you read 01 then you know its configuration was correctly set. If not you must go in a loop to try to set the configuration of 01 again. These steps seem without purpose, but they are necessary. All of these steps can be done with queue heads, which are data structures which you write with the right numbers filled in their correct fields.

After all this, usb memory sticks will be ready for work. And so will mice be ready for work.

But audio devices such as usb headphones and headsets need one or two more steps before they can possibly work. With a usb headphone or headset, you need to send them another 8 bytes setup packet to "give its interfaces an alternate setting". For example, you often have to give a headphone's interface number 01 an alternate setting of 01. You do that by sending to its endpoint 0 (the control endpoint) another setup packet which simply has these two 01 numbers in the correct fields. (in these steps I assume you have already given the headset its new device address, and so you have to put that device address into the queue head's device address, addressing the headset by that.)

And sending this setup packet turns on the headphones, turns on its sound. To get its microphone turned on, you need to send a headset a second setup packet which is supposed to give an interface an alternate setting of 01. Often it would be interface 02 that needs alternate setting of 01. It turns the microphone on. These steps are always done just by sending an 8 bytes long setup packet to its endpoint 0, the control endpoint.

Setup packets are also called "standard device requests", which is another word for "setup packets".

Whenever you send a setup packet to a usb device, you should use a queue head which contains a zero in its endpoint field, and which contains an 8, (for 8 bytes), in both its max packet length field and in its total length field. Its first buffer pointer should point exactly to the start of your setup packet.

Queue heads can be of 3 different types, (setup/input/output) depending on the number in their PID field, and it has to be the setup type. And it should have a device address number in its device address field. That device address was zero to start with, but then you have given the USB device a new device address which it keeps until it is unplugged from the computer.

So to get a memory stick ready to work takes a total of at least 5 setup packets. A first setup packet to set its device address to almost any value you want in the range of 3 to 120. A second setup packet to give it a configuration of 01. A 3rd setup packet called "get configuration" is used to double check that its new configuration of 01 has really been set.

It should now be ready, but there is also the need to read from it a so-called device descriptor and a so-called configuration descriptor. To do it takes another 2 setup packets. I have found out that with a USB memory stick you can assume that its device descriptor will almost surely say that its packet size for endpoint 0 is 40h bytes. However the reading of the memory stick's so-called configuration descriptor really is necessary now.

  Because the configuration descriptor will tell you the endpoint numbers for the memory stick's input and outputs. And it is really necessary because these two endpoint numbers for input and output are quite different for every different make of memory stick. To make any kind of memory stick work you have to find the two endpoint numbers by reading into memory its configuration descriptor, either manually or automatically.

 In the case of audio headsets, 2 more setup packets have to be sent to turn on the sound and turn on the microphone. You turn it on by using two setup packets that give so-called interfaces their so-called alternate settings.

As soon as the usb device has received its new device address, it knows whether signals sent over the usb system are intended for it or intended for some other device, by the device address. It knows when the usb signals are for it, specifically by its recognizing that its own device address is included in the signals.

A usb device normally keeps its device address until the moment when you unplug it.   Any usb device also has electronically inside itself several endpoints, parts of itself which each are addressed by a small number called "endpoint number", and these endpoint numbers are normally small numbers in the range of 0 to 9 usually in most cases.

In my own experiments I discovered a technique which I called "blank input". At first without this blank input it was sometimes difficult to set a device address and then a configuration of 01, because some of my usb memory sticks and especially headsets did not always accept the new device address or set configuration of 01. After sending it the setup packet, I tried reading an input from the device's endpoint 0, its control endpoint. Almost always the input did not even read a single byte of data, but it did something necessary because it was suddenly quick and easy to set device address and configuration. Somehow the blank input was making the usb devices pay more attention to the setup packets.

To work, the blank input Must be to endpoint 0 and it must start with the data toggle bit set Data1. That is a data toggle bit in the queue head which tries to take an input must be data1.

The different situations in different computers. I only know about 2 different situations but there must be many more which I don't know anything about. It is really a pity that different computers have different USB systems. My experiments were almost all with an Emachines laptop PC.

The laptop had 2 EHCI circuits in it, and each of them is connected to a permanently built-in Usb 2.0 hub. The laptop has No UHCI. A desktop PC which I tested had none of those Usb hubs, in stead its EHCI was directly connected to the USB sockets on the outside of the PC. But by setting the right binary bits, the outside sockets could be connected to a UHCI in stead of to the EHCI . (The UHCI would be used only for the lower speeds.)

The permanently built in USB 2.0 hubs of the laptop are directly connected to the Usb sockets on the outside. The first 1 of the 4 EHCI port status and control registers (Portsc) is permanently wired up to a USB hub. (these hubs are often like 4 way adaptors.) The other 3 Portsc registers of each of the Laptop's EHCI can never be connected to anything.

 In all my experiments it was necessary to find the address of the EHCI command register, it is at an address which is called the "**USB operational base address**". The other EHCI registers are nearby. All these registers are in the computer's normal RAM address space, they are not worked with inputs and outputs.

You program them with normal Mov instructions. But they are in an area of the RAM address space which is above the upper end of the RAM memory. In all my experiments it was necessary to use my hexadecimal viewing screen, one which shows all the memory as hexadecimal numbers and can be quickly scrolled up or down with page up/ page down keys.

I could then see clearly the EHCI registers, and even try to make changes to these registers under my typing cursor. (I had arranged that my program can increment or decrement bytes under my typing cursor). You often see the frame list pointer register running quickly. You see the PORTSC registers. At first I tried plugging in Usb memory sticks, while I looked at those registers. I was so disappointed at first, by the fact that there were no changes in the registers! The explanation for it was the built-in Usb 2.0 hub. One of the PORTSC registers looked different from the others, the first one, that was the one which is permanently plugged in to that built-in usb hub. It turned out that this built-in Usb hub was electronically almost identical to the rather cheap external USB 2.0 hubs which you can buy in shops. These hubs have one USB plug and several USB sockets which you can plug other usb things into.

 The manuals say that to enable a port, you have to reset the port. With a USB hub, you have to send it specific setup packets to reset and enable a port, which is a usb socket on its outside. The port enables automatically only if something else is plugged in to it. When nothing is plugged into the USB socket, it won't enable.

 In the different case of a desktop PC, you have direct connection of portsc registers and external usb sockets. And with my hexadecimal numbers screen I could see the PORTSC registers changing immediately whenever I plugged in and unplugged something. In this different case, you reset and enable a port by writing certain binary bits to the PORTSC register, and it enables only if something is plugged in to the socket on the outside of the computer. So depending on the arrangement inside the computer, different methods have to be used.

 This complicated things, and my experiments mostly only work with the laptop. But I noticed that sometimes, such experiments can work with a desktop that has an external usb 2.0 hub plugged in. It should not be a 1.0 hub, because only 2.0 hubs work at high speed and have in them a transaction translator to convert speeds. But really this writing is about programming my laptop. I discovered that the Bios always automatically enumerated my laptop's built in usb hubs at the moment of booting the computer, and that the Bios always gave them each a device address of 02.

They could both have that same device address of 02, because the laptop had 2 EHCI, and there is only one of the hubs for each EHCI. So there is no confusion even though they both have the same device address.

Enumeration is the process of firstly reading descriptors from a usb device, then giving the usb device a device address (which it stores in itself until it is unplugged) (and which is any small number in the range of 1 to about 120.) And then always just after giving a device address, one has to give the usb device a configuration of 01.

The whole process is called enumeration, and one definitely has to give a "configuration of 01" as the usb devices are not supposed to work until you do it. In normal programming every Usb device which is plugged in stores in itself the device address which you give to it, and then it knows whether usb signals are addressed to it or not because the usb signals contain the device address. It ignores usb signals that are not addressed to it. That must be the purpose of the device address, so that the device knows whether signals are addressed to it or not. Of course you are supposed to give every device that is plugged in a different device address to avoid confusion. I experimentally tried giving the same device address two memory sticks plugged in together. Then when my program asked them to send descriptors data there seemed to be sometimes a mix up of signals, but sometimes one of them seemed to dominate as it was faster and it would send descriptors while the other one which was slower did not do so.

The Bios of my laptop was definitely doing this process of enumeration of the permanently built in hubs exactly as you would need to do it for any other usb device including memory sticks, headphones, and external 2.0 hubs.

I relied on the Bios having already given the device address of 02 to each hub. But in one experiment I tried to reset and enumerate the hub myself, and that worked too. If you were doing more advanced programming, the ability to enumerate the built-in hubs by your own program would be important. I discovered that when you enumerate a 2.0 hub yourself, at first the hub's ports do not work because they don't yet have electrical power. You need to send the hub a series of setup packets one to each port, to turn on the ports power, and then it all works.

Usb signals are of 4 different speeds. These are called Low speed; Full speed; High speed; and Super speed. An EHCI can only create signals at High speed, that is it does only one speed. But in my laptop it seems to be able to do low speed and full speed too, though it can't really. And that is because there is inside the laptop a permanently connected USB 2.0 hub. A USB 2.0 hub contains a Transaction Translator which converts low and full speeds into high speed and does that in both directions. To make that Transaction Translator work, the Queue head or the Transfer descriptor which you use has to have some numbers in two fields which are for this purpose, the device address number of the hub, (that was given to the USB 2.0 hub when it was enumerated) and also the port number of the HUB's port, in a field of the queue head used for that purpose.

An EHCI Can't do any signals at low speed or at full speed, and there are two different ways you can create those 2 slower speeds signals.

In the desktop PC I tested with, there were several UHCI attached to the EHCI (so called companion controllers). One can program those UHCI to obtain low speed and full speed, the 2 slower speeds only.

The other way of doing it is to use a USB 2.0 Hub, because the 2.0 type of hubs contain a "Transaction translator" which can convert high speed into either low speed signals or full speed signals.

With my laptop the permanently built-in USB hubs do this. Mice are usually low speed devices which only work with the low speed signals. Headphones and headsets are often full speed devices, which is slower than high speed. (The sound data has to be sent by isochronous transfer descriptors pointed to with a frame list).

Signals coming out from the EHCI are always "high speed" data, and these signals can spread in an apparently simple way to all of the 4 or so ports, which may be directly connected the Usb sockets on the outside of the computer in the case of many desktop PCs. (But not in my laptop).

"High speed" signals can also spread out to reach all the enabled ports of a USB 2.0 hub simultaneously. But it is different with the 2 slower speeds. The situation is different and signals go to only one port at a time then. Because a field in the Queue head or transfer descriptor addresses a specific port number for conversion of speed to one of two lower speeds. When the EHCI sends signals intended for low speed devices such as mice, or full speed devices (which are slower than high speed), there has to be a USB 2.0 hub attached, signals go to a specific port in the hub, not to all the ports. When there is no 2.0 hub then the two slower speeds cannot work without the hub, and operating systems must use UHCI programming instead. And when there is a 2.0 hub there, (external separate or built-in) the Queue heads or transfer descriptors which you write have to contain in a field the device address which was given to the 2.0 hub and as well the specific port number of the hub's port that you want the slower signals to go to. Because these signals have to address the Transaction Translator in the hub that changes signal speeds to and from high to low speed or full speed.

I can only try to write down a small fraction of the information which one might want to know.

It is important that one should find and download the free PDF document called "Intel Specification for the Extended Host Controller Interface". And you need to print out most of it on paper. The clear information in this pdf document about EHCI registers and about Queue Heads is absolutely necessary if you want to program it.

You need to print out pages about queue heads and look at Intel's diagram of a Queue Head constantly when you try to program the EHCI.

To send and receive USB signals you write some data structures called "Queue heads" with blank queue element transfer descriptors. To understand how to write queue heads you have to download and print out on paper the Intel specification about the EHCI. This is easy to find with Google and completely free to download.

There is a page in the Intel manual which is a kind of yellow diagram of the queue heads with the binary bit positions of all the different fields in the queue heads.

I needed to look at that page constantly while I tried to program. The Queue heads are obviously just like forms in which different pieces of information are written in different places. The queue heads contain detailed information on how the EHCI should send USB signals. The Intel manual for the EHCI is written well but I could not remember for long the details of queue heads in my head, so I always had to re read the specification every time I did a bit of programming to find out how to write information into the correct fields of queue heads.

The EHCI knows the address of your first queue head because you tell it the address by writing the address into the "Asynchronous current address register."

I found that it was necessary that with every queue head there also had to be a blank "queue element transfer descriptor." (qeTD). A pointer field in the queue head points to that. With my hexadecimal view screen I could see that as the EHCI runs it writes some things into that blank transfer descriptor automatically.

For a while I was not sure that I was using the right technique, but it turned out it was. With experiments I found there are 2 techniques which you can use when writing queue heads:

There is a single binary bit in a queue head called a DTC bit, and depending on whether this binary bit is set, you have to either write "all the information in your queue head" and leave your queue element transfer descriptor "blank", or, you have to write only part of the necessary information in the queue head, and fill in part of the qeTD with the rest of the information. I am sure that I prefer to make the dtc bit=0 and leave the qeTD blank. I did a timing test to measure the speed of both ways. I found out that both techniques take exactly the same time. I definitely prefer writing all the information into the queue head and leaving the qeTD blank, because it was easier for me. And so I always make the dtc bit=0.

The USB system is obviously full of unnecessary complexity which makes programming more difficult than it should be. Lots of things would work in a simpler way. As examples of how things could be designed to make programming simpler: The step of giving all USB devices a configuration of 1 should be completely unnecessary. That change would mean that 2 setup packets, set and get configuration, would be avoided to make programming shorter. In the queue heads, the method of buffer pointers is crazy. There should be only one buffer pointer which should be a single normal 32 bit address. The step of giving a USB hub setup packets to turn on ports power should not be necessary.

More importantly, the system could use Endpoint Numbers more, in a standard way so as to make programming simple. To read and write sectors to a Memory stick, it should not be necessary to send a Command Block Wrapper, as instead of that there could be 4 fixed and standard endpoints, and you would only have to adjust the endpoint number in a queue head. One standard endpoint number could be for the absolute sector address. One endpoint number could always be for input of sectors data. One other endpoint could always be for output of sectors data. The 4th endpoint could always be for reading status, and reading it should not be necessary. It would make programming a lot easier and you would never need CBWs. With USB headsets, endpoint numbers could obviously be used in a standard way to make all the programming simpler. The step of turning on headset speakers by giving an interface an alternate setting of 01 should not be necessary, and step of turning on a headset microphone, by giving another interface an alternate setting of 01 should never be necessary either. The whole of the programming could be smaller. And these were a few ideas on how hardware could be different.

The **Intel specification for the EHCI** is interesting, and you need to download it and read it for essential information on the EHCI registers and on the fields of queue heads. This is the most important document to download and print out. The only things it lacks are any examples of programming, and the details of setup packets. I find that at least one simple example of computer programming was necessary for me to get started with programming the EHCI.

Information of setup packets is in the USB 2.0 specification which can be downloaded for free when you use Google. In that the setup packets are called standard device requests, and all of them are 8 bytes long.

A Queue Head is of course a data structure in which there are many fields which you have to fill in with the right numbers. A Queue Head can be written almost anywhere in the computer's normal RAM memory, except for the rule that the lowest 5 binary bits of the address of where the Queue Head starts have to be zeroes. Making the lowest 5 binary bits of an address zeroes was called aligning.

A 4 bytes number is a 32 bit number and that can also be called a dword, (doubleword). Something confusing is that "dw" is written when you mean data word or 2 bytes. The first dword of a queue head is called its **horizontal link pointer.** It is a 32 bit address. The lowest 5 binary bits of it should be the code number 02, not part of the address, which means that it is pointing to another queue head. (As this 32 bit number is used as an address the lowest 5 bits are ignored and assumed to be zeroes, but you have to write in them the code 02). All the other binary bits of the 32 bit horizontal link pointer are an address. The address should point either to another queue head or to the same queue head, which means you can make the address point exactly to itself! The Intel manual says there can be several queue heads, the horizontal link pointer of each one can point to the next queue head in the series, except for the last queue head whose horizontal link pointer can point to the first queue head. That means the queue heads are in a circle. The EHCI or Host Controller then works with the first queue head, (which it finds because you write its address into the asynchronous list current address register, which is the register at USB operational base address +18h) and when it has finished working on one queue head it follows the horizontal link pointer to get to the next queue head.

You stop the EHCI (stop the so called asynchronous schedule) by writing 80001h into its command register (the register exactly at the USB operational base address) and then you write the address of the 1st queue head into the asynchronous list address register (At USB operational base address +18h), then you re-start the EHCI by writing 80021h into the USB command register. The EHCI or Host Controller then finds your 1st queue head immediately, and it works on that queue head.

While the EHCI works on that queue head, it does automatically write changes into that queue head. As an example of the changes it makes, the queue head's total length field may go down to zero, and it's buffer pointer loading address may be increased forward by the same amount that the total length field was decreased.

Then as the EHCI feels that it has finished working with that queue head, the binary bit in it which is called the "Active bit", is automatically cleared to 0. This binary bit has to be set to 1 by you to show that the queue head is active. When the active bit is cleared to 0, this prevents the EHCI from doing any more work with this queue head. I experimented many times setting this active bit to binary 1 again, and this did get the EHCI to work with the queue head again. Before you re-activate a queue head by setting its active bit to 1, you need to firstly re-write a number into its total length field. And you need to re-write its buffer pointers, (its loading address).

When the EHCI has finished working with a queue head and when it clears to 0 its active bit, the EHCI immediately tries to follow the Horizontal Link Pointer to the next queue head. As I said the horizontal link pointer can point exactly to itself. Or it can point to another queue head. And when it points to another queue head the EHCI or Host controller immediately starts working on this other queue head as soon as it has finished with the first one.

When the horizontal link pointer points to itself, the EHCI continuously looks at the queue head but does nothing with it when the Queue head's "active" binary bit is 0. In my own programming, I frequently wrote a setup queue head and an inputs queue head. (A small field in a queue head determines whether its type is Setup/Input/Output. Only the 3 types exist.) Its horizontal link pointer pointed to itself. I made the EHCI start working with the setup queue head to send an 8 bytes setup packet. After it has done that, the EHCI continuously looks at the setup queue head, but does nothing more with it because it has cleared to 0 the active binary bit as soon as it had finished sending the setup packet. Then my program went in a small loop to make a time delay of a few milliseconds, because USB devices like memory sticks often need a few milliseconds time to get ready when they have received a setup packet.

Then after a few milliseconds, my program wrote over the queue head's horizontal link pointer writing in it the address of the 2nd queue head. Immediately the EHCI sees that the link pointer has changed, and it automatically goes to work on the 2nd queue head. The 2nd queue head was often an inputs queue head, for example, to read descriptors as an input from the USB memory stick's endpoint 0.

So the First dword of a queue head is a horizontal link pointer. The 2nd dword of a queue head has 9 fields. Binary bits 0 to 6 of the 2nd dword, are the "Device address" field. This is where you write the important device address, which lets USB devices know whether signals sent from the EHCI are addressed to them or not. Binary bit 7 is called the "inactive on next transaction" bit. For work with any high speed devices like memory sticks it must be zero, I made it zero. Binary bits 8 to 11 are the endpoint number field. The endpoint number must be zero whenever sending setup packets and zero is called the control endpoint. The endpoint number is intended to tell USB devices which part of them the signals are intended for.

In many cases you need to read the configuration descriptor to find out what are the right endpoint numbers to use. Binary bits 12 and 13 (still of the second dword of a queue head) are called the EPS field for endpoint speed.

The field should contain 01 for low speed, 00 for full speed, and 02 for high speed. (Because of its binary bit position the 02 actually looks like a 20h). Very often a USB Mouse is low speed, a USB headset is full speed, and a USB Memory stick is high speed. In reality the EHCI can only create signals which are high speed, and so its signals would go with the EPS field of 02, which looks like 20h. When this EPS number in the queue head is 01 or 00, it gets a bit more complicated because then the 3rd dword of the queue head has to address a transaction translator (or TT) inside a USB 2.0 Hub. It needs the device address of the 2.0 hub in the 3rd dword plus the port number, and really signals from the EHCI are high speed but the hub converts them into low or full speed in that case. For a USB memory stick the EPS field should be 02 and the situation is simpler because in the high speed case the 3rd dword of the queue head is mostly ignored and can mainly be zeroes. Binary bit 14 of the 2nd dword of a queue head is called the DTC bit, for data toggle control. This dtc bit is Not the data toggle, but something else, and I always make it 0.

When you look at the queue heads running you see the EHCI automatically filling in parts of the blank queue element transfer descriptor. I do not understand what the EHCI is actually doing there, but I think the Intel specification said it uses the blank transfer descriptor partly as a scratch pad automatically which stores temporary information? Binary bits 16 to 26 of the 2nd dword, are the max packet length field. (The USB signals all go in packets. Often it is compulsory that these packets should have a certain length, in bytes. You should fill in the max packet length field with the correct packet length. For example it is 8 for 8 bytes if you are sending a setup packet, and it should be always 200h when you are reading or writing sectors to a USB memory stick.) Binary bit 27 is the "C" bit. Intel says it should only be set to 1 when the device is Not high speed and it is also for a control endpoint. Otherwise it should be 0. Binary bits 28-31 are the RL field.

The Buffer Pointers.

See **on Page 146** the call "do_buffer_pointers:"
There is something important which you need to know about the buffer pointers.

The loading address for data is the apparently normal 32 bit number at offset +1Ch relative to the start of the queue head. In a setup queue head this is a normal 32 bit address of where your setup packet is located, because the setup queue head only sends 8 bytes of data.
When you write an INPUT queue head to input data from a USB device, you write at offset +1Ch the first buffer pointer as a simple 32 bit address of where you want the data to be loaded to. When it is an OUTPUT queue head you write there the address of the data which you wish to send to a USB device.

But they have designed a strange thing. The problem was solved quite easily, and filling in the buffer pointers can be done easily and always in the same way. But, I want to explain that there was something very strange and obviously crazy about the design of this area of Queue Heads and transfer descriptors, called buffer pointers.

These buffer pointers are the data loading address. Obviously a computer programmer would always want the loading address to be a simple 32 bit or 64 bit number. Specifically you don't want it to be complicated.

While the EHCI is using the queue head, you can see that the EHCI reads and writes changes in some fields of the queue head to follow its progress.
At first it uses the simple 32 bit number you have written into the first buffer pointer, at offset +1ch.

As the queue head works to input or to output data, this works normally if the length of the data is very short, but if the data is slightly longer, then as soon as there is, or would be a normal carry-over from the 3rd hexadecimal digit of the address into the 4th hexadecimal digit of the address, a funny thing happens, and suddenly, the upper 5 hexadecimal digits of the (8 digit) number no longer count.
Now, they don't count and it is THE SECOND buffer pointer which gives the upper 5 hexadecimal digits to the whole address. The lower 3 hexadecimal digits continue to come as before from the first buffer pointer. (which has been following the loading). (A small field of the queue head called current page or C_Page, increments +1 to track this switch, and so points the EHCI to the next buffer pointer).

So a normal arithmetic carry over from the 3rd hex digit to the 4th hex digit does not happen, and instead of that an unusual change in the system gets triggered which makes the upper 5 hex digits of the loading address come from the next buffer pointer. The actual 8 digit loading address then comes from the upper 5 digits of the 2nd buffer pointer together with the lower 3 digits of the first buffer pointer.
 (The normal carry over from third to fourth hexadecimal digit is worth 4K and is equal to 1000h)

As the loading of data goes on, there would be again another normal arithmetic carry over from the 3rd hex digit in the 1st buffer pointer into the 4th hex digit.
But instead of that normal thing happening a change is triggered again and suddenly the upper 5 hexadecimal digits of the loading address has to come from the 3rd buffer pointer.

(The second buffer pointer no longer counts) This continues with the series of 5 buffer pointers until the queue head has sent up to its maximum capacity of data. (I think 7FFFh bytes is the maximum capacity of the total length field, yet 5 buffer pointers each doing up to 1000h bytes must be a maximum of 20K bytes?.)
Obviously the complexity of that system is wrong, and anyway no computer programmer could ever want that system, since a single simple 32 bit address would work better.
This system is definitely not useful. Perhaps Microsoft wanted the system of fragmented buffer pointers to discourage other companies just by seeming difficult?
I found that there is a simple way to deal with these buffer pointers. You can deal with the buffer pointers in exactly the same way every time you write queue heads and it is not difficult. The call shown below here "do_buffer_pointers:" does it OK. (See page 130)

What I do is to start out with a simple, normal 32 bit address and put it into the EAX register. Then call do_buffer_pointers, and it will write that simple number directly as the first buffer pointer. It is the address where I want loading to start. Then while the number is in a register it adds exactly 1000h to that number, and it uses logical AND AX,0F000h to clear the lower 3 hexadecimal digits of it to zero, and then it writes it into the second buffer pointer (The 2nd buffer pointer is at offset +20h). Then it adds 1000h to the number again, and writes it to the 3rd buffer pointer (The third buffer pointer is at offset +24h).

Then it adds 1000h to it again, and writes it to the 4th buffer pointer (at offset +28h). And then add 1000h again and write it into the fifth and last buffer pointer at offset +2Ch). Then it has finished.
 This works and since the method is always the same it is not difficult for my program to do. The adding of 1000h in each step is like an exact **substitute for the normal "carry over"** which should happen in arithmetic from the 3rd hex digit to the bottom of the 4th hex digit. While the program writes the queue heads it can always fill in the buffer pointers with this same method, or instead a separate call can fill them in after writing the queue head. So this is not actually discouraging or difficult.

The buffer pointers must all be done before the queue head gets used for more than very short data.
 If the length of the data which a queue head deals with is very short, for example when you are sending an 8 bytes setup packet, then only the first buffer pointer is necessary and it seems alright for the other buffer pointers to be zeroes. But, as soon as the length of the data becomes longer, it is essential to fill in all the buffer pointers properly. When you are using an input queue head and you forget to fill in the other buffer pointers, the computer itself will always crash, and the computer will need to be switched off.
 The reason for it is that if the other buffer pointers are zeroes, then as soon as they become active the EHCI must start loading the inputted data into the lowest parts of the computer's memory. This must over-write the computer's interrupt vector table, its BIOS area too, and crash.

Starting USB programming and reading in the configuration space.

I have done hundreds of experiments programming the EHCI (Extended Host Controller Interface) with my laptop. Nearly all my experiments were with one laptop. The EHCI can send data from any address in the computer's memory to a USB device, such as writing data to a USB memory stick or sending sound through a hub to a USB headset. I was able to send good quality sound to my USB headphones and a headset, and take sound track recordings from a headset's microphone, which was interesting. And my program could read and write files to memory sticks.

The most necessary document was the Intel Specification for the EHCI. It is easy to find this document with Google search, and I needed to print out most of it on paper. When I did any programming I had to look at this document all the time, and could not have done any programming without it. The Intel specification for the EHCI has in it complete details of the EHCI operational registers, and all the structure of Queue Heads (Queue heads are used for setup or control operations and for memory sticks) and isochronous transfer descriptors (which are used for sound output to headsets). There is also the USB 2.0 specifications, which you should download too. That should be enough, except that the information used for "Audio devices" like headsets is unnecessarily complex and at least 7 different USB specifications documents are necessary if you want all of it, which can be found on Google search.

They have made the system complicated, and there was no way for me to make it simple. The first thing which you need to do to be able to start programming the EHCI in your computer is to find its USB **operational base address.** This address is quite different for different computers so you need to find it. This is the address where most EHCI registers can be reached. Its command register is exactly at the operational base address, and the other registers are a little bit further on.

The EHCI registers are reached in the same normal address space as the computer's RAM memory, but at a high address which does not actually have RAM memory.

To find the EHCI's Operational Base Address, you have to read the PCI Configuration Space. You can either read the configuration space yourself with a hexadecimal screen, or you can write a short program which will search through it automatically to find the USB operational base address automatically. The base address can then be saved as a variable for other parts of your program to use. I am going to give some examples of how to do that here.

In every computer there is a "**Configuration space**". The configuration space is an address space which you can read from using two different methods. With modern computers the configuration space can be read from at very high addresses inside the normal RAM address space, as well as being able to use the configuration mechanism. With older and modern computers, the configuration space can also be read from by using the so called configuration mechanism, which is different from the normal address space.

When you read it using that mechanism, you see that the configuration space has 256 bytes long zones which each belong to a different integrated circuit inside the computer. You can see that these zones are spaced at varying distances apart, with the empty areas between the zones solidly filled with the hex number FFFFh. At a certain offset in each of those zones there is a number called a class code and a subclass code which you can use to recognize which kind of integrated circuit each zone belongs to. There are websites which have a free list of the different class codes which you can use to identify which integrated circuit is there.

In the zone which belongs to an EHCI, at offset +9 there is the class code 0C0320H and if you find this number, you have found the EHCI zone. Actually I have read this at offset +8 and making the lowest byte zero I find the code 0C032000H. For a UHCI the class code is 0C0300H at offset +9.

(I think a different zone with the class code of 3000000h at offset +8 belongs to the graphics accelerator, and I think that the start address of the high resolution screen memory can probably be read from offset +18h inside this zone).

You have to look through the configuration space to find the zones which belong to the EHCI integrated circuits, and read from the zone a 32 bit number at offset +10h relative to the start of the zone, which is called the "USB Base address."

You have to put the USB Base address into a 32 bit address register, and then you can read from exactly that address a 1 byte number which is called caps length. You then have to add this 1 byte number to the 32 bit USB base address, and the result of that sum is the USB Operational base address. Which is what you have to find. (This is because the 1 byte number is the length of some read-only registers called capabilities registers which give information about the particular version of the EHCI. I did not find the capabilities registers very interesting. Immediately beyond them the important operational registers start.)

The mechanism for reading the Configuration space.

You select an address by sending it with an output to port 0CF8h, and then you read or write the data with port 0CFCh. The port number should be in DX. The highest binary bit of an 32 bit address, bit 31, has to be always set to 1. Setting b31 to 1 was called enabling access to configuration space. In hexadecimal the set bit 31 looks like an 8 followed by seven zeroes. To set b31 to 1 you can for example use the operation OR EAX,80000000H. The lowest 2 binary bits of the address have to be used differently from the others. And to make it simple the lowest 2 bits should be zero and you should read 4 bytes at a time.

You have to select an address with an Output operation to port 0CF8h. And then you can read or write configuration space data through data port 0CFCH. For example, these operations will read 4 bytes from the configuration space at the address specified in the EAX register and sent with an output to port 0CF8h.

```
OR EAX,80000000h            ;assume the address is already in EAX, and set binary bit31
MOV DX,0CF8h                ;
OUT DX,EAX                  ;
MOV DX,0CFCh
IN EAX,DX                   ;configuration space data is read into EAX.
```

Apparently if you want to read only 1 byte at a time from the configuration space, then you have to separate the lowest 2 binary bits of the address, use them to select one of the 4 data ports 0CFCh to 0CFFh and then take an input by IN AL,DX. While in the output of an address to port 0CF8h, the lowest 2 binary bits of the address have to be cleared to zero. So it is simpler to read 4 bytes at a time. You can also write to the configuration space with the same mechanism. To write to the configuration space you output a 4 bytes address to address port 0CF8h and then output 4 bytes of data to port 0CFCh. The lowest 2 binary bits of an address should be zero.

When I tried writing to the configuration space, I found that only some of the registers in these integrated circuits zones are writable, and when you write to them without knowing what you are doing it can crash the computer.

Look at the short program Find_EHCI:

It uses the EHCI class code to find it, and its purpose is to save the USB Operational base address for other parts of the program to use later.

```
;============================================ =========
```

Find the USB operational base address automatically.

An Automatic Search through the Configuration Space.

;This is important since it gets the USB operational base address. It searches through the Configuration Space for the class code of 0c032000h of areas belonging to an EHCI. Then it takes the USB base address and by adding caps length to it it finds the USB operational base address, which is the address of the EHCI command register. The other registers are near. This address is used by other parts of the program, and in this example happens to be saved in [50050h]. The computer had 2 EHCI circuits in it, and the second USB Operational base address belonging to the second EHCI happens to get saved in [50054h]

Find_EHCI:
```
find_usb:   mov esi,50050h          ;where to write the two found USB op base addresses.
            mov dword [esi],0
            mov dword [esi+4],0
            Pushad                  ;Binary bit 31 should be set to address the configuration space

            mov ecx,80000008h       ;bit 31 set, ecx to address the configuration space
fh1:        mov dx,0cf8h            ;port 0cf8h the configuration space address register
            mov eax,ecx
            out dx,eax              ;output to select an address. assembler does not allow out dx,ecx
            mov dx,0cfch            ;0cfch is the configuration space data I/O register
            in eax,dx               ;input reads from the selected address.
            mov al,0                ;isolate class and sub class code
            cmp eax,0c032000h       ;EHCI Class code is 0c032000h
            jnz fh2
            mov cl,10h              ;cl =10h so ECX addresses USB base address
            mov dx,0cf8h ;
            mov eax,ecx
            out dx,eax          ;select the address
            mov dx,0cfch
            in eax,dx               ;read "USB Base address number"
            mov edx,0
            mov dl,[eax]            ;read caps length  in DL
            add eax,edx             ;make "USB Operational base address" number by adding caps length
            mov [esi],eax           ;record the Op base address for other parts of the program to use.
            add esi,4
            mov cl,8                    ;offset +8 for reading  a class code
fh2:        add ecx,100h                ;+100h to next zone within the configuration space.
            cmp ecx,80010000h       ;go up searching maybe to 1 or 2 x64k
            jb fh1                      ;fh1 to another turn of this loop
            popad                       ;After finding the EHCI, look for an UHCI
            ret         ;
```

; offset 20h-23h uhci i/o base address, but clear its b0
;UHCI class code 0c030000h EHCI class code 0c032000h

```
find_uhci:  mov esi,4ff00h              ;where to write the found uhci i/o addresses
            mov word [esi],"NO"         ;it should say NO when does not find an UHCI.
            pushad

            mov ecx,80000008h           ;bit 31 set, ecx to address the configuration space
fh4:        mov dx,0cf8h
            mov eax,ecx
            out dx,eax                  ;select an address. assembler does not allow ecx here
            mov dx,0cfch
            in eax,dx                   ;read configuration space at selected address
            mov al,0                    ;isolate class and sub class code
            cmp eax,0c030000h           ;+09-0bh. 00 for UHCI 20h for EHCI. was for ehci =0c032000h
            jnz fh6
            mov cl,20h                  ;cl so ecx addresses usb base address
            mov dx,0cf8h
            mov eax,ecx
            out dx,eax
            mov dx,0cfch
            in eax,dx                   ;read UHCI i/o base address number
            mov edx,0
            and al,0feh                 ;remove bit0 to get real i/o base number
            mov [esi],eax               ;record the i/o base address of UHCI (this erases the NO)
            add esi,4
            mov cl,8
fh6:        add ecx,100h                ;to next zone in the configuration space
            cmp ecx,80010000h           ;go up to 1 or 2 x64k
            jb fh4
            popad
            ret
```

;===

;Tests of the program pieces.

Be warned that if you try any of these programs it may not work. It would only work under a special set of circumstances. Which is, the computer is a laptop with similar configuration to mine.
Additionally, there are large gaps in the information I have here, and it could only be useful if you study many other documents about USB.
They might not work either because something is missing from the start, or because an error was added when they were rearranged for clarity.
Call Find_EHCI   ;; To automatically find the **USB operational base address** and save that in [50050h]
 if there is one, and save a second USB operational base address in [50054h] if there is a second one.
After the call you can look at that spot to see whether a base address has appeared.
;------------------------------------
Call find_uhci   ;To automatically find out whether the computer has an UHCI. The word "NO"
                        ;should appear at address [4ff00h] if none is found.
;--
To test giving a USB memory stick a device address of 09 and a configuration of 01, you can call these if there is a HUB inside the computer, as there was in my Emachines laptop:
Call Find_EHCI   ;get the necessary USB operational base address.
Call reset_enable_of_hub_ports   ;call this only if a USB Hub is set in between the EHCI and the USB sockets.
Call set_get_configuration   ;If configuration was set then you should see the number 01 appear in [50400h]
ret
;-----------------------------
The same test bit if there is No Hub, and if the EHCI ports are directly connected to the USB sockets on the outside of the computer. As it was with a certain desktop PC.
Call Find_EHCI
Call reset_of_EHCI_own_ports
Call set_get_configuration   ;;If configuration was set then you should see the number 01 appear in [50400h]
ret
;---
To test reading of 7 different kinds of **descriptors** from a USB memory stick or from other "high speed" devices
Before the device has been enumerated:
Call Find_EHCI
Call find_uhci
Call which_kind_of_ports_to_reset   ;?? (Either Hub ports, or EHCI own ports, one or the other but not both.)
Call read_before_enumeration   ;If this works a series of different descriptors should appear in the memory.
ret
;---
The same test of reading descriptors from a USB memory stick or from other "high speed" devices, but
After giving it a device address of 9 (and its configuraton of always 01)
Call Find_EHCI
Call find_uhci
Call which_kind_of_ports_to_reset   ;?? Alternatively call from here to reset & enable one type of port.
Call set_get_configuration   ;gives a device address of 9 and configuration of 01.
Call read_after_enumeration   ;If this works a series of different descriptors should appear in the memory.
ret
;--------------------------
;One kind of reset and enable should be used, never both. And if nothing works when you try one kind, try the
;other kind of reset and enable.
;Also, if BIOS has given the memory stick a device address, one should unplug the memory stick for
;a moment and then plug it back in. (So as to reset the device address to 0). That was often necessary.

To Test **reading of sectors** from the USB Memory stick, for example to read its boot sector.
Call Find_EHCI
Call reset_enable_hub_ports   ;The one I use for the laptop. (other one would work for a certain desktop)
Call set_get_configuration   ;gives a device address of 9 and configuration of 01.
Call read_after_enumeration   ;Descriptors should appear in the memory. Need them to find endpoint numbers.

```
Mov esi,31000h                        ;to address 3 variables
mov word [esi+22h],4                  ;Length in sectors to read,
mov dword [esi+28h],0                 ;Start sector number. Number 0 when for the boot sector.
mov dword [esi+24h],45000h            ;Any 32 bit loading address for loading the sectors data.
Call read_sectors_first_time          ;reads the sectors.
;-- Example to read some more sectors.
Mov esi,31000h                        ;to address 3 variables.
mov word [esi+22h],10                 ;Length in sectors to read,
mov dword [esi+28h],020h              ;Start sector number.
mov dword [esi+24h],46000h            ;Any 32 bit loading address for loading the sectors data.
Call read_more_sectors                ;reads more of the sectors, called after the first time.
 ret
;================================================================
```

One can try the 2 different kinds of port reset, but only 1 kind should be used since if there is a Hub then reset of the EHCI's own ports would probably erase the Hub's enumeration making the hub not ready and making its device address go back to 0. So when the type of reset does not work the computer would need to be rebooted, or alternatively you can try to add to the program the ability to enumerate a hub.
The "Call which_kind_of_ports_to_reset" might be able to jump to do the right type of reset?? This call might be able to decide which type of reset to jump to? Because I noticed that sometimes when a computer has a UHCI as a companion controller that means that its EHCI ports have a direct connection to the USB sockets on the outside of the computer.

;--
My laptop has two EHCI circuits in it, and each EHCI is permanently connected to an internal USB 2.0 Hub. (I think this type of hub is described in the USB 2.0 specification. Anyway one should download and look at the specification.) These hubs have to be programmed exactly like the external USB hubs you can buy in the shops, (They are like 4-way adaptors with 1 USB plug and about 4 USB sockets). But these 2 hubs are permanently hidden inside my Emachines laptop, and the BIOS enumerates them automatically at the time the laptop is switched on.
On my laptop one EHCI with one hub works for a left side USB socket, and the other EHCI with the other hub works for two right side USB sockets on the outside of the laptop. Hub Ports having a specific port number apply to the external USB sockets. The Hub ports are disabled to begin with and do not work even when a USB device is plugged into them. And the ports have to be "enabled" by resetting them.

When you reset a port the port should enable automatically if a USB device is plugged in. When nothing is plugged in the port stays disabled. There is no other way of enabling the ports, they only enable when you reset them.
This concept of a port becoming enabled if you reset it, would apply to the EHCI's own ports as well. But reset & enable of EHCI's own ports would apply mainly in the case of some different kind of computer which does not have a built-in hub. The Hub ports are reset & enabled in a different way from the EHCI ports.
The Hub ports are given Reset & Enable by sending the hub a "setup packet" which contain the port number, one setup packet for each port you want to reset & enable. But the EHCI's own ports are given Reset & Enable by writing the right numbers to the PORTSC registers that belong to the port. (PORTSC stands for Port Status and Control).
I enjoyed a lot programming the EHCI in my own laptop PC, and so almost all of my thousands of tests were with only that laptop. It seemed frustrating that my progams might not work with other computers, because of the differences.
The problem is the fact that the circuitry of the USB system is different in different computers. Almost all my experiments were with one Emachines laptop. Very old PCs only have a UHCI, more modern computers have an EHCI or sometimes a super speed controller. I have never tried to program the super speed.

I firstly discovered that my Emachines Laptop computer has two EHCI and that for each of them there is a permanently built-in 2.0 Hub. It has no UHCI. The permanently built in hubs come in between the EHCI and the USB sockets on the outside of the laptop, and therefore until you learn how to program these hubs they are almost like an obstacle or obstruction which stops signals from the EHCI reaching the sockets on the outside of the laptop. When I began programming, signals from the laptop's EHCI did not reach the sockets on the outside of the computer, and I had to firstly do Reset & Enable of the Hub port that corresonded to the external USB socket. Then signals from the EHCI did reach the external sockets.

I did a lot with my laptop, but I only tested a few programs with a desktop PC a few times. I don't know about the differences in the system with other computers. In the desktop PC the EHCI's ports were **directly** connected to the USB sockets on the outside of the computer.

And as I looked at the EHCI registers with my hexadecimal screen, I could see immediately that whenever I plugged a memory stick or any other USB device into the sockets on the outside of the computer, there was a corresponding change in the corresponding EHCI PORTSC register.(All the EHCI operational registers can be easily seen with a hexadecimal screen because they are in the computer's normal RAM address space, but at a high address above the normal RAM. For example, [0d4405c20h] was the USB Operational base address for one of the two EHCI in my laptop PC.)

With my laptop, I would see no change at all in any of the PORTSC when a memory stick was plugged in to the computer. At first this was frustrating because I wanted to see a change. Instead I could only see with the hexadecimal screen that a single one of the EHCI ports, the first port, at offset +44h, was permanently connected to something (the built-in hub) and the others were never connected to anything at all.

With my Emachines laptop signals have to get through the hub to reach the outside sockets, whereas with the desktop PC there is a direct connection to the outside sockets.

The desktop PC had both EHCI and UHCI as companion controllers, and setting the right binary bit in the EHCI PORTSC registers can give an external USB socket temporary connection to the UHCI if you want that.

With the desktop PC programming is simple if the USB device is specifically "high speed" (as memory sticks usually are) but you are supposed to program the UHCI for the two slower speeds.

With the laptop, the built-in USB 2.0 hubs can be used to interconvert the two slower speeds into high speed and the reverse. This works because USB 2.0 hubs all contain a transaction translator (TT) which automatically converts the speed of slower signals to and from High speed. To make that transaction translator convert speeds, you only have to fill in a few extra fields of your queue heads including the endpoint speed field and a second device address field with the device address of the hub itself.

Getting signals to get through the built-in 2.0 hubs is not so difficult, especially since the BIOS in my laptop reliably enumerates these hubs at the moment when the computer is switched on, always giving them a device address of 02, a configuration of 01, and always turning on their ports power. But you have to send these hubs setup packets which do the "Reset & Enable" of the right hub ports.

As soon as the built-in hub receives the setup packet for doing the reset & enable a port, the ports enable if a memory stick or something else was plugged into the corresponding USB socket on the outside of the computer.

And then high speed data packets can go freely between the EHCI and the memory stick. In the case of my Laptop and a high speed device like a memory stick, the signals coming from the EHCI always reach the port at offset +44h, that has the permanent connection to the permanent Hub, spread out through the 2.0 hub and can reach simultaneously several external USB sockets.

It is a bit more complicated when the device plugged in is not high speed, as for the two slower speeds (called slow speed and full speed), some extra fields in the queue head should be filled in that are not necessary for high speed. One of these is a second device address field addressing the built-in hub, and so that field needed to have a 2 in it.

The endpoint speed field of the queue head has to be filled in, telling the transaction translators in the hub what speed you want them to translate the high speed signals into.

With my laptop, I usually just assumed the BIOS gave the built-in hubs a device address of 02, since that always worked. But alternatively you can try experimentally erasing the enumeration of the built-in 2.0 hub, so its device address returns to zero, and then with your program enumerate the built-in hubs yourself. It worked when I tried it, and it is interesting that the built-in hubs can be enumerated in the same way as you would enumerate any external USB devices (giving them a non zero device address number such as in this case 02, and giving them a configuration always of 01.)

But then, after that enumeration, the built-in hubs are not ready to work until you also send them setup packets which turn on their "ports power". Until ports power is turned on by the setup packets, you cannot do anything, not even read their ports status or have reset& enable of the ports. I have read that with some types of hub it is enough to send one setup packet which turns on port power, and all the other ports get power turned on. But for other hubs you need to send a series of setup packets, one for each port. (All setup packets are 8 bytes long. And you sent them using a "Setup" Queue Head which has a total length field of 8, and a packet length field of 8. A Queue Setup Head is one which has in its PID field the small code which means setup.)

About the desktop PC. If your program is able to enumerate the built-in hubs of a laptop, then the same program can work with a desktop PC that has no built in hubs, but if or when you buy an external USB 2.0 hub and plug it in to the desktop PC. (They are usually like 4 way adaptors, with one USB plug and about 4 sockets) (An external 2.0 type hub plugged in to the desktop PC can perhaps work the same as a permanently built-in hub of the Laptop PC.) That worked when I tried it.

Something about USB keyboards is difficult.

The desktop PC I tried it with, had UHCI as companion controllers, and obviously the BIOS was making the (low speed) USB keyboard work using the UHCI. As soon as I did my experiment the USB keyboard stopped working, of course. I did an experiment in which my program left untouched those PORTSC registers which were given connection to the UHCI, and also the program firstly saved all the values which were in all the EHCI registers, which I knew the BIOS had been using, and then, when the experiment was finished it replaced all these values back into the EHCI registers. This seemed to work as very often the USB keyboard went on working, but unfortunately not always. Obviously you would want the keyboard to go on working. (The problem does not apply to my laptop's keyboard which is PS2 type).

If you want to test to find out if anything is plugged in to a USB socket of the desktop PC, you can test binary bits of the PORTSC registers. But to test it with my laptop, the only way is to send the built-in hub setup packets for "get port status", and then to read an input of data of port status. Testing ports was not really necessary in any of my experiments with the laptop, as I would just plug in one memory stick, just one at a time, and tried enabling all the hub ports, which simplified things.

I suppose there are many other arrangements of circuits inside computers which I don't know anything about.

```
;-----------------------------------------------------------------------
;
;reset_of_EHCI_own_ports: is not suitable for my laptop. It assumed that the PORTSC registers of the EHCI are
directly connected to the USB sockets on the outside of the computer, which was the case in a certain desktop
PC, but not for the laptop which I used much more often.

        ;Also, separately, the step of not resetting ports given to UHCI allowed USB Keyboard to go on working
        ;Assumes that a call to Find_EHCI: has found the USB operational base address and has
        ;recorded that address in [ebx+50h].

reset_of_ehci_own_ports:
        pushad
        mov ebx,50000h
        mov ebx,[ebx+50h]       ;Load in EBX the found EHCI operational base address.
        mov cl,8                ;for 8 EHCI  port status and control registers which are at +44h+4n
        push ebx                ;test 1000h for some computers only?, = port power on too.
rese:   mov eax,[ebx+44h]       ;look for PORTSC binary bit 13 =2000h which means port to UHCI
        test ax,2000h
        jnz rese5               ;nz would mean port goes to UHCI and should not  be reset now.
        mov eax,1100h           ;reset and enable port.  100h=binary bit 8 set for resetting.
        mov [ebx+44h],eax       ;reset the EHCI own port which start at operational base +44h.
rese5:  add ebx,4               ;to the next EHCI own port
        dec cl
        jnz rese
        pop ebx
        mov eax,4000000h
rese2:     dec eax              ;64 milliseconds? how long does it have to wait?
        jnz rese2
        mov cl,8
        push ebx
rese3:     mov eax,[ebx+44h]    ;read from a PORTSC register
```

```
            test ax,2000h                    ;do not reset/end reset when it goes to a low speed through UHCI
            jnz rese6
            mov eax,1004h                    1000h for port power on some EHCIs?
            mov [ebx+44h],eax                ;end port reset, writing into a PORTSC register
   rese6:   add ebx,4                        ;address +4 to do the next EHCI PORTSC register
            dec cl
            jnz rese3
            pop ebx
            mov eax,4000000h
   rese4:   dec eax
            jnz rese4
            popad
            ret
;--------------------------------------------------------------------------------
```
;This was working with my laptop, which does not have a UHCI, in which case it went down to send the built-in hub several set-up packets for reset & enable the hub ports.
;This assumed that when there is an UHCI as well as an EHCI in the computer, then the EHCI ports are directly connected to the USB sockets on the outside of the computer, but assuming that is not necessarily right.

If it found an UHCI it would jump to reset & enable the EHCI own ports, but any reset of EHCI ports had to be avoided with my laptop. Because with my laptop I often relied on the fact that BIOS has already enumerated its built-in hubs, and has already given the hubs a device address of 02. When you rely on that, you should specifically avoid resetting the EHCI's own ports, so that the built-in hubs are sure to keep their device address of 02. But alternatively, one can enumerate built-in hubs with one's own programming. I mainly tried this with the laptop, and with the laptop the computer jumped down to run the reset_loop here which sends a series of setup packets to the built-in USB 2.0 hub, each set-up packet for the reset & enable of a Hub port.

```
   which_kind_of_ports_to_reset:
            push esi
            mov esi,4ff00h    ;
            cmp word [esi],"NO"                        ;With my laptop PC the NO is there.
            pop esi
            jnz ehci_own_ports_reset
            jmp reset_enable_hub_ports
```
;assumes that when there is a UHCI then there is no USB 2.0 hub, But is that right??
;Down here to do the reset+enable of USB 2.0 hub ports.
;my laptop has built-in USB 2.0 hubs and has no Uhci, so it always used this below.

```
   reset_enable_hub_ports:
            pushad
            mov ebx,50800h
            mov cx,100h                     ;for erasing an area where the queue head will be written.
            mov al,0
     clear1: mov [ebx],al                   ;write zeroes which are a part of the queue head.
            inc ebx
            dec cx
            jnz clear1
            mov ebx,50000h
;------------ for resetport
                                 ; 00040323h   ;Write a set-up packet for "set port feature(port  reset)
                               ; resetting a port should enable it automatically only when something is plugged in to it

            mov dword    [ebx+7c0h],00040323h                    ;write a set-up packet
            mov dword    [ebx+7c4h],0000001h                     ;set-up packet for port 1.
            Mov cx,6                                             ; a 6 for up to 6 hub ports
```

```
Reset_loop:        push cx

                   call resets_port              ;Tries resetting 6 ports together.

                   call waits
                   pop cx
                   add byte [ebx+7c4h],1         ;inc +1 in set-up packet for the next port

                   dec cx
                   jnz reset_loop

                   popad
                   ret

resets_port:       pushad
                   mov ebx,50000h

;Write a setup Queue Head, used to send a setup packet of reset port.
;It assumed that the hub had been enumerated and given a device address of 2 and ports power before this runs.
;If the BIOS has given a hub a different device address, you need to find it and substitute the right device address for 2.
                   mov dword  [ebx+800h],050802h      ;At +0, Link pointer pointing to ITSELF.
                                                     ;At +4, 02 = Device address of hub; 20h=high speed;08=packet length
                   mov dword  [ebx+804h],82002h
                                                     ;At +8 is not really used now, ignored because
                                                     ;memory stick is high speed.
                   mov dword  [ebx+808h],41020000h    ;4=mult .
                                                     ;At +0ch, an necessary pointer to a Blank Queue element TD
                   mov dword  [ebx+80ch],0508c0h
                   mov dword  [ebx+810h],01           ;01 means pointers are unused
                   mov dword  [ebx+814h],01
                                                     ; then at +18h, 80h=Active; 02=PID of "Setup"; 0=cerr ; and
                                                     ; 08=total length of 8 bytes

                   mov dword  [ebx+818h],080280h

                                                     ;at +1ch the first buffer pointer must point to your setup packet.
                   mov dword  [ebx+81ch],0507c0h     ; Point to setup packet.

                                                     ;Write an Blank Queue element Transfer Descriptor.

                   mov dword  [ebx+8c0h],01
                   mov dword  [ebx+8c4h],01

                                                     ;Take into EBX the USB Operational base address which
                                                     ; has been found and saved.
                   mov ebx,[ebx+50h]                 ;(One USB Operational Base was for example =0d4405c20h)
                                                     ;write 80001h into the EHCI Command register, to leave
                                                     ; run/stop on run, but stop asynchronous.
                   mov dword  [ebx],80001h           ;Stops the "asynchronous schedule"
                   mov ecx,10000h
             pk10: dec ecx
                   jnz pk10
                                                     ;Asynchronous address register loaded while it is
                                                     ; stopped, with the address of the queue head.
```

```
                mov dword   [ebx+18h],50800h
                mov dword   [ebx],80021h              ;Starts the asynchronous schedule
                mov ecx,10000h
        pk11:   dec ecx
                jnz pk11

                popad
                ret
```

;==

You need to use your programming to make a hexadecimal view screen which can show you the memory and which lets you scroll the memory view up and down, with for example the page up / page down keys, in order to see what is happening.

Set_get_configuration worked in my experiments to enumerate memory sticks. (Then my program would read and write whole files to them). I also wrote another similar routine which worked faster, but I lost it.

Only one memory stick was plugged in at a time. It gives the memory stick a device address of 9 in this example, and then it gives it a configuration which should always be 01, and then it double checks to make sure the configuration is set to 01. If not, it tries once more but using the other USB operational base address for the other EHCI. It does this with a queue head that sends the setup packets.

After a short time delay, it over-writes the horizontal link pointer at the start of the first queue head, making it point to the second queue head. And the second queue head then runs, it is an input queue head which tries to take an input from endpoint 0 and with data1.

I called this operation a blank input, and for some reason this makes the memory sticks pay more attention to the setup packet.

The call ets2 writes the two queue heads, and the call "run_qh" needs to use the USB Operational base address, when it firstly turns off the EHCI's asynchronous schedule by writing 80001h into its command register, and then it writes the address of the first queue head into the EHCI's current asynchronous address register and then it restarts the EHCI asynchronous schedule by writing 80021h into the command register. As it does it the first queue head starts working.

```
        set_get_configuration:
                        push eax                ;####    NOTE extra long delays only necessary for ""The Week"" stick
                        push edx
                        mov cx,4
        cd00:           push cx         ;

                        call ehci_reset_port
                        mov eax,1400000h                        ;16 milliseconds minimum are essential after reset port.
        cd16:           dec eax
                        jnz cd16

                        mov ebx,50000h
                        mov byte [ebx+40h],9            ;The new device address will be 9.
                        mov dl,[ebx+40h]                ;take a device address no for the stick. DL=09
        cd10:           call ets2                       ;ets2 writes 2 queue heads. A setup QH and an Input QH.
                        mov byte [ebx+104h],0           ;Write device address of 00 into both queue heads
                        mov byte [ebx+304h],0
                        mov dword [ebx+100h],50102h             ;make sure link pointer points to itself
                        mov dword [ebx+0160h],0090500h          ;This writes a setup packet
                        mov dword [ebx+0164h],0h                ; try to set device address
                        mov [ebx+0162h],dl              ;new device address =9 from dl into setup packet.
                        call run_qh
                        mov eax,4000000h                ;A wait time of 3 to 64 milliseconds is often necessary?
        cd2: dec eax
```

```
            jnz cd2                                      ;next the link pointer of the first queue head is Changed
                                                         ; to point to the second queue head.
;
            mov dword [ebx+100h],50302h       ;Link pointer pointing to second QH.
                                                         ;the Ehci sees the new link pointer and follows
                                                         ; the address to work on the second queue head, input
            mov eax,2000000h
      cd6: dec eax                             ;The new device address of 9 should be set by now.
            jnz cd6
            call ets6
;----------------------------
                  ; Assuming that a device address of 9 has been set. Now to set configuration to 01.
            call ets2                          ;ets2 writes 2 queue heads
            mov byte [ebx+104h],dl             ;the new device address =09 into Both queue heads
            mov byte [ebx+304h],dl
            mov dword [ebx+100h],50102h        ;horizontal link pointer of first queue head
            mov dword [ebx+0160h],00010900h    ;write a setup packet for set config to 01
            mov dword [ebx+0164h],0h              ;this worked well.
            call run_qh
            mov eax,4000000h                   ;The wait has to be longer for some memory sticks
      cd3: dec eax   ;
            jnz cd3
;next, the horizontal link pointer of the first queue head is over-written to make it point to the
; second queue head. Its input made devices pay more attention to the set-up packets for some reason.

            mov dword [ebx+100h],50302h        ;For blank input
            mov eax,2000000h
     cd11: dec eax
            jnz cd11
            call ets6
            call ets2  ;ets1
            mov dword [ebx+100h],50102h        ;link pointer of first queue head points to itself
            mov byte [ebx+104h],dl             ;device address written into both queue heads
            mov byte [ebx+304h],dl

            mov dword [ebx+31ch],50400h        ;loading address into input qh.
            mov byte [ebx+400h],20h            ;erase there to see it set.

            mov dword [ebx+0160h],00000880h    ; set-up packet for "get configuration"
            mov dword [ebx+0164h],10000h
            call run_qh
            mov eax,3000000h
      cd4: dec eax
            jnz cd4                            ;after a delay over-write the link pointer of the first QH
            mov dword [ebx+100h],50302h             ;to make it point to the second queue head.
            mov eax,3000000h                   ;the second queue head should actually input 1 byte data.
     cd14: dec eax
            jnz cd14

            call ets6
            pop cx                    ;with the compare, look to see whether 1 byte data inputted =01?
            cmp byte [ebx+400h],01        ;has configuration been set?
            jz cd15                       ;If Yes, then it is finished. The computer has two EHCI's
            mov eax,[ebx+50h]             ;If No, then try the other EHCI.
```

```
            mov edx,[ebx+54h]
            mov [ebx+54h],eax
            mov [ebx+50h],edx       ;exchange the two USB operational base addresses

            dec cx
            jnz cd00                ;try again with the other EHCI for left side usb socket.
            pop edx
            pop eax
            mov cx,9999h            ;error signal to make caller exit.
            ret
    cd15:   pop edx                 ;jumps to here when configuration 01 has been set.
            pop eax
            ret

;================================================================
    run_qh: push ecx                ;this call starts the Ehci and leaves it running.
            push ebx                ;(One computer's USB operational base address was 0d4405c20h).
            mov ebx,[ebx+50h]       ;The saved USB Operational base address goes into EBX.
            mov dword [ebx],80001h  ;Write into EHCI Command register
                                    ;The 80001h stops asynchronous but leaving run/stop on run.
            mov ecx,40000h          ;.
    pk1j:   dec ecx                 ;(You only write into asynchronous address register while it is stopped.)
            jnz pk1j
            mov dword [ebx+18h],50100h   ;set asynchronous address register to 1st queue head.
            mov dword [ebx],80021h       ;starts asynchronous schedule with the command register
            mov ecx,100000h              ;Here wait for it to have time to react to setup packet.
    pk1k:   dec ecx         ;
            jnz pk1k
            pop ebx                 ;pop recover EBX pointing to the queue heads
            pop ecx
            ret
```

To read descriptors I had written my setup packet for "get descriptor" very close to
the first of two queue heads. It might actually be a good idea to move it a bit further away.
The call to ets2 writes two queue heads, a setup queue head, and an input queue head.
Looking at the call ets2:
As it writes the two queue heads, it takes a device address which it assumes I have saved in [ebx+40h], and
writes that device address into both the queue heads as 1 byte at offset +04.
Reading descriptors is possible even before enumeration, and when a device address is still zero.
The horizontal link pointer of each queue head, at offset 00, points exactly to itself. Wherever you write the
queue heads, make it point to itself.
The first queue head is made to be a setup queue head by its having a PID field of 2. It has a packet length field
of 8 and a total length field of 8, because the setup packets it sends are all 8 bytes.
Its first buffer pointer has the address of my setup packet in it, it happens to be 50160h
in this example.
Now looking at the call to ets3:
The call to ets3 stops the asynchronous schedule of the EHCI by writing 80001h into its
Command register. (The register which is at exactly the USB operational base address).
It then writes the address of the first queue head, (the setup queue head), into the asynchronous list address
register.(Which is at USB operational base +18h)
   Then it re-starts the asynchronous schedule by writing 80021h into the command register. Then it waits for a
time delay of about 2 milliseconds, for it to work.
   Then it over-writes the horizontal link pointer of the first queue head to make that pointer point to the second
queue head. It means that after the deliberate time delay, the EHCI which I assume had finished working on the
setup queue head, will always **see and follow** the new horizontal link pointer, and it will immediately work on
the second queue head. (When the EHCI finishes working on a queue head, it clears to zero the queue head's

"Active" binary bit. It then looks at the horizontal link pointer and follows the pointer. When that horizontal link pointer points to itself, the EHCI simply looks at it over and over again, while doing nothing.
   That goes on until your program either sets to 1 the "Active" bit in the queue head, or instead over-writes the horizontal link pointer making it point to a different queue head.)
The second queue head is an inputs queue head. The EHCI works with that taking an input. Then the program waits for another delay of about 6 milliseconds. The call to ets3 ends.
Now call ets6 simply stops the asynchronous schedule with 80001h written to the command register.
   This assumed that before calling these things the program has automatically looked through the configuration space to find the address of the EHCI, and that it has saved the USB operational base address in [ebx+50h].
   (In my laptop the usb operational base address happened to be [0d4405c20h], but it is different for other computers).

The series of 3 calls, ets2, ets3, et6, is repeated to read more descriptors. Each time the first 4 bytes of the setup packet for "Get descriptor" is rewritten for a different descriptor.

;===

;---
;   ; Writes at an address that happened to be [ebx+160h] a setup packet for "Get descriptors".
;Actually this setup packet was written very close to the first queue head, and it would
;have been better to have written the setup packet further away from queue heads.
;Its first 4 bytes contain a number for the descriptor type and index.
;Its second 4 bytes get re-used, and only had to be written once. In the re-used area,
;the number 0c0h is in the length field, any length greater than the longest descriptor is ok.
;In this case there is no blank input, but sometimes a blank input before trying to read each descriptor would make it all work much better.

;A call to ets2 writes two queue heads. It writes a Setup queue head at [ebx+100h], and
;it writes a Input queue head at [ebx+300h]. Separately write a setup packet at [ebx+160h].
;The first buffer pointer of that setup queue head points to the setup packet at [ebx+160h]
;The first buffer pointer (= loading address) in the second queue head is over-written with the address where ;you want the descriptor to be loaded to. You should see the descriptor appearing at that address.

;**To be able to do any of these tests, it was essential to firstly make my own dual text/hexadecimal**
; **view-screen program to be able to see the memory** in hexadecimal. I made a dual view
; screen with normal alphabetical text on the left side of the screen and memory in
; hexadecimal on the right side. To test this it was essential to be able to see the
; descriptors appearing, and also see changes in the queue heads.

   ;-------------------------- To read most of the descriptors
read_before_enumeration:
                mov ebx,50000h
                mov byte [ebx+40h],0   ;zero to the device address byte.??
                jmp read_descriptors2
   read_after_enumeration: ;assuming that enumerating gave the device address of 9
                mov ebx,50000h
                mov byte [ebx+40h],9   ;assume memory stick has a device address of 09 now.
   read_descriptors2:
                mov byte [ebx+60h],0   ;a starting data toggle for reading sectors
                mov byte [ebx+62h],0   ;another starting data toggle

                call ets5   ;ets5= just erase descriptors area

                mov dword [ebx+160h],1000680h   ;Type 1 =device descriptor.

```
                mov dword [ebx+164h],0c00000h                    ;re-used part of setup packet.
                call ets2                            ; Call ets2 writes 2 queue heads
                                    ;Now rewrite the address (the first buffer pointer ) in the
                                    ;input queue head, making it point to where you want descriptors.
                mov dword [ebx+31ch],50420h       ;to make device descriptor appear in [50420h]
                call ets3
                                    ;ets3=run (Stop asynchronous schedule, load -
                                    ;asynchronous address register then start it running)
                call ets6           ;ets6=wait then stop asynchronous while run/stop still running
                call ets2                           ;ets2=write main part of 2 queue heads
            mov dword [ebx+160h],2000680h       ;Now type 2.= for configuration descriptor.
            mov dword [ebx+31ch],50460h         ;To make configuration descriptor appear in [50460h]
                call ets3
                call ets6
                mov al,[ebx+474h]           ;Read one of the 2 bulk IN or OUT endpoint numbers.
                mov ah,al
                and ah,7                    ;remove binary bit 7 from copy in ah
                cmp al,80h          ;A set binary bit 7 is a signal that it was an INPUT endpoint no.
                jb rec_output
                mov [ebx+410h],ah           ;save the INPUT Endpoint number, it will be used.
                mov ah,[ebx+47bh]           ;Read the other one, of the 2 endpoint numbers.
                mov [ebx+411h],ah           ; Save the  Output Endpoint number
                jmp recdone

    rec_output:     mov [ebx+411h],ah           ;Save the OUTPUT Endpoint number in [ebx+411h]
                mov ah,[ebx+47bh]   ;Read the Input endpoint number from configuration descriptor.
                and ah,7                    ;remove its set binary bit 7
                mov [ebx+410h],ah           ; Save the INPUT endpoint number in [ebx+410h]
        recdone:
;-------------------------------------------------- on to read more descriptors.
                call ets2
                mov dword  [ebx+160h],3010680h          ;Type 3 = string type, with index 1
                mov dword  [ebx+31ch],504a0h            ;rewrite pointer in inputs queue head.
                call ets3
                call ets6                       ;ets6 = 5 milliseconds then stop the asynchronous.
;----
                call ets2
                mov dword  [ebx+160h],3020680h          ; Now type 3 with index 2
                mov dword  [ebx+31ch],504e0h            ;rewrite pointer in inputs queue head.

                call ets3
                call ets6           ;ets3 then writes over H link pointer to point to second QH
;----
                call ets2
                mov dword  [ebx+160h],3030680h          ;type 3 with index 3
                mov dword  [ebx+31ch],50520h            ;rewrite pointer in inputs queue head.
                call ets3
                call ets6

                call ets2
                mov dword  [ebx+160h],6000680h          ;type 6 was also = device?
                mov dword  [ebx+31ch],50560h            ;rewrite pointer in inputs queue head.
                call ets3
                call ets6
                call ets2
```

```
                    mov dword   [ebx+160h],7000680h        ;type 7  was also = configuration?
                    mov dword   [ebx+31ch],505c0h          ;rewrite pointer in inputs queue head.
                    call ets3
                    call ets6
                    ret
```
;--
;note: descriptor type 6 was similar to type 1. Descriptor type 7 was similar to type 2. THE Memory stick's
important two endpoint numbers can be read from either the descriptor type 2 or type 7. But normally from 2.
;after reading descriptors, record the Memory stick's endpoint numbers. These two endpoint numbers are used
when reading and writing   sectors.

;---------------- A certain Verbatim memory stick only worked when it had received request_sense

;--
```
ets3:   push ebx
        mov ebx,[ebx+50h]              ;Read the found and saved USB operational base address into ebx
        mov dword   [ebx],80001h       ;Write into command register to turn off asynchronous schedule.
        mov ecx,40000h
  apk1: dec ecx
        jnz apk1
                                       ; At  op base +18h the asynchronous address register is loaded
                                       ;with the address of Setup Queue Head
        mov dword   [ebx+18h],50100h   ;Write the address of the first queue head.

        mov dword   [ebx],80021h       ;Re-start the EHCI's asynchronous schedule
        mov ecx,200000h                ; Wait for memory stick to have time to react to the setup packet
  apk16: dec ecx
        jnz apk16
        mov ebx,50000h
        mov dword [ebx+100h],50302h    ;over-write horizontal link pointer to point to 2nd QH.
        mov ecx,600000h                   ;Waits again
  apk18: dec ecx
        jnz apk18
        pop ebx
        ret
```

This is a drawing of a Memory stick's Configuration Descriptor.

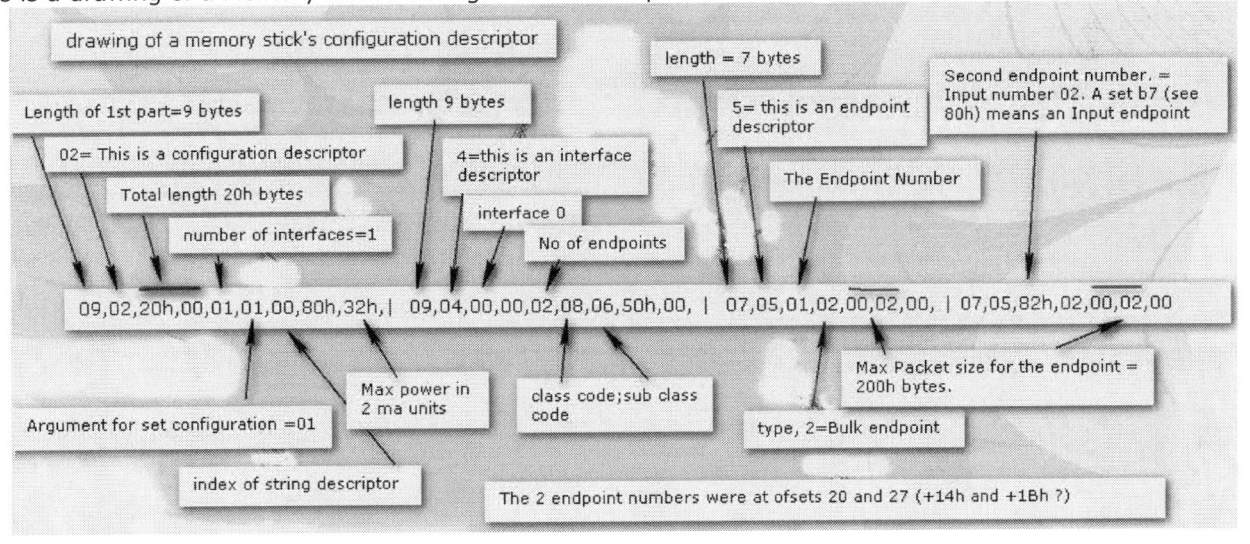

drawing of a memory stick's configuration descriptor

Length of 1st part=9 bytes
02= This is a configuration descriptor
Total length 20h bytes
number of interfaces=1
Argument for set configuration =01
index of string descriptor
Max power in 2 ma units

length 9 bytes
4=this is an interface descriptor
interface 0
No of endpoints
class code;sub class code

length = 7 bytes
5= this is an endpoint descriptor
The Endpoint Number
type, 2=Bulk endpoint

Second endpoint number. = Input number 02. A set b7 (see 80h) means an Input endpoint
Max Packet size for the endpoint = 200h bytes.
The 2 endpoint numbers were at ofsets 20 and 27 (+14h and +1Bh ?)

09,02,20h,00,01,01,00,80h,32h, | 09,04,00,00,02,08,06,50h,00, | 07,05,01,02,00,02,00, | 07,05,82h,02,00,02,00

Reading and writing sectors of USB memory sticks.

USB devices are not ready to work immediately, and some of the complexity is obviously unnecessary.

They have this complexity with unnecessary things, but you have to program it or else it won't work. The first step was to enumerate the memory stick by giving it a device address of non-zero, (I gave it a device address of 09) and then giving it a configuration of 01, as usual,. And then a double check that the configuration has been set to 01,. And then reading descriptors from the memory stick. Or actually you can read the descriptors firstly while device address is still zero.

From reading the descriptors you find the important endpoint numbers which you need. You need the input and the output endpoint numbers for bulk input and output. They are usually small numbers, either 1 or 2, and they are different for every different make of memory stick. One memory stick had 02 for both its input and its output endpoints. Another had 01 for input and 02 for output. Another had the reverse.

To read and write sectors from the memory sticks, you need to put the right endpoint number for input or for output into the endpoint number field of a queue head, use the queue head to send the memory stick a read(10) or a write(10) command in a 31 bytes long command block wrapper (CBW); put the right endpoint number in a queue head again, and read or write the data. For the data the queue head should have 200h in its max packet size field, while the total length field should be set to a correct total length. And then just afterwards read from the memory stick a 13 bytes long command status wrapper (CSW). The CSW's last byte should be zero when no errors.

The program may look at the total length field of the queue head to see when that field goes down to zero, and its going down to zero indicates that the data has all been sent. The program can also read the queue head's "active" binary bit to see when that gets cleared to zero. (The EHCI should automatically change several numbers in the queue heads, especially the total length field which goes down, the buffer pointer fields, and the status field if only to clear to zero its "active" bit when work is finished).

A few years ago I worked on my bootable program to get it to read and write whole files to USB memory sticks, as well as other things, and after a lot of experimenting and a lot of work it was able to read and write long files to the memory sticks of either Fat16 or Fat32 file format. It worked reasonably quickly. I tested it over and over again by reading and viewing Windows bitmap pictures with the program (.bmp) and saving the file back to the memory sticks again and loading it again. A test was to reload the bitmap image and view it to see whether the picture was all there or whether parts of it were missing. After a long time I got it working perfectly. Files saved to a memory stick by my program were properly compatible with Windows, but they had to have short file names since I only tried using the older type of file name which has to have up to 8 characters all in capitals.

I am only going to try to explain the reading and writing of sectors. My file program specifies three variables: 1) The sector number of the sectors it wants to read or write to the memory stick, 2) the length in sectors which it wants to read or to write at a time. 3) It also specifies the memory address in the computer's memory, where it wants to load the data.

Then the program pieces which I want to explain here do reading and writing of specified sectors. As my longer bootable program starts to read or write files, it starts with the above process of enumerating the memory stick and of finding the 2 important endpoint numbers, called the bulk input endpoint and the bulk output endpoint, and then, it saves the two endpoint numbers as 2 variables. And they are used, to go into the queue heads, during reading and writing of sectors and files.

129

In this text the words "input", and "output" are always from the point of view of the computer.

I had tried Read(6) and read (12) commands, but only Read(10) worked.

This is the format of a Command Block Wrapper for the Read(10) command.

A Command Block Wrapper (CBW) for Read(10)

Length.	Offset	Hex value		
4	0	43425355H	"USBC"	The fixed word USBC
4	+4	Anything. Any letters of your choice, to get reflected in CSW		
4	+8	Length in bytes, a multiple of 200h, normal Little-endian way round.		
1	+12	80h	Direction flag. 80h=read direction; 00= write direction.	
1	+13	00	zero	
1	+14	0AH	Always 0Ah	
1	+15	28h	28h=Read(10) command/ 2Ah = Write(10) command	
1	+16	00	zero	
4	+17	Absolute sector number, Big-endian way round.		
1	+21	00	zero	
2	+22	Length in sectors, Big endian way round		
7	+24	00	7 Bytes of zeroes	

A Command block wrapper is always 31 bytes long, and it is padded with binary zeroes at its end. 31 bytes which is 1Fh bytes in hex. Many commands look shorter, but their ends have to be padded with a number of zeroes. When you send a CBW to a memory stick, you should put the number 1Fh into the packet length field of your queue head, and also into the total length field of the queue head.

The Command Block Wrapper has to be sent to the bulk OUTPUT endpoint of the memory stick. The queue head has to have the bulk out endpoint number in its endpoint field. The words input and output are always from the point of view of the computer. This is the same output endpoint to which you send data for writing sectors, but a memory stick is supposed to recognize that it is a CBW. Both the packet length field and total length fields of the queue head should contain 1fH, as a USB memory stick is supposed to automatically recognize this length and know from that this is a CBW. A memory stick might also automatically recognize the letters "USBC" in the first 4 bytes.

In a CBW for the Read(10) command or the Write(10) command, the length which you want to read or write should be specified TWICE. At offset +8 bytes, you have to write the length of the data in bytes, a normal 4 bytes number, and in the computer's normal little endian way round. It should be a multiple of 200h. This is the way round with least significant bytes on the left, as is normal for computers. But at offset +22d bytes (= offset +16h bytes) you have to write the length of the data in sectors, as a 2 bytes number, but you have to write it Big-endian way round. Each memory stick sector is always 200h bytes long.

For example, when you want to read/write 4 sectors, you know 4 sectors are 800h bytes, so you have to fill in the CBW at its offset +8 with the normal number 800h, and at the same time fill in at offset +16h the number 0004 as a 2 bytes number, BUT written in the unusual Big endian way round. The big endian way round means that the order of the two bytes has to be swapped so that the 04 is actually written at offset +17h and the zero at +16h.

You have to write into the CBW the absolute sector number, of the starting sector which you want to read or write in the memory stick. At offset +17d bytes, (= +11h). This sector number is of 4 bytes long, and it also needs to be written in the unusual Big-endian way round. Now the more significant bytes are on the left. That means that the 4 bytes of it have to be swapped around before being written. You can use the assembly language operation "Bswap eax" to do that. The rest of the CBW is padded with zeroes, making 31 bytes length.

So you take the number of sectors to be read or written, multiply that by 200h, and write it as a normal little-endian 4 bytes number at offset +8. And the same number but just in sectors, (not x 200h), has to be Bswapped and written in the big endian way round as a 2 bytes number at offset +16h.

I think the way two of the numbers have to be big-endian way round is difficult and I had trouble doing that.

After sending the Command Block Wrapper, for either read(10) or write(10), I write a queue head for either input or output of the sectors which the CBW has asked for. The queue head must have a max packet length field of 200h, so that it works with 200h bytes long data packets. It has to have a total length field filled in with a right total length. It has to have a packet ID field of 01 as the code for Input, or 00 as the code for Output. (The packet ID field is at offset +19h relative to the start of the queue head. It determines the type of the queue head, as there are 3 types. 0=Output, 1=input, 2=setup.)

And it's very important to fill in properly all the buffer pointers of the queue head, with the loading address of where you want the data to be in the computer's memory. If you take an input without doing all the buffer pointers, the input could load accidentally into the lowest area of the computer's memory, causing a crash.

The queue head's starting data toggle bit must be correct. The data toggle bit is binary bit 7 of the byte at offset +1Bh relative to the start of the queue head. So if it is a "1" it looks like an "80h." For every data packet which the EHCI sends or receives, the data toggle should alternate automatically 1 or 0. One has to keep track of the data toggle somehow in order to know which value to start with, a 80h for data1 or a 0 for data0? Every data packet which is sent includes a data toggle bit, and when any data packet is sent and received without error both the EHCI and the memory stick's own internal memory of data toggle for each endpoint, alternates it with every data packet.

The memory stick remembers a separate data toggle for each of its 3 endpoints. As every data packet is sent and received, the data toggle bit which goes with the next data packet is automatically toggled. And one has to keep track of that somehow. That is difficult and if you make a mistake you can notice the first data packet goes missing, or sometimes strange effects. The queue head always has to be activated, by setting its active binary bit to 1. The "active" binary bit is bit 7 of the byte at offset +18h relative to the start of the queue head. The "active" bit therefore looks like an 80h. The EHCI does nothing at all with the queue head until its active bit is set.

And if the EHCI is looking at the queue head, it will immediately notice whether you have set the active bit to 1, and it starts working on the queue head only if it sees the bit is set.

But just before I send a CBW to a memory stick, my program attempts to take a "blank input" from the memory stick's endpoint 0 using data toggle of data1. For some reason, a memory stick pays much more attention to a CBW if just before sending the CBW you attempt to take an input from its endpoint 0. It has to be with the data toggle in the input queue head at data1 and its endpoint field at 0. The attempted input does not seem to actually read any data at all, but it works, and it makes the program run much better, more reliably. The below example is how I took this blank input. First the call to ets2 writes 2 queue heads, only the first one is used at all now. Two loads prepare the queue head. The address of where the queue head is in memory is loaded into EAX register, and the call to ets7 gives the EHCI the address of the queue head and then makes it start running.

I wonder whether the blank input is really inputting some information which I have not noticed? There was nothing at the loading address. The same blank input can also make memory sticks and other USB devices pay more attention to setup packets, and so it's useful when you are sending setup packets too.

```
test3:
        pushad                              ;test3 = blank input.

        call ets2                                   ;Calling test3 improved the file saving program
        mov dword [ebx+11ch],52000h                 ;change loading address to unused space.
        mov dword [ebx+118h],80080180h      ;Active=80h, Input pid=01, and length 08,data1=80h at m.s.

        mov eax,50100h          ;EAX=address of queue head. Above changed the PID to INPUT from setup.
        call ets7               ;ets7 stops, after 1 milliseconds runs queue head at [eax], waits 1 millisec

        call ets8               ;   ets8  waits 1 milliseconds then stops
        popad
        ret
```

The next thing is the program which I used to send the CBW to the memory stick:

```
;--------------------------------------------------
;
send_cbw_data1: mov cl,80h          ;put data toggle in CL, 80h=data1
                jmp overs
  send_cbw:     mov cl,0            ;put data toggle in CL, with 0 for start data0
   overs:       call ets2           ;call ets2 writes 2 queue heads but only the second QH is used
                mov edi,50900h      ;address of the CBW into edi for Queue head
   overs4:                          ;This queue head is to send the CBW

                                    ;edi= Address to my Command block wrapper
                                    ;written into the first buffer pointer of the queue head.

        mov dword [ebx+31ch],edi

        mov dword [ebx+304h],1f2209h        ;packet length 1fh, 20h=high speed, 09 = device address.
        mov dword [ebx+318h],1f0080h        ;Data0. And total length 1fh bytes.
                                    ; 00=Out PID makes it become an output queue head.
                                    ;80h=active, does activate the queue head
        or [ebx+31bh],CL            ;data1 or data 0 by OR to the prepared CL register.

        mov al,[ebx+411h]           ;get Output endpoint number which was found from descriptor
        OR al,20h                   ;OR,20h for high speed. (the byte is now usually 21h or 22h here)
        mov [ebx+305h],al           ;Endpoint number and high speed into queue head at +5.

        mov eax,50300h              ;EAX loaded with address of my 2nd Queue Head.
        call ets7                   ;load Async reg with address in EAX, and start running of Queue head
        call waitn_cbw ;
        call ets8                       ;stop running
        ret
```

The data toggle bit happened to go into the CL register, where it looked like either 0 or 80h, and it is ready to go into the queue head. Next the call to ets2 writes 2 queue heads, but only the second of those queue heads is used in this case. The queue head happens to start at address 50300h. The EDI register happened to be loaded with the address of the CBW, and this is then written directly into the queue head's first buffer pointer, which is at offset +1Ch relative to the start of the queue head. Since it is for sending a very short length of only 1Fh bytes data, only the first of the queue head's buffer pointers has to be filled in, with a loading address pointing to the CBW. (When a longer length of data is going to be sent, it is very important to fill in all the buffer pointers properly).

Next a load of the number 1f2209h into the queue head at offset +04, gives it a "max packet length" of 1fh bytes (31 bytes in decimal) , (and the 1fh itself is actually into offset +06.) And it also writes a 20h at offset +05, which stands for high speed. Next it loads the number 001f0080h into the queue head at offset +18h relative to the start of the queue head. This gives it data0, and a total length field of 1fh. (The total length field and the max packet length field are the same now).

And the 80h at offset +18h is the "active bit" which makes the queue head activated. Next the CL register, which in this spot may contain either 00 or 80h, gives the queue head either data1 or data0, by logical OR operation at the offset of +1bh. Next the correct output endpoint number for the USB memory stick, which was found out from the descriptors, goes into the AL register, and it is combined with a 20h for high speed, and goes into the queue head at offset +05h. Then the address of the queue head goes into EAX and the call to ets7 starts it running. The result should be that the memory stick receives the CBW.

;===

Writing some sectors to a memory stick:

Step1: Do a blank input (to make the memory stick pay more attention to the CBW). Step2: Write a CBW for Write(10) command. Step3: Send the CBW to the memory stick's bulk Output endpoint (Both max packet size field and total length field can be value 1fh for this). Step4: After a short delay to give the memory stick time, send the memory stick all of the sectors the CBW asked for, to its bulk output endpoint. (Until you send all of those sectors, the memory stick won't want to do anything else). Step5: read from the memory stick's bulk input endpoint, a CSW (Command status wrapper). This CSW is always 0dh bytes long (13 bytes long) and its thirteenth byte should be 0 if there is no errors. This is the end of writing the sectors.

Reading some sectors from a memory stick:

Step1: My program does a blank input. (It makes the memory sticks pay more attention to the CBW). Step2: Write a CBW for Read(10) command. Step3: Send the CBW to the memory stick's bulk output endpoint. Step4: read all the sectors you have asked for from the memory stick's bulk input endpoint. (You have to read All the sectors which were asked for as the memory stick will not want to do anything else until you do). Step5: Read a CSW from the bulk input endpoint. This finishes operations for reading some sectors from the memory stick.

I tried it with about 12 different kinds of memory sticks. One type of memory stick, called I-Poco, did not work at first, until I tried sending it a CBW for the "Test unit ready" command. After sending it the Test unit ready command twice, it turned on and started working. Another memory stick, of the Verbatim brand name, did not work at first, until I tried sending it a CBW for the "Request sense" command. Then it turned on, and went on working. Some of the memory sticks were very easy to make work. A free memory stick called "The Week", was slow to set a device address, and needed a time delay of at least 0.1 seconds? A non secure Sandisk memory stick worked easily, but a secure version of the Sandisk never worked at all. The Sandisk which worked was the only memory stick that did not check automatically that the two length of data fields in the CBW were equivalent, as it worked anyway.

;============

Writing the Read(10) and Write(10) Command Block Wrapper.
;----------   To Call with CX=length in sectors and EAX= First sector number.
write_cbw_write(10):
        call write_cbw_read(10)   ;CBW is of length 1fh bytes = 31 bytes.

        mov byte   [ebx+90ch],0   ;b7=0=flag for write
        mov byte   [ebx+90fh],2ah   ;write(10) op-code is 2ah.
        ret   ;CBW for read(10) was here converted into write(10)
;================================
;---------- To Call with CX=length in sectors and EAX= absolute First sector number.

write_cbw_read(10):   mov ebx,50000h   ;CBW is of length 1fh bytes = 31 bytes.

        mov dword   [ebx+900h],43425355h   ; The CBW signature
        mov dword   [ebx+904h]," DHR"   ; A tag gets reflected back in csw.
                                              ;(4 bytes byte length at +908h filled in last)
        mov byte   [ebx+90ch],80h   ;flag bit 7, 80h= direction is READ
        mov byte   [ebx+90dh],0   ; 0
                                              ; command block area
        mov byte   [ebx+90eh],0ah ;   ;length of the following command block.
        mov byte   [ebx+90fh],28h   ;read (10) op-code =28h, starts at +0fh
        mov byte   [ebx+910h],0   ;lun number bits 5 to 7 should be 0

        bswap eax   ;eax=absolute sector number of first sector to be read.
        mov [ebx+911h],eax   ;Bswap it because it is the Big Endian way round
        mov byte   [ebx+915h],0   ;a reserved 0

        mov [ebx+916h],ch   ;Data length field measured in sectors, here big-endian way
        mov [ebx+917h],cl   ;swap to other way round. 1=1 sector of 512 bytes

        mov dword [ebx+918h],0   ;reserved bytes 0
        mov dword [ebx+91ch],0   ;pad end with zeroes? Length sent=31 bytes.

        push edx   ;Both lengths fields should correspond but *200h
        and ecx,0ffffh   ;clear extended part
                                               ;multiply number of sectors by 200h
        move eax,200h   ;Imul ecx multiplies eax by ecx
        Imul ecx   ; Result of imul ecx should be in edx:eax
                                               ; Last, write the first of the two length fields.
                                               ;It is length in bytes, and it is in normal little endian way round.
        mov [ebx+908h],eax   ;Data length in bytes field is normal way round.
        pop edx   ;recover edx which imul has changed

        ret

;---
Save_sectors_the_first_time:
        mov ebx,50000h
        mov byte [ebx+62h],1   ;???
        mov byte [ebx+60h],0

        ;;; call test_unit ;was only necessary for I-Poco memory sticks

Save_more_sectors: ;calls to here to write more sectors to the memory stick

```
                mov ebx,50000h
                mov esi,31000h                  ;esi addressed variables in usb files writing

                mov cx,[esi+22h]                ;cx length field in sectors, at first normal way round
                mov eax,[esi+28h]               ;eax=start sector number to write sectors
                call write_cbw_write(10)        ;Read(10) converted into write(10)
    diw:        call test3                      ;a blank input call test3 improved the program a lot
                test byte [esi+60h],1           ;test keep track of data toggle
                jz tk7
                call send_cbw                   ;if data toggle data0 send the CBW to the memory stick
                jmp tk8

    tk7:
                call send_cbw_data1             ;if data toggle data1 send the CBW to the memory stick
        tk8:    call output_sector              ;Does the loading address, writes a series of sectors.
                mov eax,300000h                 ;does about 3 milliseconds
    tk8b:       dec eax
                jnz tk8b

                call removes                    ;# To read the CSW, but is it a good way of reading that?

                ret
;-----------------------------------
;The total length field of the queue head is 15 binary bits at offset + 1Ah.
;Whenever number of sectors to do is at least 20h, then start with 40000080h which
;means total length field of queue head has 4000h. (200h bytes per sector times 20h)
;And it goes through cycles of transferring 4000h bytes per cycle.
;When number of sectors to be done falls below 20h, then the small number
;of remaining sectors goes into the uppermost byte of edx, which is then doubled,
;(effect of it is x200h) when to go into the queue head's total length field for the last time.

    output_sector:              ;writing sectors onto usb memory stick, after a CBW has been sent,

                mov eax,[esi+24h]               ;The simple 4 byte loading address goes into EAX.
                mov ebx,50000h
                mov cx,[esi+22h]                ;The number of sectors to write at once goes into CX
        inst5:

                cmp cx,20h                      ;CMP,20h  no-borrow when it has to do several cycles
                jnb inst10                      ;if no borrow, does a 4000h length of data.

                mov DL,CL                       ;in the last cycle
                bswap edx                       ;Swap from lowest byte to highest byte

                add edx,edx                     ;(here when it needs to do one cycle or a last cycle)
                and edx,7e000000h               ;upper edx will go into the total length field of a Q.H
                add edx,80h                     ;80h is the queue head's "active" binary bit.
                jmp inst11    ;
    inst10:     mov edx,040000080h              ;to here to do 4000h bytes when it will need to do several cycles.
                                                ; to go into queue head.  0= OUT PID.
                                                ;Total length field of 200h x 20h bytes Data0

    inst11:     push eax                        ;push EAX= address for loading
```

```
                    push ecx                 ;push CX=count down of sectors to do
                    mov cl,0                 ;Cl a different use, 0 for data0

                    test byte [esi+60h],1
                    jz tk10
                    mov cl,80h               ;CL=80h for start data1

tk10:               call inst2         ;called enough times, but a separate call to read the CSW after that.
                    ;----------------------------------------
                    pop ecx      ;
                    pop eax
                    mov dl,[ebx+318h]        ;Read the status field of the queue head, it is at +18h.
                    and dl,78h
                    jz inst7b                ;Zero when no status errors? This exit improved it.
                    ret

  inst7b:           add eax,4000h            ;move up loading address 4000h = 20h packets of 200h bytes.
                    sub cx,20h                ; count down, does 20h sectors at every turn
                    jz inst6
                    jnb inst5                ;inst5 to the next turn of a loop,
        inst6:
                    ret
```

```
;------------------------------------------------------
;
;the whole of the data asked for has to be transferred or a memory stick stops working
;------------------------------------------------------------------------------
;
inst2:   push eax                     ;EAX=the loading address to go into the buffer pointers
         call ets2                    ;writes 2 queue heads, but only the second queue head is used.
         pop eax                      ;then do all the buffer pointers properly
         call do_buffer_pointers      ;call with EAX= the loading address,
         mov byte [ebx+304h],9          ;write the device address of 09 into queue head at +4

         mov al,[ebx+411h]            ;get bulk Output Endpoint number found from descriptors
         or al,20h                    ;include 20h for high speed
         mov [ebx+305h],al            ;write Endpoint number and 20h into queue head at +5.
         mov word [ebx+306h],200h     ;Packet length of 200h bytes written at offset +6.

;Next prepared EDX, has to go in +18h the 80h="active" bit; at +19h the 00 for "output";
;at +1ah the 2 bytes total length; at +1bh it should have 80h/00 the starting data toggle.

         mov [ebx+318h],edx           ; prepared EDX has total length. 00=OUT PID, 80h=active
         OR [ebx+31bh],cl             ;CL writes the starting data toggle at offset +1bh
         mov eax,50300h               ;the address of the second queue head
         call ets7                    ;call to start it running
         call waitn_out               ;makes ax=3333h if an error
         call ets8                    ;stop running
         ret
```

;--
The call to write sectors a first time, had to firstly call several other calls, which finds the USB operational base address of the EHCI(the address of its command register) by looking through the "Configuration space". You should choose one of two different kinds of ports reset, to decide which kind of port should undergo "reset+enable", and that is a difficult thing as with my laptop only the hub ports should be reset, and with a desktop PC there was no such hub and so only the Ehci ports should be reset. And then the Ehci experiment

should enumerate the memory stick giving it a device address of 9 in the example and a configuration of 01, and then read from it the descriptors mainly to be able to find the 2 right endpoint numbers for bulk input and output.

The call to inst2 calls to write 2 queue heads, but only the second of the queue heads is used at all. It happens to start at address 50300h. To get this queue head ready, the number 2002109h is written into it at offset +4. This gives it a data packet length of 200h bytes,
And a device address field of 9. The endpoint field is going to be overwritten. Next a number prepared in EDX goes into the queue head at offset +18h. This included the total length field of the queue head, the 00 for output pid, and an 80h =active bit. Next CL which holds either 00 or 80h, puts the starting data toggle into the queue head at offset +1Bh.
A call do_buffer_pointers, with EAX= the loading address, writes correctly all the queue head's buffer pointers. Next it reads the Output endpoint number which was found out by reading descriptors, and which just happens to have been saved at [ebx+411h]. This goes into the queue head with 20h for high speed, at offset +5. Next the address where the queue head starts, 50300h, goes into EAX so that a call ets7 will start it running. A call waitn_out waits for the memory stick to have time to work, and then call ets8 stops it running. This cycle of writing sectors is over, but inst2 is usually called again for more. It was a good idea for the total length field of the queue head to have exactly the right total length in it, so that the subroutine waiting for it to work can read the total length field and wait for that to automatically go down to 0.

;--

Next when all the sectors are written to the Usb memory stick, you have to read a Command Status Word from the memory stick's bulk Input endpoint. This CSW is always 13 bytes long, and its thirteenth byte should be zero when there are no errors, a non-zero in the thirteenth byte would mean there was an error. My programming experiments did not really use it, but you have to read the CSW for the memory sticks expect you to read it away. The number 0dh for 13 should preferably be written in both the packet length and the total length field of the queue head.
The program below is not necessarily the best way of reading the CSW, and if I continue the experiment I will look for a better way of doing it.

```
removes:      pushad                        ;Note this was to read away a CSW (The Command Status Wrapper)
              mov cl,80h
              test byte [ebx+62h],1
              jnz remo2
              mov cl,0
remo2:
              call ets2                     ;ets2 draws two queue heads, but only using the second one.

                                            ;packet length now 0dh bytes.  20h=high speed,
                                            ; 1= endpoint 1 ;9=device address

              mov dword  [ebx+304h],0d2109h
              mov dword [ebx+318h],0d0180h  ;00dh=total length field 01=IN pid, 80h=active
              or [ebx+31bh],cl              ;set data0 or data1 by OR with CL
              mov eax,54200h                ;A loading address to go into buffer pointers.
              call do_buffer_pointers       ;Then over-write its endpoint number

              mov al,[ebx+410h]             ;get Input endpoint number found from descriptors
              or al,20h                     ;20h for high speed
              mov [ebx+305h],al             ;overwrite endpoint number into queue head.

              mov eax,50300h
              call ets7
              call waitn_removes
```

```
                    call waits
                    call ets6
                    inc byte [ebx+62h]
                    popad
                    ret
;-----------------------------------------------------------------
```
;**This normal method for filling in the buffer pointers is important!**
; It does the buffer pointers of the second queue head, which starts at address [ebx+300h]
;One can always use the same method for filling in the buffer pointers of any other Queue head.
;If buffer pointers not done, it can load onto lowest memory RAM and so crash.

;Call it with EAX containing the 32 bit loading address.

```
     do_buffer_pointers:    mov [ebx+31Ch],eax         ;At +1Ch, the simple loading address= buffer pointer 0.
                            and ax,0f000h                ;(And ax,0f000h is the Same as and eax,0fffff000h)
                            add eax,1000h                 ; 1000h is 4K
                            mov [ebx+320h],eax          ;write buffer pointer 1
                            add eax,1000h
                            mov [ebx+324h],eax          ; write buffer pointer 2
                            add eax,1000h
                            mov [ebx+328h],eax           ;write buffer pointer 3
                            add eax,1000h
                            mov [ebx+32Ch],eax          ;write buffer pointer 4;  the last one of the 5.
                            ret


;-------------------------------------------------
 waitn_removes:    push ecx
           push eax
           mov ecx,100000h
   waitn11:   dec ecx
           jz waitn10
           mov al,[ebx+318h]             ;get status field
           and al,78h                    ;take sta
           jnz waitn10

           mov al,[ebx+318h]
           test al,80h
           jz waitn10                     ;active bit, read and test the "active bit" of the queue head.

           mov ax,[ebx+31ah]       ;read total length field to see when it goes to zero.
           and ax,7fffh
           jnz waitn11
   waitn10:   pop eax
           pop ecx
           ret



;------------------------------------------------------------
;It called set-get config And get descriptors and get boot sector then usb the first time
;it called only direct-r every time after the first time.
```
read_sectors_first_time: ;??
```
 usb:                mov ebx,50000h
                     mov byte [ebx+60h],0     ;A byte at +60h kept track of the input endpoint's data toggle.

;;; call test_unit ;test-unit was only necessary for I-POCO and harmless to the others.
```

```
read_more_sectors:        ;
                mov ebx,50000h
                call test3                              ;test3= a blank input improved it a lot.

                mov esi,31000h                          ;esi addressed variable in usb files reading

                mov cx,[esi+22h]                        ;length field in sectors, normal way round at first

                mov eax,[esi+28h]                       ;start absolute sector number, sector to be read
                call write_cbw_read(10)                 ;call with cx and eax pre loaded.

                test byte [esi+60h],1                   ;keep track of the data toggle !
                jz tk3
                call send_cbw
                jmp tk4

         tk3:   call send_cbw_data1  ;
         tk4:   call input_sector    ;

                ret
;------------------------------


;================================================================
;make a queue head become a bulk input queue head to read data blocks from a memory stick.

    input_sector:                                       ;called when reading usb stick file from file name.

                mov eax,[esi+24h]                       ;new 4 byte simple loading address
                mov ebx,50000h

                mov cx,[esi+22h]                        ;into cx number of sectors to be read at a time

         inst4: cmp cx,20h                              ; offset to make 256 cubed. +22h-3 = +1fh
                jnb inst8

                mov DL,CL
                bswap edx                               ;swap from lowest byte to highest byte

                add edx,edx                             ;times 256 cubed and then times 2.
                and edx,7e000000h                       ;I think edx is at a maximum value here
                add edx,180h
                jmp inst9  ;

         inst8: mov edx,40000180h                       ;To go into queue head.
                                ; Total length field of 200h x 20h = 4000h bytes, and Data0
         inst9: push eax                                ;push address for loading
                push ecx
                mov CL,080h         ;Data1 in CL it will go just 1 binary bit above the total length field.

                test byte [esi+60h],1                   ;Test keeping track of the right data toggle.
                jz tk5
                mov cl,0                                ;Data0 in CL.
```

```
        tk5:    call inst1
                                            ;called enough times to read 1 cluster, plus read the CSW after that.
                pop ecx
                pop eax
                add eax,4000h
                                            ;move up loading address for 20h packets of 200h bytes each.
                                            ;An Even no of packets.
                sub cx,20h                  ;For short files, it needs jz?.
                jz inst7
                jnb inst4                   ;detect nb not z because want 1 more input for CSW
                                            ;An extra input is essential,
;------------------- to read a csw
        inst7:  test byte [esi+60h],1       ;test the data toggle
                mov cl,80h
                jz inst20
                mov cl,0
        inst20: mov edx,0d0180h
                mov eax,54000h              ;loading address into eax
                call inst1
                ret
;----------------------------------------------------------


        ;---------------------------------
        inst1:  push eax                    ;reading sectors call to inst1 here.
                call ets2

                pop eax                                 ;NOTE should read a CSW after reading sectors
                mov dword [ebx+304h],2002109h           ;packet length 200h bytes,
                                            ; 2=high speed, 1= endpoint 1

                mov [ebx+318h],edx          ;edx was prepared, to go in second queue head
                or [ebx+31bh],cl            ;  ;set data0 or data1 by OR with the CL register
                                            ;A loading address has to be ready in eax
                                            ;for calling do buffer pointers.
                call do_buffer_pointers     ;eax was prepared for this call

                mov al,[ebx+410h]           ;get Input endpoint number from descriptors
                or al,20h                   ;20h code for high speed
                mov [ebx+305h],al           ;overwrite endpoint number into second queue head.
                mov eax,50300h              ;eax= address of my second queue head
                call ets7
                call waitn_in
                call ets8
                ret
;-----------------------------------------

;==========================================================
  waits:    mov eax,900000h                 ;It was necessary to lengthen this for i-poco?.
    waii:   dec eax                         ;increasing this wait from 3milsec to 9milsec stopped errors.
            jnz waii
            ret
```

```
waitn_in:    mov eax,39054h                    ;an input of usually 200h x10h bytes
             jmp waitn1
waitn_out:   mov eax,39056h                    ;an output of usually 200h x10h bytes
             jmp waitn1
waitn_cbw:   mov eax,39058h                    ;an output of a 1fh bytes cbw

waitn1:      push ecx
             push eax
             mov ecx,2a000000h                 ; HAD TO BE INCREASED.
    waitn2:  dec ecx
             jz waitn3
             mov al,[ebx+318h]
;
             and al,78h                        ;AND to take status area
;take status bits   Now when status field error, does not see total length field error if there is one
             jnz waitn4

             mov al,[ebx+318h]
             test al,80h
             jz waitn7                         ;active bit

             mov ax,[ebx+31ah]                 ;read total length field to see when it goes to zero.
             and ax,7fffh
             jnz waitn2
    waitn7:  pop eax
             pop ecx
             ret

    waitn3:  pop eax
             inc word [eax]
             mov eax,1ffff4h
             inc word [eax]       ;VISIBLY RECORD HOW MANY TIMES TIME EXPIRES.
             pop ecx
             mov ax,3333h
             ret
    waitn4:  pop eax
             add eax,10h          ;39064h,  39066h,  39068h
             inc byte [eax]
             pop ecx
             mov ax,3333h
             ret
```

;--------------------------------------

To learn about Queue Heads, one should download Intel's free specification for the EHCI.
This call with label ets2 writes 2 queue heads which can be modified for different purposes.
The **first** of them is a **setup** queue head. This queue head is made for sending a setup packet, which is always 8 bytes long. The queue head therefore has an 8 in both its packet length field and in its total length field.
 At offset +04 the device address field needs to be rewritten with the device address that you have given to the USB device, the one you want to send the setup packet to. At offset +1ch relative to the start of the queue head there is the pointer which points to the setup packet, it happens to be address [50160h] in this example.

The **second** queue head is an **input** queue head. It can be changed for different purposes, and at first I used it for taking a blank input from endpoint 0. It can be changed into an **output** queue head just by changing the small PID field at offset +19h to a 00 for output.

```
;===========================================================

        ets1:       call ets5
                    call ets2
                    call ets3
                    call ets6
                    popad
                    ret    ;end

        ets5b:      push ebx
                    mov ebx,50940h              ;erase area where to read blocks from usb stick memory
                    mov cx,400h
                    mov al,0
        ets4b:      mov [ebx],al
                    inc ebx
                    dec cx
                    jnz ets4b
                    pop ebx
                    ret


        ets5:       push ebx
                    mov ebx,50420h              ;erase area where to read descriptors.
                    mov cx,0160h
                    mov al,0
              ets4: mov [ebx],al
                    inc ebx
                    dec cx
                    jnz ets4
                    pop ebx
                    ret
                                      ; Write a Setup Queue Head first, used to send a setup packet
ets2:                   mov ebx,50000h
                        mov dword   [ebx+100h],050102h   ;Horizontal link pointer pointing to ITSELF.
;At +4h A wrong dev address of 2, the 820 means for packet size=8 bytes, 20 for high speed.

                        mov dword   [ebx+104h],82002h
                                                          ;+108h (Unused in this case)
                                                         ;For Hub's device address=02 and Port
                                                         ; number=2 But the 2 looks like 1 (Not used)
                        mov dword   [ebx+108h],41020000h

                        mov dword   [ebx+10ch],0501c0h   ;Essential pointer to a Blank Queue Element TD
                        mov dword   [ebx+110h],01   ;
                        mov dword   [ebx+114h],01
;next, 8 bytes length, current page=0 ; 2=pid of setup+0=cerr  ;lower 80h= Active
                        mov dword   [ebx+118h],080280h   ;the total length field is 15 binary bits at + 1Ah.
                        mov dword   [ebx+11ch],050160h    ; First buffer pointer Point to set-up packet.

                        mov dword   [ebx+120h],0
```

```
            mov dword    [ebx+124h],0
            mov dword    [ebx+128h],0
            mov dword    [ebx+12ch],0
            mov dword    [ebx+130h],0
            mov dword    [ebx+134h],0         ;zeroes fill 64 bit area.
            mov dword    [ebx+138h],0
            mov dword    [ebx+13ch],0
            mov dword    [ebx+140h],0                     ;1st queue head done

            mov al,[ebx+40h]                   ;at [50040h]a test device address
            mov [ebx+104h],al                  ;write it into the queue head

            mov dword    [ebx+1c0h],01        ;Write an Blank Queue element Transfer Descriptor.
            mov dword    [ebx+1c4h],01        ;
            mov dword    [ebx+1c8h],0h
            mov dword    [ebx+1cch],0h
            mov dword    [ebx+1d0h],0
            mov dword    [ebx+1d4h],0
            mov dword    [ebx+1d8h],0
            mov dword    [ebx+1dch],0

;Write an INPUT Queue Head. Its horizontal link pointer points to itself.
            mov dword    [ebx+300h],050302h
            mov dword    [ebx+304h],0402002h    ;Length sometimes 08 but now making it 40h.
            mov dword    [ebx+308h],41020000h   ;unused dword now
            mov dword    [ebx+30ch],050360h     ;Pointer pointing to an blank Queue Element TD.
            mov dword    [ebx+310h],01
            mov dword    [ebx+314h],01
                                                 ;At +318h, 90h bytes, 01=pid=IN
                                                 ; lower 80h=active ; higher 80h= Data1
            mov dword    [ebx+318h],80900180h   ;the total length field is 15 binary bits at + 1Ah.
            mov dword    [ebx+31ch],050420h     ;pointer to where it should read descriptors to.
            mov dword    [ebx+320h],0
            mov dword    [ebx+324h],0
            mov dword    [ebx+328h],0
            mov dword    [ebx+32ch],0
            mov dword    [ebx+330h],0
            mov dword    [ebx+334h],0
            mov dword    [ebx+338h],0
            mov dword    [ebx+33ch],0
            mov dword    [ebx+340h],0           ;2nd queue head done

            mov al,[ebx+40h]                    ;at [50040h] a test device address
            mov [ebx+304h],al                   ;write it into 2nd queue head

            mov dword    [ebx+360h],01         ;Write an Blank Queue element Transfer Descriptor.
            mov dword    [ebx+364h],01         ;
            mov dword    [ebx+368h],0h  ;
            mov dword    [ebx+36ch],0h
            mov dword    [ebx+370h],0
            mov dword    [ebx+374h],0
            mov dword    [ebx+378h],0
            mov dword    [ebx+37ch],0
            ret
```

```
;==============================

ets8:   push ebx
        push ecx
        mov ecx,100000h
  pk82: dec ecx
        jnz pk82
        mov ebx,[ebx+50h]              ;load the USB operational base adress. In laptop was =0d4405c20h
        mov dword   [ebx],80001h       ;Stop asynchronous by writing into Command register
        mov ecx,100000h                ;
  pk83: dec ecx
        jnz pk83
        pop ecx
        pop ebx
         ret

ets7:   push ebx                       ; stop, restart with queue head of address from eax
        mov ebx,[ebx+50h]              ;call here with eax pre loaded with queue heads address.
        mov dword   [ebx],80001h
        mov ecx,100000h
  pk14: dec ecx
        jnz pk14
        mov dword   [ebx+18h],eax      ;    call only with EAX ready
        mov dword   [ebx],80021h            ;start async running
        pop ebx
        ret

ets6:   push ebx                       ; Just delay then stop. About 5 milliseconds
        mov ecx,500000h                ;These ecx delays were essential for some memory sticks.
  pk12: dec ecx
        jnz pk12
        mov ebx,[ebx+50h]
        mov dword   [ebx],80001h       ; Stop the asynchronous
        mov ecx,40000h                 ;    Some delay were necessary              ;
  pk13: dec ecx
        jnz pk13

        pop ebx
         ret
;----------------------------------------------------------------------------------
;
```

One Experiment with an external Samsung USB-DVD writer drive.

I have bought my Samsung USB DVD writer drive because I wanted to play with writing and reading sectors to DVDs and to make them bootable. Firstly, exactly the same program which can enumerate a USB memory stick and read its descriptors can also enumerate the DVD writer drive and read its descriptors. The same bit of program which finds the input and output endpoint numbers of a memory stick, can also do it with this DVD writer drive. Because the endpoint numbers are in exactly the same spot in the descriptor.

I found that almost the same read(10) command and write(10) command CBWs (Command Block Wrapper) which you can use to read and write sectors to a USB memory stick, also works with the DVD writer drive. But there was an important difference, which is that with a DVD the sector size is 800h bytes (it was 200h bytes for any memory stick).

Every read(10) or write(10) CBW has in it 2 length fields which have to be written so that they correspond to one another. The first length field at offset +8 relative to the start of the CBW, has to have the length **in bytes** which you want to read or write. This length field has to be written in the little-endian way round. The second length field is at offset + 16h relative to the start of the CBW, and it has to contain the length **in sectors** which you want to read or write. This second length field has to be written in the big-endian way round, which is sometimes a bit confusing since I am used to computers working with numbers in the little endian way round. That did not affect the experiment, since I always used less than 255 sectors at a time.

When you read or write 1 sector to a USB memory stick, the first length field has to contain 200h, but when you read or write to the DVD writer drive, the first length field has to contain 800h because one DVD sector is 800h bytes. This was the difference.

I wrote a short piece of a program which takes the sectors length field and multiplies it by 800h and then writes it into the bytes length field at offset +8, so as to make sure that whatever the number of sectors you read or write the two length fields are corresponding. A BSWAP operation can undo the big-endian way round to make it little-endian, but I did not use it as I assumed the length would be less than 255 sectors. Exactly as with a USB memory stick, the "Sector address" number (the number of the sector you want to either read or write) has to be in the CBW of the Read(10) or the Write(10) command as a 4 bytes number at offset + 11h relative to the start of the CBW, and this sector number has to be written in the big-endian way round. I thought it a bit confusing that the number has to be in the big-endian way round while I am used to numbers in computers being in the little-endian way round. A BSWAP EAX operation can be useful if you want to turn a little endian number into the big endian way round.

The USB DVD drive started working slowly and when it was turned on I had to wait for about 15 seconds for it to be ready. As far as I can tell, the USB DVD needs to be sent the command "Test Unit Ready" to make it start working. Sending it this command seems to turn on something inside it, as it was necessary. The USB DVD drive could be started by sending it the command "Request Sense" instead. It never worked until I sent it either of these 2 commands, to get it to start.
Whenever I tried to read or write sectors to the DVD disc, it would not work the first time and I had to patiently wait for a few seconds and then try again. It worked the second time. I assumed that this was because the DVD drive takes a few seconds to get ready, as its lens has to move to the right track and its motor has to start turning. When the drive seems to have written sectors to the DVD, you have to wait patiently for a few seconds longer for it to actually write.

To try to make it work more easily, I got my program to try every read and write twice automatically, and in between tries my program waits in a time delay for about 4 seconds. Then in that way I got it to read or write sectors to the DVD first try. Reading and writing were slightly different. To read sectors I firstly took a blank input from endpoint 00 with data toggle starting data1. As usual, doing that 'blank input' made the device seem to react to the next CBW more reliably. I send the CBW, and after a short time delay input the data with a input queue head. Having the correct length of data in the total length field of the queue head improved it. Then my program reads the CSW which the USB DVD drive sends. The CSW is always 13 bytes long, and it is normally necessary to read it.

Writing sectors to the DVD using the usual Write(10) command, was a bit more difficult than the reading of sectors, and I do not know the reason why. I do not understand why, but to write sectors I had to send the Write(10) CBW twice, once before outputting all the data, then once again after wards. My program sends the CBW, then outputs all the data, then with the data toggle changed sends the same CBW a second time. It then waits for a time delay of several seconds for it to have time to write the sectors and then it inputs the CSW which the drive sends to the computer.

All of my experiments so far firstly enumerate the USB DVD drive, and automatically find from reading the descriptor its 2 important endpoint numbers, its IN and its OUT endpoint numbers. (The words IN and OUT are always relative to the computer.) Also, just before any read or write sectors test, my program gives the drive its configuration of 01 again (using a setup queue head to send the "Set configuration" setup packet another time.) Giving the configuration of 01 when the drive has already got it, was intended to set the drive's two endpoint's data toggles to a known state, but I am not sure whether it does that. If you are trying to do more advanced computer programming, then you are surely supposed to keep track of both IN and OUT data toggles by keeping in the memory a binary bit for each endpoint, which keeps track of whether they are data 1 or data 0.
In that case you can avoid giving the drive its configuration of 01 again. Keeping track of data toggle seems difficult, but one should always do it.
 I noticed that there is a single difference between the DVD drive and a USB memory stick, which is that because the memory stick has 200h bytes sectors, and because the USB data packet size(for high speed devices) is 200h bytes as well, whenever you read or write an odd-number of sectors to the memory stick there is also an odd-number of USB data packets.
And that means the data toggle has to be changed (data1 or data0) for the start of the next operations using IN or OUT endpoint. When the number of sectors is even-numbered, the data toggle did not have to be changed with the USB memory stick. The DVD drive is simpler, since the USB DVD drive has 800h bytes long sectors, and since the 800h is 4 of the 200h bytes long USB packets, which is an even-number, the DVD drive always does an even-number of USB packets and so the data toggle is not changed by the normal data IN or OUT.
But, of course, when sending a CBW, the data toggle does have to change for the next time. Because the CBW has to be sent as 1 data packet always 31 bytes long, sending a CBW is always sending an odd-number of packets, which means that the data toggle has to be changed at the start of the next OUT operation. Also reading the CSW has to change the Input endpoint's data toggle since the (13 bytes long) CSW is an odd number of packets.

My experiment firstly tries to read a blank input from endpoint 00 and with data1, to try to make the drive react more reliably to the CBW. Then it sends a CBW to the drives data OUT endpoint. It sends it with a queue head in which both the packet length and the total length fields are 1fh for 31 bytes. For Read(10), after waiting for a delay it inputs all the data with a queue head from the drives IN endpoint. And then after a long delay, it reads the 13 bytes CSW from the same IN endpoint as the data.
For writing sectors to the DVD with Write(10), it does the same blank input from endpoint 0, then it sends a Write(10) CBW to the drives OUT endpoint, Then after a delay it sends all the data to be written onto DVD

sectors to the same OUT endpoint, with the data toggle starting as the opposite data toggle from when sending the CBW. (Since the CBW is an odd-number of packets.) For example if the CBW was sent data1, the output of data had to start with data0. Then after a long delay, the program sends the same CBW a second time. (with the same data toggle as the start of the data, since the data was an even-number of packets and does not change the next data toggle.) Then the program waits again to make sure the drive had time to write to the DVD. Then it reads the CSW which the drive sends. This worked. I do not know why it was necessary to send the CBW a second time, and there is maybe a different way of doing it? It could have been a data toggle mistake, but I thought it was not. In the case of writing sectors, the CSW was definitely not a way of telling whether it had succeeded in writing the data to the DVD sectors. I do not know why, but I could not tell whether this had worked by looking at the CSW. It did write the sectors and gave a CSW in which the last byte was 00 which means "command passed".

Made in United States
Orlando, FL
02 November 2023